# **FREE** Study Skills Videos/DVD Offer

Dear Customer,

Thank you for your purchase from Mometrix! We consider it an honor and a privilege that you have purchased our product and we want to ensure your satisfaction.

As part of our ongoing effort to meet the needs of test takers, we have developed a set of Study Skills Videos that we would like to give you for FREE. These videos cover our *best practices* for getting ready for your exam, from how to use our study materials to how to best prepare for the day of the test.

All that we ask is that you email us with feedback that would describe your experience so far with our product. Good, bad, or indifferent, we want to know what you think!

To get your FREE Study Skills Videos, you can use the **QR code** below, or send us an **email** at studyvideos@mometrix.com with *FREE VIDEOS* in the subject line and the following information in the body of the email:

- The name of the product you purchased.
- Your product rating on a scale of 1-5, with 5 being the highest rating.
- Your feedback. It can be long, short, or anything in between. We just want to know your impressions and experience so far with our product. (Good feedback might include how our study material met your needs and ways we might be able to make it even better. You could highlight features that you found helpful or features that you think we should add.)

If you have any questions or concerns, please don't hesitate to contact me directly.

Thanks again!

Sincerely,

Jay Willis
Vice President
jay.willis@mometrix.com
1-800-673-8175

**Mometrix**
TEST PREPARATION

# Mometrix
TEST PREPARATION

# CDL

## Study Guide 2023-2024

**675** Practice Test Questions

Secrets Prep for the Commercial Driver's License Exam with Detailed Answer Explanations

5th Edition

Copyright © 2022 by Mometrix Media LLC

All rights reserved. This product, or parts thereof, may not be reproduced, stored in a retrieval system, or transmitted in any form or by any means—electronic, mechanical, photocopy, recording, scanning, or other—except for brief quotations in critical reviews or articles, without the prior written permission of the publisher.

Written and edited by the Mometrix CDL Test Team

Printed in the United States of America

This paper meets the requirements of ANSI/NISO Z39.48-1992 (Permanence of Paper).

Mometrix offers volume discount pricing to institutions. For more information or a price quote, please contact our sales department at sales@mometrix.com or 888-248-1219.

Mometrix Media LLC is not affiliated with or endorsed by any official testing organization. All organizational and test names are trademarks of their respective owners.

Paperback
ISBN 13: 978-1-5167-2267-9
ISBN 10: 1-5167-2267-1

# Dear Future Exam Success Story

First of all, **THANK YOU** for purchasing Mometrix study materials!

Second, congratulations! You are one of the few determined test-takers who are committed to doing whatever it takes to excel on your exam. **You have come to the right place.** We developed these study materials with one goal in mind: to deliver you the information you need in a format that's concise and easy to use.

In addition to optimizing your guide for the content of the test, we've outlined our recommended steps for breaking down the preparation process into small, attainable goals so you can make sure you stay on track.

We've also analyzed the entire test-taking process, identifying the most common pitfalls and showing how you can overcome them and be ready for any curveball the test throws you.

Standardized testing is one of the biggest obstacles on your road to success, which only increases the importance of doing well in the high-pressure, high-stakes environment of test day. Your results on this test could have a significant impact on your future, and this guide provides the information and practical advice to help you achieve your full potential on test day.

### Your success is our success

**We would love to hear from you!** If you would like to share the story of your exam success or if you have any questions or comments in regard to our products, please contact us at **800-673-8175** or **support@mometrix.com**.

Thanks again for your business and we wish you continued success!

Sincerely,
The Mometrix Test Preparation Team

# Table of Contents

| | |
|---|---|
| Introduction | 1 |
| Secret Key #1 – Plan Big, Study Small | 2 |
| Secret Key #2 – Make Your Studying Count | 3 |
| Secret Key #3 – Practice the Right Way | 4 |
| Secret Key #4 – Pace Yourself | 6 |
| Secret Key #5 – Have a Plan for Guessing | 7 |
| Test-Taking Strategies | 10 |
| General Information | 15 |
|     Getting Your CDL | 15 |
|     Serious Violations | 19 |
| General Knowledge | 20 |
| Basics of Controlling Your Vehicle | 28 |
| Communication | 32 |
| Space Management | 34 |
| Hazardous Conditions | 43 |
| General Knowledge Practice Test #1 | 54 |
| Answer Key and Explanations for Test #1 | 60 |
| General Knowledge Practice Test #2 | 64 |
| Answer Key and Explanations for Test #2 | 70 |
| General Knowledge Practice Test #3 | 74 |
| Answer Key and Explanations for Test #3 | 80 |
| General Knowledge Practice Test #4 | 84 |
| Answer Key and Explanations for Test #4 | 90 |
| Air Brakes Endorsement | 95 |
| Air Brakes Endorsement Practice Test #1 | 104 |
| Answer Key and Explanations for Test #1 | 107 |
| Air Brakes Endorsement Practice Test #2 | 109 |
| Answer Key and Explanations for Test #2 | 112 |
| Air Brakes Endorsement Practice Test #3 | 114 |
| Answer Key and Explanations for Test #3 | 117 |

| | |
|---|---|
| CARGO AND TRANSPORT VEHICLES ENDORSEMENT | 119 |
| TANK VEHICLES ENDORSEMENT | 123 |
| CARGO AND TANK ENDORSEMENT PRACTICE TEST #1 | 125 |
| ANSWER KEY AND EXPLANATIONS FOR TEST #1 | 128 |
| CARGO AND TANK ENDORSEMENT PRACTICE TEST #2 | 130 |
| ANSWER KEY AND EXPLANATIONS FOR TEST #2 | 133 |
| CARGO AND TANK ENDORSEMENT PRACTICE TEST #3 | 135 |
| ANSWER KEY AND EXPLANATIONS FOR TEST #3 | 138 |
| COMBINATION VEHICLES (DOUBLES AND TRIPLES) ENDORSEMENT | 140 |
| INSPECTING COMBINATION VEHICLES | 144 |
| COUPLING AND UNCOUPLING COMBINATION VEHICLES | 147 |
| DRIVING COMBINATION VEHICLES | 154 |
| COMBINATION VEHICLES ENDORSEMENT PRACTICE TEST #1 | 158 |
| ANSWER KEY AND EXPLANATIONS FOR TEST #1 | 161 |
| COMBINATION VEHICLES ENDORSEMENT PRACTICE TEST #2 | 163 |
| ANSWER KEY AND EXPLANATIONS FOR TEST #2 | 166 |
| COMBINATION VEHICLES ENDORSEMENT PRACTICE TEST #3 | 168 |
| ANSWER KEY AND EXPLANATIONS FOR TEST #3 | 171 |
| COMBINATION VEHICLES ENDORSEMENT PRACTICE TEST #4 | 172 |
| ANSWER KEY AND EXPLANATIONS FOR TEST #4 | 175 |
| COMBINATION VEHICLES ENDORSEMENT PRACTICE TEST #5 | 177 |
| ANSWER KEY AND EXPLANATIONS FOR TEST #5 | 180 |
| HAZARDOUS MATERIALS ENDORSEMENT | 182 |
| HAZARDOUS MATERIALS ENDORSEMENT PRACTICE TEST #1 | 201 |
| ANSWER KEY AND EXPLANATIONS FOR TEST #1 | 205 |
| HAZARDOUS MATERIALS ENDORSEMENT PRACTICE TEST #2 | 207 |
| ANSWER KEY AND EXPLANATIONS FOR TEST #2 | 211 |
| HAZARDOUS MATERIALS ENDORSEMENT PRACTICE TEST #3 | 214 |
| ANSWER KEY AND EXPLANATIONS FOR TEST #3 | 218 |
| HAZARDOUS MATERIALS ENDORSEMENT PRACTICE TEST #4 | 221 |
| ANSWER KEY AND EXPLANATIONS FOR TEST #4 | 225 |
| PASSENGER AND SCHOOL BUS ENDORSEMENTS | 228 |

| | |
|---|---|
| OPERATING THE BUS SAFELY | 229 |
| HANDLING EMERGENCIES | 231 |
| TRANSPORTING PASSENGERS | 232 |
| SAFE DRIVING WITH BUSES | 234 |
| PASSENGER AND SCHOOL BUS ENDORSEMENT PRACTICE TEST #1 | 236 |
| ANSWER KEY AND EXPLANATIONS FOR TEST #1 | 239 |
| PASSENGER AND SCHOOL BUS ENDORSEMENT PRACTICE TEST #2 | 240 |
| ANSWER KEY AND EXPLANATIONS FOR TEST #2 | 243 |
| PASSENGER AND SCHOOL BUS ENDORSEMENT PRACTICE TEST #3 | 245 |
| ANSWER KEY AND EXPLANATIONS FOR TEST #3 | 248 |
| PASSENGER AND SCHOOL BUS ENDORSEMENT PRACTICE TEST #4 | 249 |
| ANSWER KEY AND EXPLANATIONS FOR TEST #4 | 252 |
| PASSENGER AND SCHOOL BUS ENDORSEMENT PRACTICE TEST #5 | 253 |
| ANSWER KEY AND EXPLANATIONS FOR TEST #5 | 256 |
| PASSENGER AND SCHOOL BUS ENDORSEMENT PRACTICE TEST #6 | 257 |
| ANSWER KEY AND EXPLANATIONS FOR TEST #6 | 260 |
| HOW TO OVERCOME TEST ANXIETY | 261 |
|     CAUSES OF TEST ANXIETY | 261 |
|     ELEMENTS OF TEST ANXIETY | 262 |
|     EFFECTS OF TEST ANXIETY | 262 |
|     PHYSICAL STEPS FOR BEATING TEST ANXIETY | 263 |
|     MENTAL STEPS FOR BEATING TEST ANXIETY | 264 |
|     STUDY STRATEGY | 265 |
|     TEST TIPS | 267 |
|     IMPORTANT QUALIFICATION | 268 |
| TELL US YOUR STORY | 269 |
| ADDITIONAL BONUS MATERIAL | 270 |

# Introduction

**Thank you for purchasing this resource!** You have made the choice to prepare yourself for a test that could have a huge impact on your future, and this guide is designed to help you be fully ready for test day. Obviously, it's important to have a solid understanding of the test material, but you also need to be prepared for the unique environment and stressors of the test, so that you can perform to the best of your abilities.

For this purpose, the first section that appears in this guide is the **Secret Keys**. We've devoted countless hours to meticulously researching what works and what doesn't, and we've boiled down our findings to the five most impactful steps you can take to improve your performance on the test. We start at the beginning with study planning and move through the preparation process, all the way to the testing strategies that will help you get the most out of what you know when you're finally sitting in front of the test.

We recommend that you start preparing for your test as far in advance as possible. However, if you've bought this guide as a last-minute study resource and only have a few days before your test, we recommend that you skip over the first two Secret Keys since they address a long-term study plan.

If you struggle with **test anxiety**, we strongly encourage you to check out our recommendations for how you can overcome it. Test anxiety is a formidable foe, but it can be beaten, and we want to make sure you have the tools you need to defeat it.

# Secret Key #1 – Plan Big, Study Small

There's a lot riding on your performance. If you want to ace this test, you're going to need to keep your skills sharp and the material fresh in your mind. You need a plan that lets you review everything you need to know while still fitting in your schedule. We'll break this strategy down into three categories.

## Information Organization

Start with the information you already have: the official test outline. From this, you can make a complete list of all the concepts you need to cover before the test. Organize these concepts into groups that can be studied together, and create a list of any related vocabulary you need to learn so you can brush up on any difficult terms. You'll want to keep this vocabulary list handy once you actually start studying since you may need to add to it along the way.

## Time Management

Once you have your set of study concepts, decide how to spread them out over the time you have left before the test. Break your study plan into small, clear goals so you have a manageable task for each day and know exactly what you're doing. Then just focus on one small step at a time. When you manage your time this way, you don't need to spend hours at a time studying. Studying a small block of content for a short period each day helps you retain information better and avoid stressing over how much you have left to do. You can relax knowing that you have a plan to cover everything in time. In order for this strategy to be effective though, you have to start studying early and stick to your schedule. Avoid the exhaustion and futility that comes from last-minute cramming!

## Study Environment

The environment you study in has a big impact on your learning. Studying in a coffee shop, while probably more enjoyable, is not likely to be as fruitful as studying in a quiet room. It's important to keep distractions to a minimum. You're only planning to study for a short block of time, so make the most of it. Don't pause to check your phone or get up to find a snack. It's also important to **avoid multitasking**. Research has consistently shown that multitasking will make your studying dramatically less effective. Your study area should also be comfortable and well-lit so you don't have the distraction of straining your eyes or sitting on an uncomfortable chair.

The time of day you study is also important. You want to be rested and alert. Don't wait until just before bedtime. Study when you'll be most likely to comprehend and remember. Even better, if you know what time of day your test will be, set that time aside for study. That way your brain will be used to working on that subject at that specific time and you'll have a better chance of recalling information.

Finally, it can be helpful to team up with others who are studying for the same test. Your actual studying should be done in as isolated an environment as possible, but the work of organizing the information and setting up the study plan can be divided up. In between study sessions, you can discuss with your teammates the concepts that you're all studying and quiz each other on the details. Just be sure that your teammates are as serious about the test as you are. If you find that your study time is being replaced with social time, you might need to find a new team.

# Secret Key #2 – Make Your Studying Count

You're devoting a lot of time and effort to preparing for this test, so you want to be absolutely certain it will pay off. This means doing more than just reading the content and hoping you can remember it on test day. It's important to make every minute of study count. There are two main areas you can focus on to make your studying count.

## Retention

It doesn't matter how much time you study if you can't remember the material. You need to make sure you are retaining the concepts. To check your retention of the information you're learning, try recalling it at later times with minimal prompting. Try carrying around flashcards and glance at one or two from time to time or ask a friend who's also studying for the test to quiz you.

To enhance your retention, look for ways to put the information into practice so that you can apply it rather than simply recalling it. If you're using the information in practical ways, it will be much easier to remember. Similarly, it helps to solidify a concept in your mind if you're not only reading it to yourself but also explaining it to someone else. Ask a friend to let you teach them about a concept you're a little shaky on (or speak aloud to an imaginary audience if necessary). As you try to summarize, define, give examples, and answer your friend's questions, you'll understand the concepts better and they will stay with you longer. Finally, step back for a big picture view and ask yourself how each piece of information fits with the whole subject. When you link the different concepts together and see them working together as a whole, it's easier to remember the individual components.

Finally, practice showing your work on any multi-step problems, even if you're just studying. Writing out each step you take to solve a problem will help solidify the process in your mind, and you'll be more likely to remember it during the test.

## Modality

*Modality* simply refers to the means or method by which you study. Choosing a study modality that fits your own individual learning style is crucial. No two people learn best in exactly the same way, so it's important to know your strengths and use them to your advantage.

For example, if you learn best by visualization, focus on visualizing a concept in your mind and draw an image or a diagram. Try color-coding your notes, illustrating them, or creating symbols that will trigger your mind to recall a learned concept. If you learn best by hearing or discussing information, find a study partner who learns the same way or read aloud to yourself. Think about how to put the information in your own words. Imagine that you are giving a lecture on the topic and record yourself so you can listen to it later.

For any learning style, flashcards can be helpful. Organize the information so you can take advantage of spare moments to review. Underline key words or phrases. Use different colors for different categories. Mnemonic devices (such as creating a short list in which every item starts with the same letter) can also help with retention. Find what works best for you and use it to store the information in your mind most effectively and easily.

# Secret Key #3 – Practice the Right Way

Your success on test day depends not only on how many hours you put into preparing, but also on whether you prepared the right way. It's good to check along the way to see if your studying is paying off. One of the most effective ways to do this is by taking practice tests to evaluate your progress. Practice tests are useful because they show exactly where you need to improve. Every time you take a practice test, pay special attention to these three groups of questions:

- The questions you got wrong
- The questions you had to guess on, even if you guessed right
- The questions you found difficult or slow to work through

This will show you exactly what your weak areas are, and where you need to devote more study time. Ask yourself why each of these questions gave you trouble. Was it because you didn't understand the material? Was it because you didn't remember the vocabulary? Do you need more repetitions on this type of question to build speed and confidence? Dig into those questions and figure out how you can strengthen your weak areas as you go back to review the material.

Additionally, many practice tests have a section explaining the answer choices. It can be tempting to read the explanation and think that you now have a good understanding of the concept. However, an explanation likely only covers part of the question's broader context. Even if the explanation makes perfect sense, **go back and investigate** every concept related to the question until you're positive you have a thorough understanding.

As you go along, keep in mind that the practice test is just that: practice. Memorizing these questions and answers will not be very helpful on the actual test because it is unlikely to have any of the same exact questions. If you only know the right answers to the sample questions, you won't be prepared for the real thing. **Study the concepts** until you understand them fully, and then you'll be able to answer any question that shows up on the test.

It's important to wait on the practice tests until you're ready. If you take a test on your first day of study, you may be overwhelmed by the amount of material covered and how much you need to learn. Work up to it gradually.

On test day, you'll need to be prepared for answering questions, managing your time, and using the test-taking strategies you've learned. It's a lot to balance, like a mental marathon that will have a big impact on your future. Like training for a marathon, you'll need to start slowly and work your way up. When test day arrives, you'll be ready.

Start with the strategies you've read in the first two Secret Keys—plan your course and study in the way that works best for you. If you have time, consider using multiple study resources to get different approaches to the same concepts. It can be helpful to see difficult concepts from more than one angle. Then find a good source for practice tests. Many times, the test website will suggest potential study resources or provide sample tests.

# Practice Test Strategy

If you're able to find at least three practice tests, we recommend this strategy:

## UNTIMED AND OPEN-BOOK PRACTICE

Take the first test with no time constraints and with your notes and study guide handy. Take your time and focus on applying the strategies you've learned.

## TIMED AND OPEN-BOOK PRACTICE

Take the second practice test open-book as well, but set a timer and practice pacing yourself to finish in time.

## TIMED AND CLOSED-BOOK PRACTICE

Take any other practice tests as if it were test day. Set a timer and put away your study materials. Sit at a table or desk in a quiet room, imagine yourself at the testing center, and answer questions as quickly and accurately as possible.

Keep repeating timed and closed-book tests on a regular basis until you run out of practice tests or it's time for the actual test. Your mind will be ready for the schedule and stress of test day, and you'll be able to focus on recalling the material you've learned.

# Secret Key #4 – Pace Yourself

Once you're fully prepared for the material on the test, your biggest challenge on test day will be managing your time. Just knowing that the clock is ticking can make you panic even if you have plenty of time left. Work on pacing yourself so you can build confidence against the time constraints of the exam. Pacing is a difficult skill to master, especially in a high-pressure environment, so **practice is vital**.

Set time expectations for your pace based on how much time is available. For example, if a section has 60 questions and the time limit is 30 minutes, you know you have to average 30 seconds or less per question in order to answer them all. Although 30 seconds is the hard limit, set 25 seconds per question as your goal, so you reserve extra time to spend on harder questions. When you budget extra time for the harder questions, you no longer have any reason to stress when those questions take longer to answer.

Don't let this time expectation distract you from working through the test at a calm, steady pace, but keep it in mind so you don't spend too much time on any one question. Recognize that taking extra time on one question you don't understand may keep you from answering two that you do understand later in the test. If your time limit for a question is up and you're still not sure of the answer, mark it and move on, and come back to it later if the time and the test format allow. If the testing format doesn't allow you to return to earlier questions, just make an educated guess; then put it out of your mind and move on.

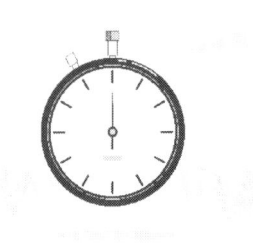

On the easier questions, be careful not to rush. It may seem wise to hurry through them so you have more time for the challenging ones, but it's not worth missing one if you know the concept and just didn't take the time to read the question fully. Work efficiently but make sure you understand the question and have looked at all of the answer choices, since more than one may seem right at first.

Even if you're paying attention to the time, you may find yourself a little behind at some point. You should speed up to get back on track, but do so wisely. Don't panic; just take a few seconds less on each question until you're caught up. Don't guess without thinking, but do look through the answer choices and eliminate any you know are wrong. If you can get down to two choices, it is often worthwhile to guess from those. Once you've chosen an answer, move on and don't dwell on any that you skipped or had to hurry through. If a question was taking too long, chances are it was one of the harder ones, so you weren't as likely to get it right anyway.

On the other hand, if you find yourself getting ahead of schedule, it may be beneficial to slow down a little. The more quickly you work, the more likely you are to make a careless mistake that will affect your score. You've budgeted time for each question, so don't be afraid to spend that time. Practice an efficient but careful pace to get the most out of the time you have.

# Secret Key #5 – Have a Plan for Guessing

When you're taking the test, you may find yourself stuck on a question. Some of the answer choices seem better than others, but you don't see the one answer choice that is obviously correct. What do you do?

The scenario described above is very common, yet most test takers have not effectively prepared for it. Developing and practicing a plan for guessing may be one of the single most effective uses of your time as you get ready for the exam.

In developing your plan for guessing, there are three questions to address:

- When should you start the guessing process?
- How should you narrow down the choices?
- Which answer should you choose?

## When to Start the Guessing Process

Unless your plan for guessing is to select C every time (which, despite its merits, is not what we recommend), you need to leave yourself enough time to apply your answer elimination strategies. Since you have a limited amount of time for each question, that means that if you're going to give yourself the best shot at guessing correctly, you have to decide quickly whether or not you will guess.

Of course, the best-case scenario is that you don't have to guess at all, so first, see if you can answer the question based on your knowledge of the subject and basic reasoning skills. Focus on the key words in the question and try to jog your memory of related topics. Give yourself a chance to bring the knowledge to mind, but once you realize that you don't have (or you can't access) the knowledge you need to answer the question, it's time to start the guessing process.

It's almost always better to start the guessing process too early than too late. It only takes a few seconds to remember something and answer the question from knowledge. Carefully eliminating wrong answer choices takes longer. Plus, going through the process of eliminating answer choices can actually help jog your memory.

**Summary**: Start the guessing process as soon as you decide that you can't answer the question based on your knowledge.

# How to Narrow Down the Choices

The next chapter in this book (**Test-Taking Strategies**) includes a wide range of strategies for how to approach questions and how to look for answer choices to eliminate. You will definitely want to read those carefully, practice them, and figure out which ones work best for you. Here though, we're going to address a mindset rather than a particular strategy.

Your odds of guessing an answer correctly depend on how many options you are choosing from.

| Number of options left | 5 | 4 | 3 | 2 | 1 |
|---|---|---|---|---|---|
| Odds of guessing correctly | 20% | 25% | 33% | 50% | 100% |

You can see from this chart just how valuable it is to be able to eliminate incorrect answers and make an educated guess, but there are two things that many test takers do that cause them to miss out on the benefits of guessing:

- Accidentally eliminating the correct answer
- Selecting an answer based on an impression

We'll look at the first one here, and the second one in the next section.

To avoid accidentally eliminating the correct answer, we recommend a thought exercise called **the $5 challenge**. In this challenge, you only eliminate an answer choice from contention if you are willing to bet $5 on it being wrong. Why $5? Five dollars is a small but not insignificant amount of money. It's an amount you could afford to lose but wouldn't want to throw away. And while losing $5 once might not hurt too much, doing it twenty times will set you back $100. In the same way, each small decision you make—eliminating a choice here, guessing on a question there—won't by itself impact your score very much, but when you put them all together, they can make a big difference. By holding each answer choice elimination decision to a higher standard, you can reduce the risk of accidentally eliminating the correct answer.

The $5 challenge can also be applied in a positive sense: If you are willing to bet $5 that an answer choice *is* correct, go ahead and mark it as correct.

**Summary**: Only eliminate an answer choice if you are willing to bet $5 that it is wrong.

# Which Answer to Choose

You're taking the test. You've run into a hard question and decided you'll have to guess. You've eliminated all the answer choices you're willing to bet $5 on. Now you have to pick an answer. Why do we even need to talk about this? Why can't you just pick whichever one you feel like when the time comes?

The answer to these questions is that if you don't come into the test with a plan, you'll rely on your impression to select an answer choice, and if you do that, you risk falling into a trap. The test writers know that everyone who takes their test will be guessing on some of the questions, so they intentionally write wrong answer choices to seem plausible. You still have to pick an answer though, and if the wrong answer choices are designed to look right, how can you ever be sure that you're not falling for their trap? The best solution we've found to this dilemma is to take the decision out of your hands entirely. Here is the process we recommend:

**Once you've eliminated any choices that you are confident (willing to bet $5) are wrong, select the first remaining choice as your answer.**

Whether you choose to select the first remaining choice, the second, or the last, the important thing is that you use some preselected standard. Using this approach guarantees that you will not be enticed into selecting an answer choice that looks right, because you are not basing your decision on how the answer choices look.

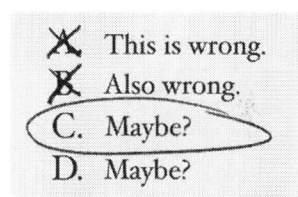

This is not meant to make you question your knowledge. Instead, it is to help you recognize the difference between your knowledge and your impressions. There's a huge difference between thinking an answer is right because of what you know, and thinking an answer is right because it looks or sounds like it should be right.

**Summary**: To ensure that your selection is appropriately random, make a predetermined selection from among all answer choices you have not eliminated.

# Test-Taking Strategies

This section contains a list of test-taking strategies that you may find helpful as you work through the test. By taking what you know and applying logical thought, you can maximize your chances of answering any question correctly!

It is very important to realize that every question is different and every person is different: no single strategy will work on every question, and no single strategy will work for every person. That's why we've included all of them here, so you can try them out and determine which ones work best for different types of questions and which ones work best for you.

## Question Strategies

### ⓥ READ CAREFULLY

Read the question and the answer choices carefully. Don't miss the question because you misread the terms. You have plenty of time to read each question thoroughly and make sure you understand what is being asked. Yet a happy medium must be attained, so don't waste too much time. You must read carefully and efficiently.

### ⓥ CONTEXTUAL CLUES

Look for contextual clues. If the question includes a word you are not familiar with, look at the immediate context for some indication of what the word might mean. Contextual clues can often give you all the information you need to decipher the meaning of an unfamiliar word. Even if you can't determine the meaning, you may be able to narrow down the possibilities enough to make a solid guess at the answer to the question.

### ⓥ PREFIXES

If you're having trouble with a word in the question or answer choices, try dissecting it. Take advantage of every clue that the word might include. Prefixes can be a huge help. Usually, they allow you to determine a basic meaning. *Pre-* means before, *post-* means after, *pro-* is positive, *de-* is negative. From prefixes, you can get an idea of the general meaning of the word and try to put it into context.

### ⓥ HEDGE WORDS

Watch out for critical hedge words, such as *likely, may, can, sometimes, often, almost, mostly, usually, generally, rarely,* and *sometimes*. Question writers insert these hedge phrases to cover every possibility. Often an answer choice will be wrong simply because it leaves no room for exception. Be on guard for answer choices that have definitive words such as *exactly* and *always*.

### ⓥ SWITCHBACK WORDS

Stay alert for *switchbacks*. These are the words and phrases frequently used to alert you to shifts in thought. The most common switchback words are *but, although,* and *however*. Others include *nevertheless, on the other hand, even though, while, in spite of, despite,* and *regardless of.* Switchback words are important to catch because they can change the direction of the question or an answer choice.

### ⊘ FACE VALUE

When in doubt, use common sense. Accept the situation in the problem at face value. Don't read too much into it. These problems will not require you to make wild assumptions. If you have to go beyond creativity and warp time or space in order to have an answer choice fit the question, then you should move on and consider the other answer choices. These are normal problems rooted in reality. The applicable relationship or explanation may not be readily apparent, but it is there for you to figure out. Use your common sense to interpret anything that isn't clear.

## Answer Choice Strategies

### ⊘ ANSWER SELECTION

The most thorough way to pick an answer choice is to identify and eliminate wrong answers until only one is left, then confirm it is the correct answer. Sometimes an answer choice may immediately seem right, but be careful. The test writers will usually put more than one reasonable answer choice on each question, so take a second to read all of them and make sure that the other choices are not equally obvious. As long as you have time left, it is better to read every answer choice than to pick the first one that looks right without checking the others.

### ⊘ ANSWER CHOICE FAMILIES

An answer choice family consists of two (in rare cases, three) answer choices that are very similar in construction and cannot all be true at the same time. If you see two answer choices that are direct opposites or parallels, one of them is usually the correct answer. For instance, if one answer choice says that quantity $x$ increases and another either says that quantity $x$ decreases (opposite) or says that quantity $y$ increases (parallel), then those answer choices would fall into the same family. An answer choice that doesn't match the construction of the answer choice family is more likely to be incorrect. Most questions will not have answer choice families, but when they do appear, you should be prepared to recognize them.

### ⊘ ELIMINATE ANSWERS

Eliminate answer choices as soon as you realize they are wrong, but make sure you consider all possibilities. If you are eliminating answer choices and realize that the last one you are left with is also wrong, don't panic. Start over and consider each choice again. There may be something you missed the first time that you will realize on the second pass.

### ⊘ AVOID FACT TRAPS

Don't be distracted by an answer choice that is factually true but doesn't answer the question. You are looking for the choice that answers the question. Stay focused on what the question is asking for so you don't accidentally pick an answer that is true but incorrect. Always go back to the question and make sure the answer choice you've selected actually answers the question and is not merely a true statement.

### ⊘ EXTREME STATEMENTS

In general, you should avoid answers that put forth extreme actions as standard practice or proclaim controversial ideas as established fact. An answer choice that states the "process should be used in certain situations, if..." is much more likely to be correct than one that states the "process should be discontinued completely." The first is a calm rational statement and doesn't even make a definitive, uncompromising stance, using a hedge word *if* to provide wiggle room, whereas the second choice is far more extreme.

### ⊘ BENCHMARK

As you read through the answer choices and you come across one that seems to answer the question well, mentally select that answer choice. This is not your final answer, but it's the one that will help you evaluate the other answer choices. The one that you selected is your benchmark or standard for judging each of the other answer choices. Every other answer choice must be compared to your benchmark. That choice is correct until proven otherwise by another answer choice beating it. If you find a better answer, then that one becomes your new benchmark. Once you've decided that no other choice answers the question as well as your benchmark, you have your final answer.

### ⊘ PREDICT THE ANSWER

Before you even start looking at the answer choices, it is often best to try to predict the answer. When you come up with the answer on your own, it is easier to avoid distractions and traps because you will know exactly what to look for. The right answer choice is unlikely to be word-for-word what you came up with, but it should be a close match. Even if you are confident that you have the right answer, you should still take the time to read each option before moving on.

## General Strategies

### ⊘ TOUGH QUESTIONS

If you are stumped on a problem or it appears too hard or too difficult, don't waste time. Move on! Remember though, if you can quickly check for obviously incorrect answer choices, your chances of guessing correctly are greatly improved. Before you completely give up, at least try to knock out a couple of possible answers. Eliminate what you can and then guess at the remaining answer choices before moving on.

### ⊘ CHECK YOUR WORK

Since you will probably not know every term listed and the answer to every question, it is important that you get credit for the ones that you do know. Don't miss any questions through careless mistakes. If at all possible, try to take a second to look back over your answer selection and make sure you've selected the correct answer choice and haven't made a costly careless mistake (such as marking an answer choice that you didn't mean to mark). This quick double check should more than pay for itself in caught mistakes for the time it costs.

### ⊘ PACE YOURSELF

It's easy to be overwhelmed when you're looking at a page full of questions; your mind is confused and full of random thoughts, and the clock is ticking down faster than you would like. Calm down and maintain the pace that you have set for yourself. Especially as you get down to the last few minutes of the test, don't let the small numbers on the clock make you panic. As long as you are on track by monitoring your pace, you are guaranteed to have time for each question.

### ⊘ DON'T RUSH

It is very easy to make errors when you are in a hurry. Maintaining a fast pace in answering questions is pointless if it makes you miss questions that you would have gotten right otherwise. Test writers like to include distracting information and wrong answers that seem right. Taking a little extra time to avoid careless mistakes can make all the difference in your test score. Find a pace that allows you to be confident in the answers that you select.

### ⊘ Keep Moving

Panicking will not help you pass the test, so do your best to stay calm and keep moving. Taking deep breaths and going through the answer elimination steps you practiced can help to break through a stress barrier and keep your pace.

## Final Notes

The combination of a solid foundation of content knowledge and the confidence that comes from practicing your plan for applying that knowledge is the key to maximizing your performance on test day. As your foundation of content knowledge is built up and strengthened, you'll find that the strategies included in this chapter become more and more effective in helping you quickly sift through the distractions and traps of the test to isolate the correct answer.

Now that you're preparing to move forward into the test content chapters of this book, be sure to keep your goal in mind. As you read, think about how you will be able to apply this information on the test. If you've already seen sample questions for the test and you have an idea of the question format and style, try to come up with questions of your own that you can answer based on what you're reading. This will give you valuable practice applying your knowledge in the same ways you can expect to on test day.

**Good luck and good studying!**

# General Information

Most states will use a multiple choice CDL test format. This means you will be given a question followed by several possible answers. Usually there will be three to four choices. You are to choose one answer and mark the appropriate selection. This is for the written test only. There will also be a practical (driving) test that will accompany your written test scores. Some states will have laws specific to their state regarding CDL acquisition. Check with your state to find out any state specific laws that they may have. You can usually find this information on your state's DMV or DPS website. This manual is not conclusive of all information required by federal and state laws to operate a commercial vehicle. You can obtain more information about the proper requirements from your respective state's transportation department. You can also seek more information from the Federal Motor Carrier Safety Administration (FMCSA).

## Getting Your CDL

When you apply for your CDL, you must show proof of your identity, social security number and residency. You must also provide your most recent medical examiner's certificate. You are required to hold a CDL instruction permit a minimum of 30 days or show successful completion of a DMV or Department of Education approved CDL driver education course. If you already have a driver's license, you can use it as proof of your identity, social security number (dependent on state), and residency. If you do not have a driver's license, you generally must provide the following:

- 2 proof of identity documents, such as a driver's license, birth certificate, government issued photo identification card, CDL instruction permit, unexpired U.S. military identification card or U.S. military discharge papers. You must provide original or duplicate documents. Photocopies will not be accepted.
- 1 proof of your social security number, such as your social security card, IRS W-2 form, payroll check or check stub, unexpired U.S. Military identification card. Photocopies will not be accepted. If you do not want your social security number to be displayed on your license, DMV will issue a control number for your use.
- 1 proof of residency, such as a payroll check or check stub, voter registration card, IRS W-2 form, U.S. or state income tax return. Residency documents must show your name and the address of your principal residence in as it appears on your application for license.

If you are required to meet FMCSA regulations, you must provide your most recent medical examiner's certificate. Medical forms are available at any DMV or DPS office. All drivers must certify that they are in compliance with the Federal Motor Carrier Safety Administration regulations, or that they do not have to comply with them. Refer to the FMCSA regulations for an explanation of these safety requirements.

### VISION STANDARDS

To operate commercial motor vehicles, you must have:

- 20/40 or better vision in each eye
- 140 degrees or better horizontal vision

These visual requirements must be met without the aid of a telescopic lens. Some drivers may be granted waivers from these vision requirements. For information concerning waivers for travel intra-state, contact your local DMV or DPS. For information concerning waivers for travel inter-state, contact the Federal Motor Carrier Safety Administration at:

Federal Vision & Diabetes Exemptions
MC-PSP Division
400 Seventh Street SW, Room 8301
Washington, DC 20590-0001

## COMMERCIAL MOTOR VEHICLE

A commercial motor vehicle is:

- any one vehicle with a gross vehicle weight rating or (GVWR) of 26,001 pounds or more
- any combination of vehicles with a gross combination weight rating of 26,001 pounds or more as long as the vehicle or vehicles being towed has a GVWR of more than 10,000 pounds
- any vehicle carrying 16 or greater passengers, including the driver
- any size vehicle that transports hazardous materials and that requires federal placarding.

## COMMERCIAL DRIVERS

Commercial drivers refer to anyone that operates commercial motor vehicles in a paid or volunteer position. Mechanics who test drive commercial vehicles must also meet commercial driver's license requirements. Commercial driver's license requirements do not apply to the following:

- emergency vehicle operators, such as EMS or firefighters
- active-duty military personnel operating military vehicles
- operators of farm vehicles when
    - operated by farmers
    - used to move farm goods, supplies, or machinery to or from their farm
    - not used as a common or contracting motor carrier
    - used within 150 miles of the farm
- vehicles operated by persons only for personal use, such as recreational vehicles and moving van rentals

## CDL AGE REQUIREMENTS

You must be at least 18 years of age to hold a CDL. Under federal law, you must be a commercial driver at least 21 years of age to drive across state lines, transport hazardous materials, or transport interstate freight within the state. Your license will have an indication that you are restricted to intrastate driving.

## CDL INSTRUCTION PERMIT

The first step in obtaining your CDL is obtaining a commercial driver's license instruction permit. It is similar to a learner's permit you may have had as a teenager. To obtain a CDL instruction permit, you must first pass a CDL general knowledge exam and any other exams for the vehicles that you plan to operate (e.g., Tanker, Passenger, HAZMAT, Triples, Doubles, etc.). Some of these endorsements may also combine to make one endorsement. Once you have been issued your permit, you are only able to use it when accompanied by a fully licensed driver with the same endorsements for which you are training. Often times when you are attending a driving school, there will be multiple permit holders and one fully licensed driver/instructor.

## CDL Classifications

The classification of what type of CDL you will need is dependent upon the vehicle you plan to operate. To determine which class pertains to you, review the following descriptions. In the following descriptions, GVWR refers to Gross Vehicle Weight Rating, and GCWR refers to Gross Combined Weight Rating.

### Class A

Any combination of vehicles with a GCWR of 26,001 pounds or more if the vehicle(s) being towed have a GVWR of more than 10,000 pounds. Vehicles in this class include:

- Tractor-trailers
- Truck and trailer combinations
- Tractor-trailer buses

If you hold a class A CDL and you have all required endorsements, you are also permitted to operate those vehicles listed in classes B and C of this section.

### Class B

Any single vehicle with a GVWR of 26,001 pounds or more. Any single vehicle with a GVWR of 26,001 pounds or more towing another vehicle with a GVWR of 10,000 pounds or less. This class includes:

- Straight trucks
- Large buses
- Segmented buses
- Trucks towing vehicles with a GVWR of 10,000 pounds or less

If you hold a class B CDL and you have all required endorsements, you are also permitted to operate those vehicles listed in class C of this section.

### Class C

Any vehicle that is not included in classes A or B that carries hazardous materials or is able to carry 16 or more passengers, to include the driver.

## CDL Endorsements

- H: Hazardous Material
- N: Tank Vehicle
- P: Passenger
- S: School bus
- T: Double/Triple Trailer
- X: Combination of N and H (as mentioned in the section on permits)

## CDL Restrictions

The letter code for restrictions will vary by state and not all states have the same amount of restriction codes. You can find out what your state's CDL restrictions are by contacting your DMV or DPS office via their website, telephone or in-person visit. Please note that in-person visits may take longer due to potential waiting times at your nearest location.

## MOVING VIOLATIONS

If you receive two or more moving violations within the average 5-year life of your CDL license (driving either a private or commercial vehicle) you must retake all written exams applicable to your CDL license.

## TAKING THE CDL TESTS

All persons seeking a CDL are required to take a written test as well as a practical (driving) test. All CDL classifications will require a general knowledge exam. You will also need to take a test for transporting cargo. If you are going to operate a vehicle with air brakes, you will need to also take a test specific to their operation. If you choose not to take the air brakes test, there will be a restriction code placed on your CDL indicating that you cannot operate any vehicle with air brakes. If the vehicle you plan to operate is a combination vehicle, you will need to complete the corresponding test. To determine which of these sections you need to focus on for your CDL, refer to the table below.

| Class A, B, C | General Knowledge/Transporting Cargo |
|---|---|
| Air Brake Vehicles | Air Brakes |
| Class A Combination | Combination Vehicles |
| T | Doubles and Triples |
| N | Tanker Vehicles |
| H | Hazardous Material |
| P | Passenger |
| S | School Bus |
| X | Tanker Vehicles/Hazardous Material |

There will be a fee to take your exams. The frequency of how often you can test for your written exams will vary by state. Some states may also have a retest fee. You can find out any testing fees and retest information by contacting your state DMV or DPS office.

The general knowledge exam will determine how familiar you are with operation commercial vehicles. You will see things similar to your first driving exam (e.g., street signs, lights, etc.). You will also encounter specific CDL questions. Using the information you learn from this guide and any experiences from a training program, try to select the best answer. Once you pass the required written exam(s), you can take the skills exams that test your practical knowledge of what you have studied. These exams include three areas:

- Pre-trip inspection (be thorough)
- Air brakes (if applicable)
- On-road driving (control, shifting, turns)

You must take the skills exams in the same type of vehicle you plan to be licensed to operate. Skills exams are not necessary for all additional endorsements, but are for some. You will need to check with your DPS office prior to testing whether or not your endorsement will require a skills test.

*Tip: When backing for your test, (GOAL) Get Out And Look before you back.*

## DISQUALIFICATIONS

If you are convicted of any of the following violations while operating a commercial vehicle, you will be disqualified or prohibited from driving commercial motor vehicles in the future. You will lose your CDL for a minimum of one year for your first offense in any of the following:

- Operating a CMV with a breath or blood alcohol concentration of 0.04 or higher
- Operating a personal vehicle or CMV while intoxicated or under the influence of any controlled substances
- Refusing to undergo breath or blood alcohol testing whether in CMV or in personal vehicle
- Leaving the scene of a collision or accident
- Committing a felony while in use of a commercial vehicle
- Driving a CMV when the CDL is suspended, revoked, cancelled, or disqualified
- Receive a second conviction for one of the violations listed above
- Causing a fatality by way of negligence while operating a CMV
- Driving a CMV in possession of a controlled substance

You will lose your CDL for the duration of at least three years if any of these offenses occur during operation of a CMV that is placarded indicating it is carrying hazardous materials. You will lose your CDL for life for a second offense, or if you use a commercial vehicle in the act of committing a felony in relation to controlled substances in any discernable way. You will be placed out-of-service for 24 hours or more if any trace amount of BAC is found less than 0.04. As you may have noticed, the limitations for CDL holders are much stricter than those that operate normal cars and trucks.

## Serious Violations

Serious traffic violations are:

- Speeding 15 mph or greater than the posted speed limit
- Reckless driving
- Capricious changing of lanes
- Following another motorist too closely
- Traffic offenses involving fatal or injury producing traffic accidents
- Driving without a CDL
- Having a CDL in the driver's possession without the proper classification of CDL or endorsements

There are many more violations for those transporting hazardous materials. These will be explained in the hazardous material section. If you operate a vehicle on some states' roadways, you agree to take a chemical test upon request to determine if you are driving under the influence of drugs or alcohol. This is called implied consent.

# General Knowledge

## INSPECTION OF VEHICLE

Safety is a vital reason to perform inspections on your vehicle. Inspecting your vehicle thoroughly for any mechanical problems can prevent breakdowns or accidents. Pre-trip inspections are required by both federal and state laws. Federal and state inspectors can inspect your vehicle at any time without your permission. The consent is implied when you obtain your CDL. If they find your vehicle to not be in safe working order, they can put you out of service until the problems have been repaired. If you are found guilty of violating an out-of-service order, your CDL may be suspended or revoked. There are three kinds of inspections:

- Pre-trip (before operating the vehicle)
- During the trip (watching gauges, mirrors and at each stop)
- Post-trip (when you have completed your driving for the day)

Things to watch for during your trip:

- Tires, wheels, and rims (check chains in snow travel)
- Brakes (can become overheated in mountain descent)
- Lights and reflectors (make sure all lights are functioning properly)
- Brake and electrical connections to the trailer
- Trailer coupling devices (check the seal on the couplings)
- Cargo covers and tiedowns (make sure hooks are secure during travel)

It's a good idea to inspect your vehicle within the first 25 miles of the trip and also every 150 miles or 3 hours on the road.

*Tip: If your couplings aren't sealing well, moisten the connections. Also make sure there is always enough grease on your 5th wheel to ensure a solid trailer connection.*

Inspect your vehicle at the end of your day. If you find any problems with your rig, report them to your dispatcher. They will usually try to find local assistance for you as soon as possible. Make note of things that could be potential issues in the future that you may need to discuss with a mechanic at your company's local yard or truck stop.

## WHAT TO LOOK FOR

- Check for proper tire pressure using an air pressure gauge or by hitting them with a mallet (you are feeling for bounce back from the mallet strike). Look for:
    - Mismatched tire sizes
    - Cuts or other damage to the tires
    - Dual tires touching
- Damaged rims or wheels
- Damage, looseness, or rust to lug nuts
- Missing clamps or spacers
- Bent or cracked lock rings

**Brakes**: Look for brake drum and shoe problems on front, rear, and trailer brakes:

- Cracks in your drums
- Oil, grease, or brake fluid on your brake shoes or pads
- Brake shoes that are worn thin, missing, or broken

## STEERING SYSTEM

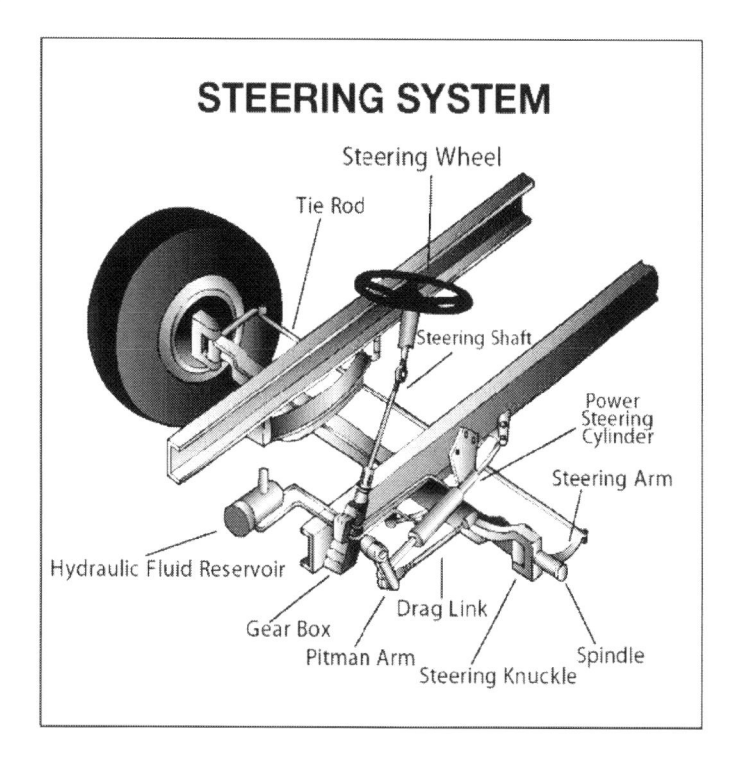

Look for:

- Missing bolts, nuts, cotter pins, or any other parts on the steering box.
- Damaged/loose parts. (i.e., steering column, gear box, or tie rods)
- If furnished with power steering, check for leaks, hoses, pumps, and fluid level.
- Free play in the steering system should not exceed more than 10 degrees (exactly 2 inches of leeway from the rim of a 20-inch steering wheel). Doing so will increase the difficulty in maneuvering.

## Suspension System

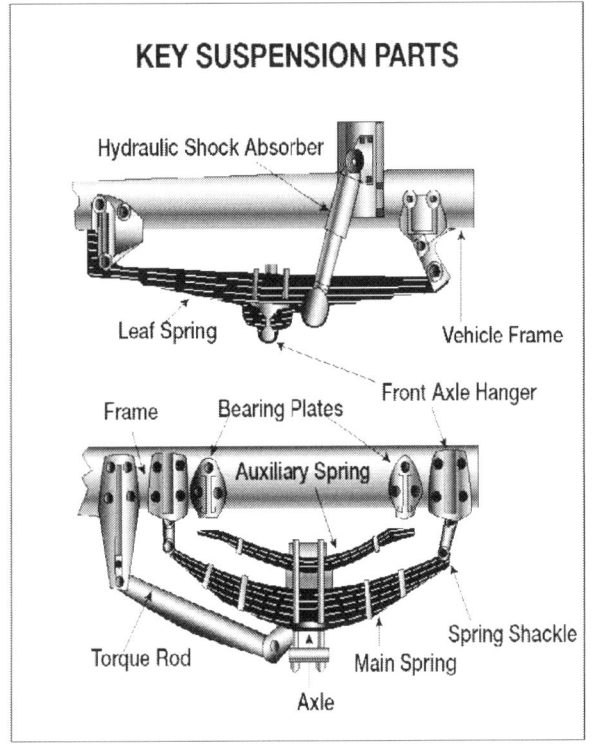

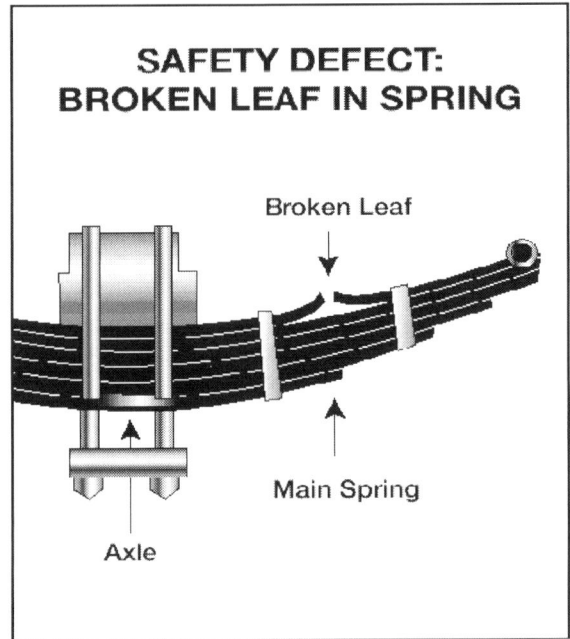

**KEY SUSPENSION PARTS**

**SAFETY DEFECT: BROKEN LEAF IN SPRING**

The function of the suspension system is to sustain the vehicle and its load, as well as keep the axles in place; this being said, broken suspensions are very dangerous. Look for front, rear, and trailer suspension defects:

- Spring supporters that give way to movement of the axle from the proper position
- Cracked or broken spring supporters
- Any leaf pieces that have missing or damaged pieces. Lacking a fourth or more will cause your vehicle could be put "out of service". But any defect is dangerous.
- Broken leaves in the multi-leaf spring or leaves that may have shifted to where they are hitting tires or other parts
- Insufficiently filled suspension absorbers (leaking).
- Radius (Torque) rod, U-bolts, spring supporters, and other axle stationing components that are cracked, damaged, or missing
- Faulty air suspension systems
- Loose, damaged, or absent frame members

Flue system defects: Damage to the exhaust system can potentially release deadly fumes into the cab or roomette.

- Loose, broken, or missing exhaust mufflers, vents, pipeage, and vertical branches
- System parts rubbing against elements of the fuel system, tires, or other mobile accessories of the vehicle.
- Loose, broken, or missing mounting brackets, clamps, bolts, or nuts.
- Any leaking parts of the exhaust system.

## Emergency Equipment

All commercial vehicles must have the following emergency equipment:

- Fire extinguisher
- Spare fuses (unless your CMV has circuit breakers)
- Three reflective triangles

Highly recommended equipment for all drivers:

- Tire chains
- Equipment to assist changing tires
- A record of emergency phone numbers
- Accident detail package (usually provided by employer)

## Cargo

Make sure your truck is not overloaded for its rating/permits. Be sure that the cargo is level and fasten in before departure. Also, if you are using load locks, make sure they are in place before transport. If carrying high-risk cargo, make sure you have all proper documents and placards for the load.

## Steps for Vehicle Inspection

Before inspecting your vehicle, make sure that you have set parking brakes and that the wheels are chocked. If you have to tilt the cab (cabover trucks), secure loose items in the cab so they will not fall.

## Step 1

Review the last vehicle inspection report. Drivers may be required to log a vehicle inspection report daily. The motor carrier must correct anything that hinders safety. The motor carrier must clarify on documentation as to whether the repairs were made or that they were unnecessary.

## Step 2

Check the engine compartment:

- Oil level
- Status of the hoses, and the coolant level in radiator
- Fluid level concerning power steering; the state of the hose if its equipped
- Fluid level of windshield washer
- Battery connections, security, and fluid level (battery location varies)
- Automatic transmission fluid level (engine must be running)
- Check belts for deterioration from wear and excessive tightness (look near alternator, water pump, air compressor)
- Learn how much "give"; each belt needs to be properly adjusted and correctly inspected
- Leaks in the engine compartment of: fuel, coolant, oil, power steering fluid, hydraulic fluid, and battery fluid
- Split, tattered electrical insulation wiring

When you have completed this part of your inspection, be sure to lower and secure the hood, cab, or engine compartment door. It is essential to make sure the latches are all secure before operation the vehicle.

## STEP 3
Start the engine and inspect the inside of the cab:

- Get in and start engine
    - Ensure the parking brake is set on both truck and trailer (red and yellow knobs), if applicable.
    - Shift the gear to neutral, or park, if your transmission provides that option.
    - Start engine and listen for anything abnormal (grinding, whining, etc.).
    - If equipped, check the Anti-Lock Braking System (ABS) indicator lights. The light on the dash should blink. If the light stays on, the ABS is malfunctioning and should be reported immediately. For trailers, there is a yellow light shining at the back left, the ABS is not working properly and should also be reported immediately.

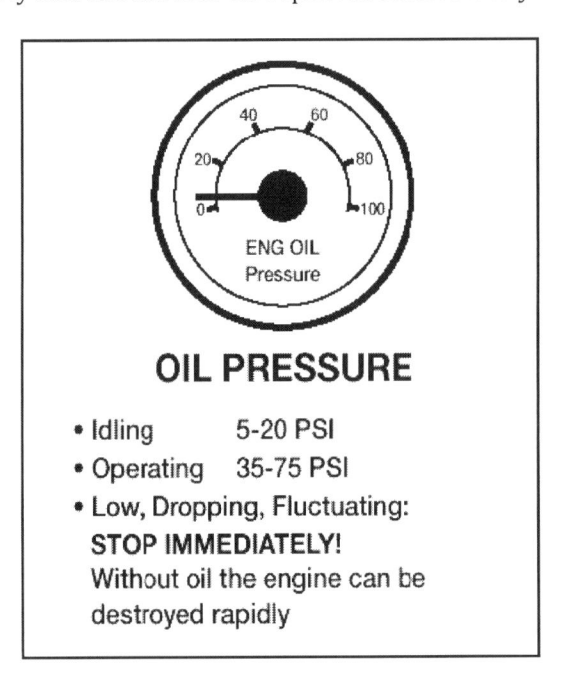

**OIL PRESSURE**
- Idling        5-20 PSI
- Operating     35-75 PSI
- Low, Dropping, Fluctuating:
  STOP IMMEDIATELY!
  Without oil the engine can be destroyed rapidly

- Check all gauges:
    - Oil pressure will take time to rise but should reach normal levels within seconds after the engine is started. Some older models may take longer.
    - Ammeter and/or voltmeter should be in normal range.
    - Engine coolant temperature should begin to gradually rise until it reaches normal levels.
    - Engine oil temperature should begin gradually rising until it reaches normal levels.
    - Most warning lights and buzzers should stop right away.
    - Air pressure should build from 50 to 90 psi within 3 minutes. Increasing the RPM will cause air pressure to rise to normal levels (around 120-140 psi).
- Check all controls for loose movement, jamming up or sticking, damage or improper setting.
    - Steering wheel
    - Clutch
    - Accelerator (gas pedal)
    - Brake controls:
        - ❖ Foot brake
        - ❖ Trailer brake (if applicable)
        - ❖ Parking brake

- o Retarder controls (if applicable)
- o Transmission controls
- o Interaxle differential lock (if applicable)
- o Horns (air and normal)
- o Windshield wiper blades and washer function
- o Lights:
  - ❖ Headlights
  - ❖ Dimmer switch
  - ❖ Turn signals
  - ❖ 4-way flashers
  - ❖ Clearance, identification, marker light switches
  - ❖ Parking lights
- Check all mirrors and windshield. Look for any cracks, dirt, smears, illegal decals or stickers, or other potential obstructions to your view. Make any necessary adjustments.
- Check all emergency equipment:
  - o Fully functional fire extinguisher
  - o Spare fuses on hand
  - o Three reflective triangles and/or road flares
- Make sure that your safety belt is not frayed or torn and that all latches work properly.
- You will also want to inspect any optional equipment
  - o Tire chains (for snowy/icy conditions)
  - o Equipment for changing tires if needed
  - o Tire chains (for snowy/icy conditions)

When you have completed all checks inside the cab, turn your engine off and test all of your lights outside of your vehicle. Make sure that your parking brakes are set and your key is removed from the ignition.

## STEP 4

Make a walk-around inspection:

- Check that all lights are working as mentioned above.
- Check the front left:
  - o Driver's door glass
  - o Door latches
  - o Left front wheel
  - o Left front suspension
  - o Left front brake
  - o Left fuel tanks (check tank straps for wear)
- Check the front:
  - o Front axle
  - o Steering system
  - o Windshield
  - o Lights and reflectors
- Check the front right:
  - o Front right checks (same areas as front left)
  - o Right fuel tanks (check tank straps for wear)
  - o Condition of all parts inspected

- Check transmission
- Check exhaust system
- Check frame and cross members
- Check air lines and electrical wiring—look for any snags, rubbing, or wearing
- Check spare tire carrier or rack:
    - Spare tire and wheel are securely held in place.
    - Spare tire and wheel are properly inflated and are the correct size.
- Check load securement:
    - Cargo is properly locked down in an acceptable fashion.
    - Tailboards are closed up and properly secured.
    - End gates are damage free and properly secured in stake sockets.
    - Protection canvas or tarp (if required) is properly secured to prevent tearing, billowing, or blocking of either the rearview mirrors or rear lights.
    - If the vehicle is oversized, check that all necessary indications (flags, lamps, and reflectors) are safely and properly in place and you have all required permits.
    - Make sure all compartment doors are securely closed, latched, or locked and that required security seals are in place.
- Check right rear:
    - Wheels and rims
    - Tires
    - Suspension
    - Brakes
    - Lights and reflectors
- Check rear:
    - Lights and reflectors
    - License plate
    - Splash guards
    - Cargo securement
- Check left side (all the same areas as the right side, plus batteries if not mounted in the engine compartment)
- Check all signal lights

## STEP 5

Start the engine and check the brake system:

- Hydraulic brakes
    - If driving with hydraulic brakes, pump the pedal 3 times.
    - Apply firm pressure to the pedal and hold steady for 5 seconds.
    - The pedal should be motionless.
    - If movement occurs, there may be problems such as a leak. This must be fixed immediately.
- Air brakes
    - If the vehicle is equipped with air brakes, build air pressure to 100-120 psi. Turn off the engine, release all brakes.
    - Press down hard on the foot brake steadily for one minute.
    - On combination vehicles, air pressure should not drop over 4 psi.
    - On single vehicles, air pressure should not drop over 3 psi.

- 
  - Turn ignition on.
  - With the foot brake, pump the air pressure down. At about 60 psi, the low air buzzer should sound.
  - Keep pumping air down with foot brake. At about 40 psi, the tractor parking brake knob and the trailer parking brake knob should pop out.
- Parking brakes
  - Set the parking brake.
  - Put the vehicle in low gear and gently release the clutch until you feel the tractor pulling against the brake.
  - The vehicle should not move.
- If operating a bus, additional things to check are:
  - Passenger entry
  - Seating
  - Emergency exits
  - Baggage compartment
- If you are driving a tractor trailer, also check:
  - Catwalk
  - All parts of the coupling system (5th wheel lower plate, etc.). You will not be able to see the lower plate if the vehicle is hooked up.
  - Trailer-front side and rear (air/electrical connections, header board, landing gear, etc.)
  - Make sure the crank handle to your landing gear is secure to avoid any potential hazards from it hanging. Also make sure your gear is lifted all the way.

If you find anything wrong during any step of your inspection, make sure it is fixed before operating your vehicle. It is against federal law to operate an unsafe vehicle. Make sure to always wear your seat belt and always watch your mirrors.

During your test, it will be required of you point out the areas of the vehicle as instructed and you may even be asked what problems that area could have during an inspection. What is tested varies by state. Key things to focus on for passing your test:

- Air brake test
- Pre-trip inspection
- Use of mirrors
- Shifting
- Turning

There are many others that are also of vital importance. These are some of the most important to make sure you know before testing.

# Basics of Controlling Your Vehicle

## Skills

To operate any vehicle safely, you must know how to control its magnitude and direction. This is especially true of CDL drivers because of the size of their vehicles. The following is a list of skills that you will need to understand extremely well before operating your vehicle:

- Accelerating
- Steering
- Shifting gears
- Backing
- Braking
- Constantly checking your mirrors

Ultimately, these skills need to be mastered, not just understood. They will ensure safe driving for you and the motorists around you. Always remember to fasten your seatbelt before operating any vehicle.

## Accelerating

Partly engage the clutch before taking your foot off the brake (unless fully automatic). Too little or too much and you will stall. Use the parking brake when on an incline to keep the vehicle in place. Release it only when you have enough power to keep from rolling back. If you are operating a tractor-trailer with a brake hand valve, you can use it to keep the object stationary. The trailer brakes can be a much safer method if equipped. You want to slowly accelerate to prevent jerking of the vehicle. If not done properly, your truck will stall. If you are pulling a trailer, the jerking can damage the coupling. Make sure to pull slowly and try to feel when the trailer has engaged. These steps are especially important in conditions where traction may be poor, such as in rain, sleet, or snow. If you do not follow these steps in these conditions, the drive wheels will spin, causing you to lose control of the vehicle. If you feel your wheels start to spin, slowly let off of the accelerator until you find traction. With the use of tire chains, chances of your drive tires spinning are decreased.

## Maneuvering

Place both hands on the steering wheel. They should be on opposite sides of the steering wheel. Avoid sharp motions to the steering wheel; this could cause your vehicle to whip due to its length.

## Shifting Gears

Correct shifting of gears is very vital. Failure to put your vehicle into the right gear while driving will mean less control, and you may have a more difficult time stopping.

## SHIFTING UP

Double clutching is the most common method used by those learning to shift. It is commonly used in truck driving schools. This is the standard process:

- Remove your foot from the accelerator. Push in the clutch and shift into neutral.
- Release the clutch
- Let the engine slow down the RPMs required for the next gear (usually 1000 RPMs slower but this can vary from truck to truck.).
- Push in the clutch and shift to the higher gear.
- Let off the clutch and push the accelerator as you would on takeoff.

This method of shifting will take a lot of repetition and practice. You can't stay in neutral too long or you will not be able to engage the next gear. If this happens, speed up your RPMs to engage the next gear. Do not force it. If you can't execute the shift, go back to your original gear and try again.

## SHIFTING DOWN

- Release accelerator, push in clutch, and shift to neutral simultaneously
- Let go of clutch
- Press accelerator, increase engine and gear speed to the rpm required in the lower gear
- Push in clutch and shift to lower gear in one movement
- Release clutch and press accelerator simultaneously

Pedal operation is very similar for shifting up or down. You just need to know when you need to shift and what the RPMs should be for each shift.

*Tip: Shifting down can help when you are having trouble stopping.*

Special conditions where you should downshift are:

- Before starting down a hill. Slow down and shift to a speed that you can control without pressing the brakes hard. Otherwise, the brakes can overheat and lose their stopping ability.
- Before entering a curve. Slow to a safe speed, and downshift before you enter the curve. This allows you to use some momentum through the curve to help the vehicle be more stable while turning. It also allows you to speed up as soon as you are out of the curve.

## BACKING SAFELY

When operating your vehicle, you are not able to see everything behind you, which makes backing very dangerous. Try to avoid backing whenever possible. When you must back, do so properly. Follow these simple steps:

- Map the path you will follow when backing. Get out and look (GOAL) is very important when backing, during your road test, and in everyday driving.
- Turn on four-way flashers and sound your horn before backing to ensure that all bystanders are clear, and to let other vehicles know that you are backing.
- Do not back fast. There is no room for error if you do. Use the lowest idler gear.
- You always want to driver's side back whenever possible. This means backing with full view of the driver's side of the vehicle. The other way is considered "blind side backing" and can lead to more accidents. Whenever possible, try to find a spotter to assist you when backing.

- Even in driver's side backing, if you have someone that can spot you in backing, utilize them. They can check all of your blind spots for you and signal directions to you. Your spotter should always stand where he or she has a view of the rear of the truck and where the driver can see them. If you lose sight of them during your backing, stop until you know their location. They may be in an area where they could be injured. Before you begin backing, agree on hand signals that the spotter will use. Audible directions are not always possible given the loud noises of the trucks and loading docks.

## BACKING WITH A TRAILER

When backing vehicles without trailers, rotate the steering wheel in the direction that you want the back of your vehicle to go. When backing with a trailer, you need to turn the steering wheel in the opposite direction. To follow the trailer during your backing, you need to turn in the direction the trailer is going. This will straighten the position of your truck with the trailer. Whenever possible, always try to back up in a straight line. If there is have no other option and must back on a curved path, always back to the driver's side so you can see the path of your trailer. Remember to back slowly. Always use your mirrors. They help you see if the trailer is staying on the proper path or not. They also make it easier to see when corrections need to be made. Whenever a correction is needed that cannot be done with small turns of the steering wheel during backing, pull up and realign your truck and trailer with your target. Pull up as often as you need to ensure that you back in properly.

## RETARDERS

Retarders help slow diesel vehicles, reducing the need for using your brakes. They diminish brake wear and offer another way to slow down. These are the types of retarders:

- Exhaust
- Engine
- Hydraulic
- Electric

All retarders can be activated by the driver. The power can also be adjusted on some vehicles. When activated, retarders reduce the engine power once you take your foot off the accelerator completely. If you are pushing the accelerator, it will not reduce power. Do not use your retarders in inclement weather where slippery conditions are present, especially if the unit is empty or lightly loaded. Because they can be loud, some city ordinances do not allow use of them within city limits. You should see signs saying "No Engine Breaks" or something similar.

## MIRRORS

Use all of your mirrors to check the traffic around you and your vehicle for any problems (flat tires, fire, cargo straps, etc.). Using your mirrors is especially vital when turning, changing lanes, or merging. Do not lose focus on the road ahead. Use your mirrors to check your tires. If you are carrying open cargo, check the mirrors to see that all of your straps or chains are still secure. Also, look for a flapping or bulging tarp. All of these things are very important to check often. Many vehicles have curved mirrors that show a wider area than flat mirrors to help with blind spots. Everything in a curved mirror appears smaller and farther away than it really is. Make sure you adjust all of your mirrors before each trip as they may have been moved at some point. They are your lifelines.

## PLANNING AHEAD

Stopping or changing lanes may take a lot of distance. You must know what the traffic is doing at all times from all sides of your vehicle. Experienced drivers plan ahead by looking far in front of them so they can estimate how much room they have to make any necessary moves in traffic. On the highway, most drivers look approximately ¼ of a mile ahead. When you plan ahead, look for traffic, road conditions, sharp pavement drop-offs and signs. Also look for slow-moving vehicles. Be especially careful when driving through work zones or when you see a law enforcement vehicle on the shoulder. Do not focus solely on what is in the distance. You want to scan constantly all around you and in the distance. Once you are accustomed to doing this, it becomes routine.

# Communication

## SIGNALING

It is important to let others know what you are doing on the road. You should always use your vehicle to communicate with other drivers. Just as you would with a car, you will use your headlights and turning signals. Signaling what you intend to do is a good safety practice. These are the general rules for signaling:

- Signal ahead
    - Signal early
    - Signal before you turn, merge, or change lanes.
    - Brake early and slow gradually for turns.
    - Flash your brake lights to warn other drivers that you need to slow down or stop. Don't stop suddenly.
    - Turn off your signal after you make the turn, merge, or lane change (not all vehicles' signals turn off automatically after the turn).
    - Use your emergency flashers when moving slowly (less than 45 mph on most freeways) or when you are parked.
    - Do not signal other drivers to pass you. They cannot see around you and it could lead to an accident.
- Always pass with caution
    - Check your side mirrors for surrounding traffic.
    - Determine if you have sufficient room to pass.
    - Use your turn signal early so that vehicles from behind know of your intentions.
    - Always check the surrounding traffic again before beginning your pass.
- Communicate your presence to others
    - Whenever you are about to pass a vehicle, pedestrian, or bicyclist, assume they don't see you.
    - Drive carefully to avoid a crash even if you would not be in the wrong.
    - At dawn and dusk and in rain or snow, you need to make yourself easier to see.
    - Use the headlights, not just the identification lights.
    - Use the low beams; high beams can irritate people in both daytime and nighttime.
    - Use your horn only when needed. Otherwise, your horn may scare others.
    - When you stop on the sides of the roadway:
        - ❖ Turn on your 4-way emergency flashers.
        - ❖ Place reflective triangles or flares within 10 minutes of stopping.
        - ❖ When putting out the triangles, hold them between yourself and the oncoming traffic for your own safety by increasing visibility. It could save your life.

## PLACEMENT OF REFLECTIVE TRIANGLES

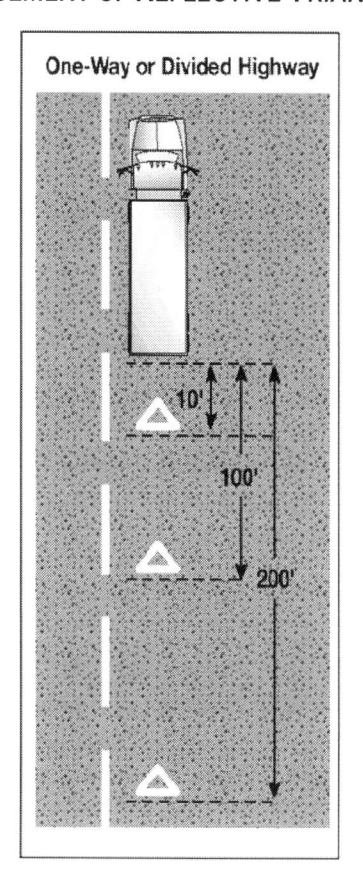

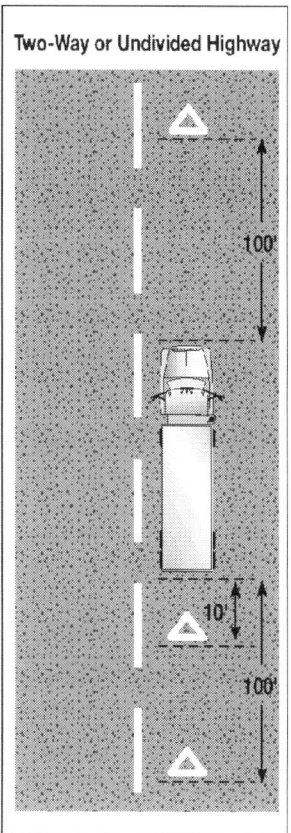

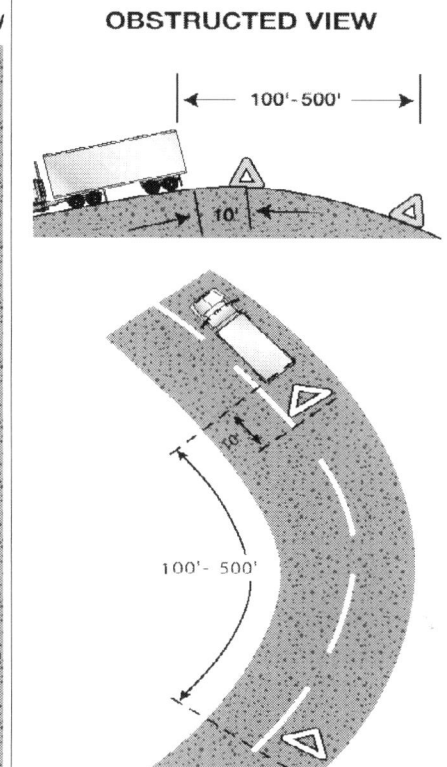

# Space Management

To be a safe driver, make sure your vehicle has plenty of space. This is because if something goes wrong, space gives you time to think and to take action. This is why you need to manage space. While this is true for all drivers, it is especially important for large vehicles. They take up more space so they require more space for stopping and turning.

## SPACE AHEAD

You need space ahead in the event of a sudden stop. According to accident reports, the vehicle that trucks and buses most frequently run into is the one in front of them. The most common cause is following too closely. Remember, if the vehicle ahead is smaller than yours, it can most likely stop faster than you. One rule says you need at least one second for each 10 feet of vehicle length at speeds below 40 mph. At greater speeds, add 1 second for safety. For example, if you are driving a 40-foot truck, you should leave 4 seconds between you and the vehicle ahead. In a 60-foot rig, you'll need 6 seconds. Over 40 mph, you'd need 5 seconds for a 40-foot vehicle and 7 seconds for a 60-foot vehicle. To know how much space you have, wait until the vehicle ahead passes a shadow on the road, a pavement marking, or some other clear landmark. Then count off the seconds like this: "one thousand- and-one, one thousand-and-two" and so on, until you reach the same spot.

Examples:

- When driving a 40-foot vehicle at speeds under 40 mph, leave 4 seconds between you and the vehicle ahead. One second for each 10 feet of vehicle length = 1×4 or 4 seconds.
- When driving a 40-foot vehicle at speeds over 40 mph, leave 5 seconds between you and the vehicle ahead. One second for each 10 feet of vehicle length plus an additional second for safety: 1×4 = 4 plus an extra second for safety = 5 seconds.
- When driving a 60-foot vehicle at speeds under 40 mph, leave 6 seconds between you and the vehicle ahead. One second for each 10 feet of the vehicle length = 1×6 or 6 seconds.
- When driving a 60-foot vehicle at speeds over 40 mph, leave 7 seconds between you and the vehicle ahead. One second for each 10 feet of vehicle length plus an additional second for safety: 1×6 = 6 plus an extra second for safety = 7 seconds.

Remember that in inclement weather, these times increase greatly.

## SPACE BEHIND

You have no control in stop others from following you too closely, but these are things that can make it safer:

- Stay on the right side of your lane. Heavy vehicles are often tailgated when they can't keep up with the speed of traffic. This regularly occurs when you're going uphill. If a heavy load is slowing you down, stay in the right lane if you can. Going uphill, you should not pass another slow vehicle unless you can get around quickly and safely.
- Handling tailgaters safely: In a large vehicle, it's often hard to see whether a vehicle is close behind you.
- You may be tailgated:
  - When you are traveling slowly, drivers trapped behind slow vehicles often follow closely.
  - When weather conditions are less than optimal, many drivers will follow closely behind large vehicles (especially when there is poor visibility on the road).

- When being tailgated, do the following to reduce chances of a wreck:
  - Proceed with caution when changing speed or direction, and signal early.
  - Increase the distance between your vehicle and the one in front of you. This allows room for error and gives a tailgater space to pass you.
  - Do not increase your velocity. It is safer to be tailgated going slowly rather than quickly.
  - Refrain from attempting tricks such as flashing brake lights to ward off tailgaters.

## SPACE TO THE SIDES

Commercial vehicles take up most of their lane, so it is important to manage safely the little space you have. This is put into practice by staying centered in your lane to keep a safe clearance between you and others driving. The dangers of driving alongside others:

- Switching lanes suddenly can lead to the other driver turning into you
- Being blocked in when you need to change lane

Always shoot for obtaining a position away from heavy traffic. This sometimes cannot be avoided, and then you should give yourself the appropriate amount of distance so that the cars can see you and both have reaction time.

### POWERFUL WINDS

Robust winds make it difficult to stay centered in your lane. This issue occurs more with lighter vehicles and those exiting tunnels.

## SPACE OVERHEAD

Be sure you have overhead clearance to avoid the risk of collision

- Don't assume that heights posted at overpasses and bridges are accurate. Re-paving or packed snow is capable of reducing the clearance of the structure.
- Weight is a factor that affects the height of a vehicle. An empty load is taller than a full one; therefore, just because you can clear a structure with cargo, doesn't mean you can with an empty bed.
- When in doubt as to whether there is a safe amount of space to pass, go slowly or take a different route. Warnings are not always posted on low-bearing structures.
- Some roads have a tendency to tilt vehicles. This can lead to a problem clearing objects near the edge of the road such as signs, trees, or bridge supports. The solution is to navigate closer to the center of the road.
- It is a good safety procedure to get out and check for overhanging objects and other hazards before backing into an area. Things such as branches and electric wires can easily be overlooked from backing while inside the truck.

## SPACE BELOW

The space under the vehicle is compact when carrying cargo and usually forgotten about. This is an issue when traveling along a dirt road or unpacked yards due to the chances of getting hung up are increased. Draining channels can cause vehicles to drag and require special care when crossing; railroads can create the same problem when traveling across with a low underneath clearance. Don't take a chance on getting hung up halfway across.

## SPACE FOR REVOLVES

Wide rotating and off tracking can cause large vehicles to collide with others. When turning right:

- By turning slowly, you offer the increase of time to avoid an issue.
- If you are unable to complete a right turn without hitting another automobile, then swing as you make the turn as shown in the diagram. To prohibit others from passing you while mid-turn, keep the rear of the vehicle in close proximity to the curb.
- Do not steer to the left when attempting this turn. The driver behind you may think you are turning left and make an effort to pass you, thus cutting you off from the right lane.
- If it is necessary to cross into another lane, watch for oncoming traffic. Allow them room to pass or stop. Do not back up for traffic. You could hit the vehicle behind you.

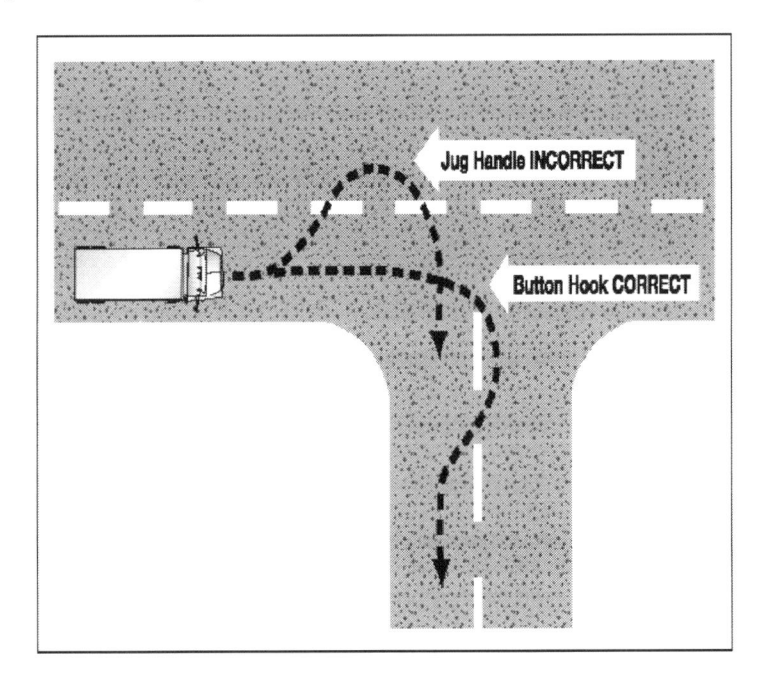

When turning left:

- Reach the middle of the intersection prior to beginning the pivot. Turning prematurely can lead to the collision with other vehicles due to off tracking.
- If there are two lanes, utilize the right side. Do not begin a left turn anywhere except the right lane. This is because you must swing right to complete the turn. You can see drivers on your left easier than those on your right.

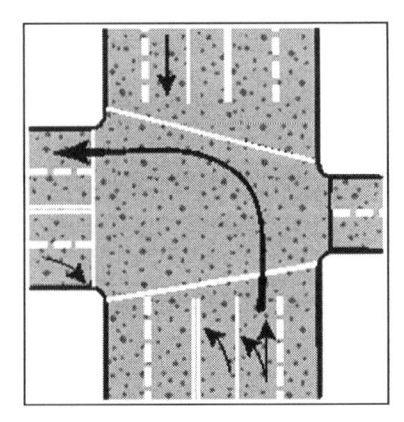

## Space to Cross or Enter Traffic

Be conscious of the size and weight of your vehicle when traveling in traffic

- A larger gap in traffic is required to enter with a pulling truck than a normal car. This is because of the slow acceleration and larger mass.
- Allow more room and adjust acceleration depending on how full your load is fully loaded.
- Before you begin across a road, make sure have safe passage to the desired location before traffic intersects.

## Controlling Speed

Driving at excessive speeds are a predominantly the causes of crashes and fatalities. Properly adjust speeds to better fit weather conditions, the road (such as hills and curves), visibility and traffic.

## Speed and Stopping

Three things make up the total stopping distance:

  Perception distance
  Reaction distance
+ Braking distance
  Total stopping distance

- Perception distance is the distance your vehicle travels from the instant your eyes recognize a threat to the moment your brain realizes it. This being said, certain mental and physical conditions can influence individuals' perception distances. This can also rely heavily on the visibility and the hazard itself. The average perception time of an alert driver is roughly 1¾ second. When traveling 55 mph covers 142 feet.
- The response distance is the interval in which you travel, in prime conditions, before having to physically apply the brakes for the oncoming hazard. An average driver has a response time between three-fourths and one second. At 55 mph this accounts for 61 feet traveled.
- Braking distance is the measure the vehicle will ideally travel while braking. For example, with good brake, traveling at 55 mph on dry pavement would take precisely 216 feet.
- The gross stopping range is the total minimum distance your vehicle has moved including perception, reaction, and braking distance until you have come to a complete stop. At speeds of 55 mph the vehicle would travel 419 feet.

Things to remember:

- When you double your speed, it takes four times as much distance to stop your vehicle, and your vehicle will have four times the destructive power in a crash.
- You cannot steer or brake a vehicle properly unless your tires have traction on the road. Traction is the friction created between your tires and the road itself. Always reduce your speed on wet and slippery roads.
- Wet roads are increasingly dangerous and can double your stopping distance. Reduce your speed by about 1/3 on a wet road. For example, slow down from 55 mph to 35 mph.
- On packed snow, reduce your speed by 1/2 or more.
- If the road is icy, reduce your speed to a crawl. Stop driving as soon as possible.
- An empty truck will require greater stopping distance. Empty vehicles have less traction due to their weight. The brakes are designed to control the maximum weight of the unit; therefore, the brakes lock up more readily when the trailer is empty or lightly loaded. This can cause skidding and loss of control.

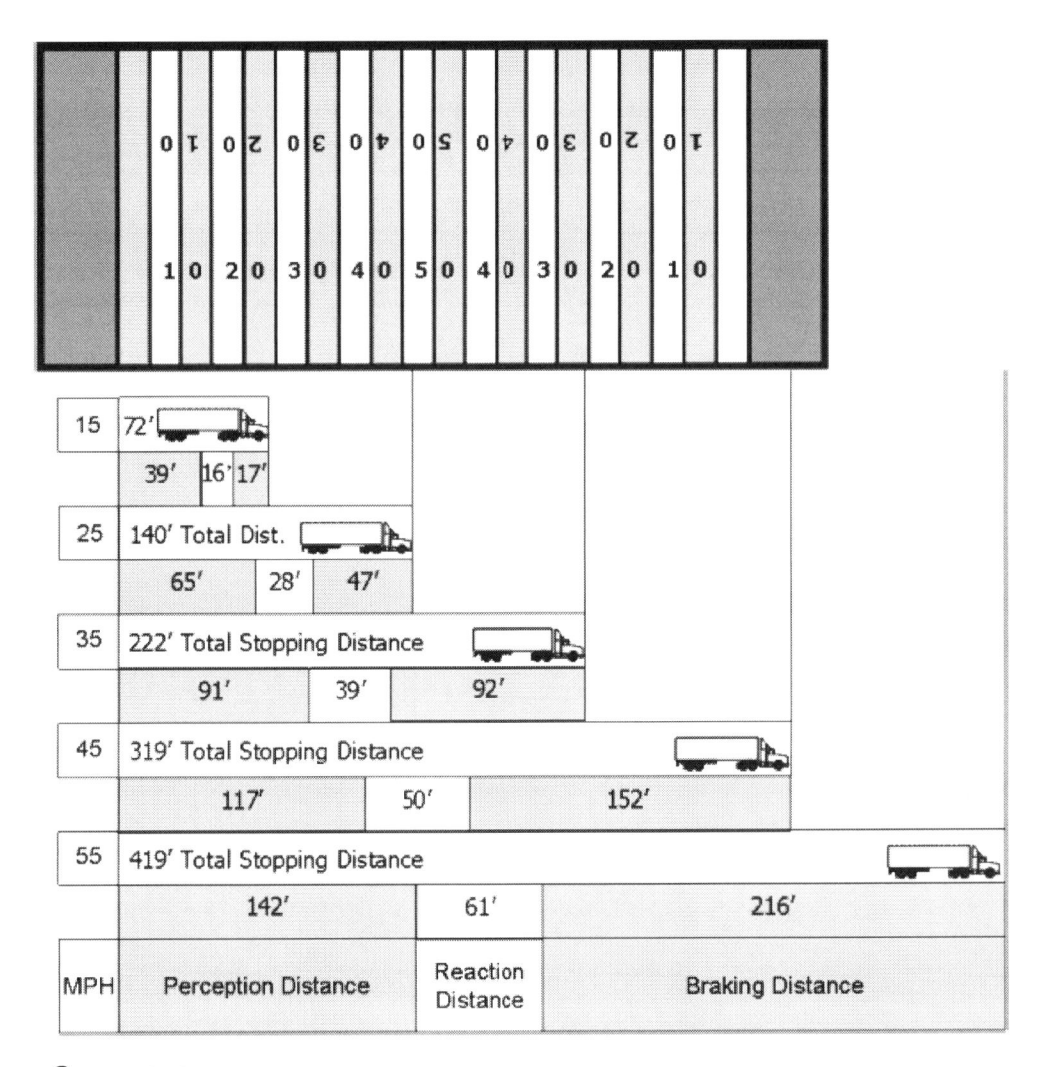

| MPH | Perception Distance | Reaction Distance | Braking Distance |
|---|---|---|---|
| 15 | \_ | \_ | 72' total, 39' / 16' / 17' |
| 25 | 65' | 28' | 47' (140' Total Dist.) |
| 35 | 91' | 39' | 92' (222' Total Stopping Distance) |
| 45 | 117' | 50' | 152' (319' Total Stopping Distance) |
| 55 | 142' | 61' | 216' (419' Total Stopping Distance) |

## SLIPPERY SURFACES

- Ice will remain on shady parts of the road after it has melted in other areas.
- When the temperature drops, bridges will ice over prior to the rest of the road. Be extra attentive when the temperature is near freezing.
- When beginning to melt, the ice becomes wet. Ice in this state is much more slippery than when it is dry.
- Black ice is when it is a thin enough layer to see the road through it creating the illusion that the pavement is wet. Be conscious of this in freezing temperatures.
- Check for ice on the road by reaching outside the window and feeling the mirror, antenna, or mirror support. If these are icy, then so is the road.
- Right when it starts to rain is when it is very dangerous to drive; the water mixes with the oil coating the road combining to form a very slippery substance. As the rain continues, the mixture gets washed off the roadway.

## GLIDING

In poor weather conditions, water or sludge gathers on the road, and can cause vehicles to hydroplane. It can be described as water skiing—the tires lose their ability to properly grip the road having no traction. This may make braking or steering uncontrollable. You can regain control by releasing the accelerator and pushing in the clutch. This will slow your vehicle and let the wheels turn freely. When hydroplaning, do not attempt to slow down by braking. If the drive wheels start to skid, push in the clutch to let them turn freely. It does not take a lot of water to cause hydroplaning. This can occur at speeds as low as 30 mph if there is a substantial amount of water present. Hydroplaning is more likely to occur if tire pressure is low, or the tread is worn. (The grooves in a tire carry away the water; if they aren't deep, they don't work well.) Road surfaces where water can collect can create conditions that cause a vehicle to hydroplane. Watch for clear reflections, tire splashes, and raindrops on the road. These are indications of standing water.

## SPEED AND CURVES

Drivers must adjust their speed for curves in the road. If you take a curve at high speeds, the tires could lose their traction, causing you to skid off the road, or keeping their grip sending the vehicle in a roll. Tests have shown that trucks with a high center of gravity can roll over at the posted speed limit for a curve. It is always best to slow to a safe speed when taking large curves. Don't ever exceed the posted speed limit for the curve; the posted safe speeds are meant for cars. Slow to a safe speed before you enter a curve. Braking in a curve is dangerous because it is easier to lock the wheels and skid across the road. Being in a gear that lets you accelerate slightly in the curve helps in maintaining control. When you must use low beams, make sure to slow down.

## SPEED AND DISTANCE AHEAD

Always be able to stop within the visible distance ahead; fog, rain, or other conditions may require that you slow down so that this can be possible. At night, high beams offer a greater range of sight than low beams.

## SPEED IN TRAFFIC

When operating in heavy traffic, it is advisable to match your speed with those of others. Vehicles traveling in the same direction seldom collide with one another. In many states, the speed limit varies up to 15 mph slower for large trucks and buses. Use extra caution when you change lanes or pass on these roadways. Drive at the speed of the traffic without going an illegal speed, and keep a safe following distance. It is an unnecessary risk to drive over the designated speed limit in hopes to save time. This increases the chances of a wreck with every car you pass and increases mental stress, which in turn leads to fatigue. Going with the flow of traffic is safer and easier.

## SPEED ON DOWNGRADES

Gravity will cause your vehicle to speed up when traveling downhill. Therefore, it is essential that you are driving at a safe speed when entering a downgrade. You must take into consideration:

- Combined weight of the cargo and vehicle
- Length of load
- Steepness of hill
- Quality of road
- Weather conditions

Do not exceed the legal speed limit and look warning signs indicating the length and steepness of the grade. You must use the braking effect of the engine as the principal way of controlling your speed on downgrades. The impact of braking on the engine is most notable when it is near the governed rpms and the transmission is in the lower gears. Shift your transmission to a low gear before starting down the grade and use the proper braking techniques.

## Work Zones

The number one cause of fatality in work zones on the roadway is speeding. Be aware of your speedometer and surroundings when going through road construction. Decrease your speed in the event of adverse weather or road conditions (even more so if the workers are on the roadway). Not only is this saving the lives of the workers, but remember that tickets for speeding in work zones are typically double that of a normal ticket. It pays to slow down.

## Braking

If someone suddenly pulls in front of you it is natural to brake, but be certain there is enough space and to apply them correctly.

### Controlled Braking

Apply the brakes without locking the wheels and maintaining command. Preform small steering movements while in this state. If you need to make a larger steering adjustment or if the wheels lock, then release the brakes. Re-apply the brakes at the earliest convenience. You never want to lose control while braking. It is important not to panic.

### Stab Braking

- Fully apply the brakes
- Release when the wheels lock
- Immediately after the wheels start rolling fully apply the brakes (It can take up to one second for the wheels to start rolling after you release the brakes. If you re-apply the brakes before the wheels start rolling the vehicle will not properly straighten out.)

Refrain from jamming on the brakes. Emergency braking does not mean slamming them as with all your strength. That would cause a lock up and a skid. If this occurs, you are unable to control the vehicle.

### Brake Failure

Brakes that are taken care of rarely falter. Hydraulics usually fail because:

- Loss of hydraulic pressure
- Failure on downgrades

Loss of hydraulic pressure: Lacking of the appropriate pressure in the system will lead to the brake pedal to feel spongy or to reach the floor. In this event, here is what you do:

- Downshifting or putting the vehicle into a lower gear will help to slow the vehicle.
- Pump the brakes; sometimes this will cause the pedal to generate enough hydraulic pressure to stop the vehicle.
- Use the parking brake. The parking brake is separate, so it will still properly function.
- Be aware of an escape route—an open field, side street, or escape ramp. Turning uphill is a good way to slow and stop the vehicle, but make sure the vehicle does not start rolling backward after you stop. Also putting the vehicle in a low gear, apply the parking brake, and rolling into an obstacle are all ways to stop it.

Brake failure on downgrades: Going slow enough and braking properly will almost always prevent brake failure on long downgrades. Once the brakes have failed, find something outside the truck to stop the movement. The best option for this is an escape ramp. If there is one available, there will be signs letting you know where each location is. Ramps can be found a few miles away from a downgrade. Every year, hundreds of drivers avoid injury by using escape ramps. Some escape ramps use soft gravel that resists the motion of the vehicle and brings it to a stop. Others turn uphill, using the hill to stop the vehicle and soft gravel to hold it in place. Any driver who loses brakes going downhill should use an escape ramp if it's available. If you don't use it, your chances of having a serious crash may be much greater. If a ramp is unavailable, the next best thing is a route such as an open field or a side road that flattens out or turns uphill. Make the move as soon as you know your brakes don't work. The longer you wait, the faster the vehicle will go, and the harder it will become to stop.

## TIRE FAILURE

Quickly recognizing you have a tire failure will give you more time to react. A few extra seconds to recall what it is you're supposed to do can be beneficial. The major signs of tire failure are:

- The loud commotion of a blowout is an easily recognizable sign. It can take a few seconds for your vehicle to react, and give the illusion that was another vehicle. Any time you hear a tire blow, it would be safest to assume it is yours and check.
- If the vehicle thumps or vibrates heavily, it may be a sign that one of the tires has gone flat. With a rear tire, that may be the only sign you get.
- If the steering feels heavy or lagging, it's probably a sign that one of the front tires has failed. Sometimes, failure of a rear tire will cause the vehicle to slide back and forth like a fishtail. However, dual rear tires usually prevent this.

Take action when a tire fails. These malfunctions jeopardize your vehicle. You must immediately:

- Grasp the steering wheel firmly. If a front tire fails, it can twist the steering wheel out of your hand. The only way to prevent this is to keep a firm grip on the steering wheel with both hands at all times.
- Keep off the brake. It's natural to want to halt in an emergency, but braking when a tire has failed could cause you to lose control. Unless you're about to run into something, stay off the brake until the vehicle has slowed down. Then brake very gently, pull off the road, and stop.
- After you've come to a stop, get out and check all the tires. Do this even if the vehicle seems to be handling right. If one of your dual tires goes out, the only way you may know it is by getting out and looking at it.

## STEERING TO AVOID CRASHING

- Stopping is not always the safest thing to do in an emergency. When you don't have enough room to pull over, you may have to steer away from what's ahead. Remember, you can almost always turn to avoid an obstacle faster than you can stop. (However, top-heavy loads and tractors with multiple trailers may flip over.)
- Keep both hands on the steering wheel. In order to turn quickly in case of an emergency, you must have a firm grip on the steering wheel with both hands. Therefore, it is best to maintain it throughout the trip.
- Do not apply the brakes while you are turning. This could cause your wheels to lock and spin you out of control.
- Do not turn any more than needed to clear whatever is in your way. The more sharply you turn, the chances of a skid or rollover increases.
- Be prepared to "counter-steer," (to turn the wheel back in the other direction) once you've passed whatever was blocking your path. Think of emergency steering and counter-steering as two parts of one driving action.

- If an oncoming driver has drifted into your lane move to your right. If that driver realizes what has happened, they will return to their own lane.
- You must be prepared for anything. If something is blocking your path, the best direction to steer will depend on the situation.

In some emergencies, you may have to drive off the road. It may be less risky than facing a collision with another vehicle. The majority of shoulders are strong enough to support the weight of a large vehicle and, therefore, offer an available escape route. Here are some guidelines, if you leave the road.

- If possible, avoid using the brakes until your speed has dropped to about 20 mph. Then brake very gently to avoid skidding on a loose surface.
- Maintain one set of wheels on the pavement to stay in control.
- If the shoulder is clear, stay on it until your vehicle has come to a stop. Signal and check your mirrors before pulling back onto the road.

## Merging on the Road

If you are forced to return to the road before you can stop, use the following procedure:

- Hold the wheel tightly and turn sharply to get back on the road safely.
- Don't try to gradually get back on the road. If you do, your tires might grab unexpectedly and you could lose control.
- When both front tires are on the paved surface, counter-steer immediately. The two turns should be made as a cohesive "steer-counter-steer" move.

## Skid Control and Recovery

A skid happens whenever the tires lose their grip on the road. Here are the four causes:

- Braking too hard and locking up the wheels, or over-braking, can lead to skids as well as when using the speed retarder when the road is slippery.
- Turning the wheels more sharply than the vehicle can turn.
- Over-acceleration. Supplying too much power to the drive wheels, causing them to spin.
- Most serious skids result from driving too fast for road conditions. Drivers who adjust their driving to conditions don't over-accelerate or have to over-brake/steer from too much speed.

## Drive-Wheel Skids

By far the most common skid is one in which the rear wheels lose traction through excessive braking or acceleration. Skids caused by acceleration usually happen on ice or snow. Taking your foot off the accelerator can easily stop them. (If it is very slippery, push the clutch in. Otherwise, the engine can keep the wheels from rolling freely and regaining traction.) Rear wheel braking skids occur when the rear drive wheels lock. Because locked wheels have less traction than rolling wheels, the rear wheels usually slide sideways in an attempt to "catch up" with the front wheels. In a bus or straight truck, the vehicle will slide sideways in a "spin out." With vehicles towing trailers, a drive-wheel skid can let the trailer push the towing vehicle sideways, causing a sudden jackknife.

# Hazardous Conditions

Driving becomes hazardous when visibility is reduced, or when the road surface is covered with rain, snow, or ice. Slow down and increase your distance gap.

## NIGHT DRIVING

You are at greater risk when you drive at night. Drivers can't see hazards as quickly as in daylight, so they have less time to respond. Drivers caught by surprise are unequipped to manage a crash. The problems of night driving involve the driver, the roadway, and the vehicle.

### DRIVER

People can't see as sharply at night or in dim light. Also, their eyes need time to adjust to seeing in dim light. Most people have noticed this when walking into a dark movie theater.

- Drivers can be blinded for a short time by bright light. It takes time to recover from this blindness. Older drivers are especially bothered by glare. Most people have been temporarily blinded by camera flash units or by the high beams of an oncoming vehicle. It can take several seconds to recover from a glare, and two seconds of glare blindness can be dangerous. A vehicle going 55 mph will travel more than half the distance of a football field during that time. Don't look directly at bright lights when driving. Look at the right side of the road. Watch the sidelines when someone coming toward you has very bright lights on.
- Fatigue (being tired) and lack of alertness are bigger problems at night. The body's need for sleep is beyond a person's control. Most people are less alert at night, especially after midnight. This is particularly true if you have been driving for an extended period of time. Drivers may not see hazards as soon, or react as quickly, so the probability of a crash is greater.
- If you are sleepy, the only safe cure is to get off the road and get some sleep. If you don't, you risk your life and the lives of others.

### ROADWAY

- Poor lighting. In the daytime there is usually enough light to see well. This is not true at night. Some areas may have bright street lights, but many areas will have poor lighting. On most roads you will probably have to depend entirely on your headlights. Less light means you will not be able to see hazards as well as in daytime. Road users who do not have lights are hard to see. There are many accidents at night involving pedestrians, joggers, bicyclists, and animals.
- Even when there are lights, the road scene can be confusing. Traffic signals and hazards can be hard to see against a background of signs, shop windows, and other lights. Drive slower when lighting is poor or confusing. Drive slowly enough to be sure you can stop in the distance you can see ahead.
- Drunk drivers and drivers under the influence of drugs are a hazard to themselves and to you. Be especially alert around the closing times for bars and taverns. Watch for drivers who have trouble staying in their lane or maintaining speed, who stop without reason, or show other signs of being under the influence of alcohol or drugs.

## Vehicle

At night, you must depend a lot on your headlights functioning to see and be seen by other motorists. Your sight is still limited at night, even with the help of your headlights. You need to make necessary adjustments for these limitations.

- Make sure you aren't going faster than it would take to stop within the distance that you can see ahead of you. With your low beams, you can see ahead about 250 feet. With your high beams, you can see ahead between 300 and 500 feet. These are approximations of course. It will vary with each driver. You should make sure you can stop between the approximate distances by adjusting your speed accordingly. This will also vary by the size of the load you are carrying and road conditions. Take everything into account when driving at night.
- Make sure that your headlights are clean and adjusted properly. Dirty headlights do not provide the same amount of light that clean ones do. Dirty headlights defeat their purpose. It makes it much harder for you to see and for others to see you. Proper headlight maintenance is very important.
- Be sure that all lights and reflectors are clean and working so that other drivers can see you. A thorough truck wash should keep you good to go for a while. You just have to continue to monitor everything to stay safe. Clean windows and lights are very important when it comes to driving in any condition. The lights you want to check include:
    - Headlights (high and low beams)
    - Tail lights
    - Turn signals
    - Brake lights
    - Marker lights
    - Clearance lights
    - Identification lights

## Fog

Fog reflects light and can reflect your own headlights back into your eyes. Use only your low beams. Look for road edge markings to guide you. Even light fog reduces your ability to see and judge distances. If possible, pull off the road and wait until the fog has lifted. If you must drive, be sure to:

- Obey all fog-related warning signs
- Reduce your speed
- Turn on all your lights (except high beams)
- Be prepared for sudden stops

## Cold Weather Driving
### Vehicle Checks

While performing your pre-trip inspection, you will want to pay close attention to a list of things. First, be sure that the following systems are working properly and that you are confident you know how to use them before operating the vehicle.

- Defrosting and heating equipment: Make sure the defrosters work. They are needed for safe driving. Make sure the heater is working, and that you know how to operate it. If you use other heaters and expect to need them (e.g., mirror heaters, battery box heaters, fuel tank heaters), check their operation.
- Make sure the lights and reflectors are clean. Lights and reflectors are especially important during bad weather. Check from time to time during bad weather to make sure they are clean and working properly.
- Remove any ice, snow, etc., from the windshield, windows, and mirrors before starting. Use a windshield scraper, snow brush, and windshield defroster as necessary. Hand Holds, Steps, and Deck Plates. Remove all ice and snow from hand holds, steps, and deck plates. This will reduce the danger of slipping.
- Remove ice from the radiator shutters. Make sure the winter front is not closed too tightly. If the shutters freeze shut or the winter front is closed too much, the engine may overheat and stop.
- Exhaust system leaks are especially dangerous when cab ventilation may be poor (windows rolled up, etc.). Loose connections could permit poisonous carbon monoxide to leak into your vehicle. Carbon monoxide gas will cause you to be sleepy. In large enough amounts it can kill you. Check the exhaust system for loose parts and for sounds and signs of leaks.
- Make sure the cooling system is full and there is enough antifreeze in the system to protect against freezing. This can be checked with a special coolant tester.
- Make sure the windshield wiper blades are in good condition. Make sure the wiper blades press against the window hard enough to wipe the windshield clean, otherwise they may not sweep off snow properly. Make sure the windshield washer works and there is washing fluid in the washer reservoir.
- Make sure you have enough tread on your tires. The drive tires must provide traction to push the rig over wet pavement and through snow. The steering tires must have traction to steer the vehicle. Enough tread is especially important in winter conditions. You must have at least 4/32-inch tread depth in every major groove on front tires and at least 2/32 inch on other tires. More would be better. Use a gauge to determine if you have enough tread for safe driving.

- Tire chains: You may find yourself in conditions where you can't drive without chains, even to get to a place of safety. Carry the right number of chains and extra cross-links. Make sure they will fit your drive tires. Check the chains for broken hooks, worn or broken cross-links, and bent or broken side chains. Learn how to put the chains on before you need to do it in snow and ice.

## DRIVING TIPS

- Drive slowly and smoothly on slippery roads. If it is very slippery, you shouldn't drive at all. Stop at the first safe place.
- Adjust turning and braking to conditions. Make turns as gently as possible. Do not brake any harder than necessary, and don't use the engine brake or speed retarder. (They can cause the driving wheels to skid on slippery surfaces.)
- Adjust speed to conditions. Don't pass slower vehicles unless necessary. Go slowly and watch far enough ahead to keep a steady speed. Avoid having to slow down and speed up. Take curves at slower speeds and don't brake while in curves. Be aware that as the temperature rises to the point where ice begins to melt, the road becomes even more slippery. Slow down more.
- Adjust space to conditions. Don't drive alongside other vehicles. Keep a longer following distance. When you see a traffic jam ahead, slow down or stop to wait for it to clear. Try hard to anticipate stops early and slow down gradually. Watch for snowplows, as well as salt and sand trucks, and give them plenty of room.

## WET BRAKES

When driving in heavy rain or deep standing water, your brakes will get wet. Water in the brakes can cause the brakes to be weak, to apply unevenly, or to grab. This can cause lack of braking power, wheel lockups, pulling to one side or the other, and jackknife if you pull a trailer. Avoid driving through deep puddles or flowing water if possible. If not, you should:

- Slow down and place transmission in a low gear.
- Gently put on the brakes. This presses linings against brake drums or discs and keeps mud, silt, sand, and water from getting in.
- Increase engine rpm and cross the water while keeping light pressure on the brakes.
- When out of the water, maintain light pressure on the brakes for a short distance to heat them up and dry them out.
- Make a test stop when safe to do so. Check behind to make sure no one is following, then apply the brakes to be sure they work well. If not, dry them out further as described above. (CAUTION: Do not apply too much brake pressure and accelerator at the same time, or you can overheat brake drums and linings.)

## Hot Weather Driving
### Vehicle Checks
Do a normal pre-trip inspection, but pay special attention to the following items.

- Tires: Check the tire mounting and air pressure. Inspect the tires every two hours or every 100 miles when driving in very hot weather. Air pressure increases with temperature. Do not let air out or the pressure will be too low when the tires cool off. If a tire is too hot to touch, remain stopped until the tire cools off. Otherwise, the tire may blow out or catch fire.
- Engine oil: The engine oil helps keep the engine cool, as well as lubricating it. Make sure there is enough engine oil. If you have an oil temperature gauge, make sure the temperature is within the proper range while you are driving.
- Engine coolant: Before starting out, make sure the engine cooling system has enough water and antifreeze according to the engine manufacturer's directions. (Antifreeze helps the engine under hot conditions as well as cold conditions.) When driving, check the water temperature or coolant temperature gauge from time to time. Make sure that it remains in the normal range. If the gauge goes above the highest safe temperature, there may be something wrong that could lead to engine failure and possibly fire. Stop driving as soon as safely possible and try to find out what is wrong. Some vehicles have sight glasses, see-through coolant overflow containers, or coolant recovery containers. These permit you to check the coolant level while the engine is hot. If the container is not part of the pressurized system, the cap can be safely removed and coolant added even when the engine is at operating temperature. Never remove the radiator cap or any part of the pressurized system until the system has cooled. Steam and boiling water can spray under pressure and cause severe burns. If you can touch the radiator cap with your bare hand, it is probably cool enough to open. If coolant has to be added to a system without a recovery tank or overflow tank, follow these steps:
    - Shut engine off.
    - Wait until engine has cooled.
    - Protect hands (use gloves or a thick cloth).
    - Turn radiator cap slowly to the first stop, which releases the pressure seal.
    - Step back while pressure is released from cooling system.
    - When all pressure has been released, press down on the cap and turn it further to remove it.
    - Visually check level of coolant and add more coolant if necessary.
    - Replace cap and turn all the way to the closed position.
- Engine belts: Learn how to check v-belt tightness on your vehicle by pressing on the belts. Loose belts will not turn the water pump and/or fan properly. This will result in overheating. Also, check belts for cracking or other signs of wear.
- Hoses: Make sure coolant hoses are in good condition. A broken hose while driving can lead to engine failure and even fire.

### Driving Tips
Watch for bleeding tar. Tar in the road pavement frequently rises to the surface in very hot weather. Spots where tar "bleeds" to the surface are very slippery. Go slowly enough to prevent overheating. High speeds create more heat for tires and the engine. In desert conditions the heat may build up to the point where it is dangerous. The heat will increase chances of tire failure or even fire, and engine failure.

## Mountain Driving

In mountain driving, gravity plays a major role. On any upgrade, gravity slows you down. The steeper the grade, the longer the grade, and/or the heavier the load--the more you will have to use lower gears to climb hills or mountains. In coming down long, steep downgrades, gravity causes the speed of your vehicle to increase. You must select an appropriate safe speed, then use a low gear, and proper braking techniques. You should plan ahead and obtain information about any long, steep grades along your planned route of travel. If possible, talk to other drivers who are familiar with the grades to find out what speeds are safe. You must go slowly enough so your brakes can hold you back without getting too hot. If the brakes become too hot, they may start to "fade." This means you have to apply them harder and harder to get the same stopping power. If you continue to use the brakes hard, they can keep fading until you cannot slow down or stop at all.

## Safe Speed

When selecting a speed for your vehicle, you must consider all of these factors:

- Total weight of the vehicle and cargo
- Length of the grade
- Steepness of the grade
- Road conditions
- Weather

Essentials for controlling your speed include:

- If a speed limit is posted, or there is a sign indicating "Maximum Safe Speed," never exceed the speed shown. Also, look for and heed warning signs indicating the length and steepness of the grade.
- You must use the braking effect of the engine as the principal way of controlling your speed. The braking effect of the engine is greatest when it is near the governed RPMs and the transmission is in the lower gears.
- Save your brakes so you will be able to slow or stop as required by road and traffic conditions.
- Shift the transmission to a low gear before starting down a grade. Do not try to downshift after your speed has already built up. You will not be able to shift into a lower gear. You may not even be able to get back into any gear and all engine braking effect will be lost. Forcing an automatic transmission into a lower gear at high speed could damage the transmission and also lead to loss of all engine braking effect.
- Use the proper braking technique. Use your brakes on a long downgrade plus the braking power of your engine. When your vehicle is in the proper low gear, use this braking technique.
- Know where the escape ramps are located on your route. Escape ramps have been built on many steep downgrades. They are made to stop runaway vehicles without injuring drivers and passengers. Escape ramps use a long bed of loose soft material to slow runaway vehicles. Use them if you lose your brakes.

## Railroad Crossing

At many highway-rail grade crossings, the crossbuck sign has flashing red lights and bells. When the lights begin to flash be sure to stop, because a train is approaching. You are required to yield the right-of-way to the train. If there is more than one track, make sure all tracks are clear before crossing. Many railroad-highway crossings also have gates with flashing red lights and bells. Stop when the lights begin to flash and before the gate lowers across the road lane. Remain stopped until the gates go up and the lights have stopped flashing. Proceed when it is safe. Never attempt to race a train to a crossing. It is extremely difficult to judge the speed of an approaching train.

- Speed must be reduced in accordance with your ability to see approaching trains in any direction, and speed must be held to a point which will permit you to stop short of the tracks in case a stop is necessary.
- Because of noise inside your vehicle, you cannot expect to hear the train horn until the train is dangerously close to the crossing.
- You should not rely solely upon the presence of warning signals, gates, or flagmen to warn of the approach of trains.
- Double tracks require a double check.
- Remember that a train on one track may hide a train on the other track. Look both ways before crossing.
- Vehicles that have low ground clearance, such as drop frame trailers and car carriers can cause your vehicle to hang up on railroad crossings with steep approaches. If you get hung up on a railroad crossing, call 911 immediately so that the scheduled trains can be notified to stop.
- Be sure you can get all the way across the tracks before you begin to cross.
- Do not shift gears when crossing railroad tracks.
- Fully stop when:
    o The nature of the cargo makes a stop mandatory under state or federal regulations.
    o Such a stop is otherwise required by law.
- When stopping be sure to:
    o Check for traffic behind you while stopping gradually. Use a pullout lane, if available.
    o Turn on your four-way emergency flashers.

## EQUIPMENT FAILURES
### BRAKE FAILURES
Brakes kept in good condition rarely fail. Most hydraulic brake failures occur for one of two reasons:

- Loss of hydraulic pressure
- Brake fade on long hills

When the system won't build up pressure, the brake pedal will feel spongy or go to the floor. Here are some things you can do:

- Downshift. Putting the vehicle into a lower gear will help to slow the vehicle.
- Pump the brakes. Sometimes pumping the brake pedal will generate enough hydraulic pressure to stop the vehicle.

### AIRBRAKE FADING OR FAILURE
Excessive use of the service brakes results in overheating and leads to brake fade. Brake fade results from excessive heat causing chemical changes in the brake lining, which reduce friction, and also causing expansion of the brake drums. As the overheated drums expand, the brake shoes and linings have to move farther to contact the drums, and the force of this contact is reduced. Continued overuse may increase brake fade until the vehicle cannot be slowed down or stopped. Brake fade is also affected by adjustment. To safely control a vehicle, every brake must do its share of the work. Brakes out of adjustment will stop doing their share before those that are in

adjustment. The other brakes can then overheat and fade, and there will not be enough braking available to control the vehicle(s). Brakes can get out of adjustment quickly, especially when they are hot. Therefore, check brake adjustment often.

## TIRE FAILURE

The sooner that you realize that a tire has failed, the more time you will have to react to the situation. The recognizable signs of tire failure are:

- Sound. You may hear a loud bang that often accompanies a blowout. However, you may mistake the noise for another vehicle as yours will not have an immediate effect on your driving. It is best to always assume it was one of yours and to use your mirrors to check.
- Vibration. If your vehicle vibrates, you may have a tire failure. With a rear tire, this may be the only sign you get as tandem wheels often compensate for the failed tire.
- Feel. If it becomes harder than usual to control your steering, one of the front tires has probably failed.

If a tire fails, take the following steps:

- Maintain a solid grip on the steering wheel. If a front tire fails, it can cause the wheel to twist out of your hands. Keep both hands on the wheel at all times.
- Stay off the brakes. If you brake during a tire failure, it could cause you to lose control of the vehicle. Unless it is necessary for the safety of you or fellow drivers, stay off the brake until the vehicle has slowed down on its own (engine brakes can help this). Then, brake gently and pull off the road.
- Check the tires even if the vehicle seems to be handling normally. Many times, you won't know that a dual tire is flat unless you look at it.

## CRASHES

As a professional driver, if you are in a crash and not seriously hurt; you need to take three steps to prevent further damage or injury to yourself or others.

- Protect the scene (keep people away):
    o Protect the area to prevent another crash. This is the first thing you need to do.
    o If your vehicle is involved in the crash, try to move it out of the roadway. This will help prevent additional crashes.
    o If you are stopping to help at the scene of a crash, park far away from the crash. The area around the crash will be needed by emergency vehicles.
    o Put on your flashers.
    o Set out reflective triangles to warn other traffic. Make sure that other drivers will see them in time to avoid another crash by following the same distance rules as if you were stalled on the side of the road.
- Notify the authorities as soon as possible (inform them of your cargo if it is hazardous):
    o If you have a CB radio or cell phone, put out a call over the emergency channel or dial 911 before leaving your vehicle.
    o If you have no way to contact authorities, wait until the crash scene has been protected, then call or send someone to call the police.
    o Remember to determine where you are before contacting anyone so you can provide an accurate location of the crash.

- Care for the injured (never move them unless they are able to move themselves):
    - If a qualified person is helping the injured, stay out of their way unless you are asked to assist. Otherwise, make every effort to help anyone who could be injured.
    - Don't move a severely injured person unless there is a danger of fire or passing traffic makes it necessary
    - Stop heavy bleeding by applying direct pressure to the wound.
    - Keep the injured person warm.

## FIRES

You might have to control minor truck fires on the road. However, unless you have the training and equipment to do so safely, don't fight hazardous materials fires. Dealing with hazardous materials fires requires special training and protective gear. When you discover a fire, call for help. You may use the fire extinguisher to keep minor truck fires from spreading to cargo before firefighters arrive. Feel trailer doors to see if they are hot before opening them. If hot, you may have a cargo fire and should not open the doors. Opening doors lets air in and may make the fire flare up. Without air, many fires only smolder until firemen arrive, doing less damage. If your cargo is already on fire, it is not safe to fight the fire. Keep the shipping papers with you to give to emergency personnel as soon as they arrive. Warn other people of the danger and keep them away. If you discover a cargo leak, identify the hazardous materials leaking by using shipping papers, labels, or package location.

Do not touch any leaking material--many people injure themselves by touching hazardous materials. Do not try to identify the material or find the source of a leak by smell. Toxic gases can destroy your sense of smell and can injure or kill you even if they don't smell. Never eat, drink, or smoke around a leak or spill. If hazardous materials are spilling from your vehicle, do not move it any more than safety requires. You may move off the road and away from places where people gather, if doing so serves safety. Only move your vehicle if you can do so without danger to yourself or others.

## HAZARDOUS MATERIALS
### RULES FOR ALL COMMERCIAL DRIVERS

Hazardous materials are products that pose a risk to health, safety, and property during transportation. The term often is shortened to HAZMAT, which you may see on road signs, or to HM in government regulations. Hazardous materials include explosives, various types of gas, solids, flammable and combustible liquids, and other materials. Because of the risks involved and the potential consequences these risks impose, all levels of government regulate the handling of hazardous materials. The Hazardous Materials Regulations (HMR) is found in parts 100–185 of title 49 of the Code of Federal Regulations. The common reference for these regulations is 49 CFR 100–185. The table below lists 9 hazard classes:

| Class | Division | Name of Class or Division | Example |
|---|---|---|---|
| 1 | 1.1 | Explosives (Mass Detonations) | Dynamite |
|   | 1.2 | Projection Hazards | Ammunition for Cannons |
|   | 1.3 | Mass Fire Hazards | Display Fireworks |
|   | 1.4 | Minor Hazards | Small Arms Ammunition |
|   | 1.5 | Very Insensitive | Blasting Agents |
|   | 1.6 | Extremely Insensitive | Explosive Devices |
| 2 | 2.1 | Flammable Gases | Propane |
|   | 2.2 | Non-Flammable Gases | Helium |
|   | 2.3 | Poisonous/Toxic Gases | Fluorine, Compressed |

| Class | Division | Name of Class or Division | Example |
|---|---|---|---|
| 3 | --- | Combustible and Flammable Liquids | Gasoline, Diesel Fuel, Fuel Oil |
| 4 | 4.1 | Flammable Solids | Ammonium Picrate, Wetted White |
|   | 4.2 | Spontaneous Combustible | Phosphorus |
|   | 4.3 | Dangerous When Wet | Sodium |
| 5 | 5.1 | Oxidizers | Ammonium Nitrate |
|   | 5.2 | Organic Peroxides | Methyl Ethyl Ketone Peroxide |
| 6 | 6.1 | Poison (Toxic Material) | Potassium Cyanide |
|   | 6.2 | Infectious Substances | Anthrax Virus |
| 7 | --- | Radioactive | Uranium |
| 8 | --- | Corrosives | Battery Fluid |
| 9 | --- | Miscellaneous Hazardous Materials | Polychlorinated Biphenyls (PCB) |

You must follow the rules for transporting hazardous materials. These rules ensure safe drivers and equipment. They also tell you how to contain the product and how to communicate its risk. The regulations require vehicles transporting certain types or quantities of hazardous materials to display diamond-shaped, square on point, warning signs called placards. You must have a commercial driver license (CDL) with a hazardous materials endorsement before you drive any size vehicle that is used to transport hazardous material as defined in 49 CFR 383.5. You must pass a written test about the regulations and requirements to get this endorsement.

## CONTAINMENT RULES

Transporting hazardous materials can be risky. The regulations are intended to protect you, those around you, and the environment. They tell shippers how to package the materials safely and drivers how to load, transport, and unload the material. These are called "containment rules."

## COMMUNICATING THE RISK

To communicate the risk, shippers must warn drivers and others about the material's hazards. The regulations require shippers to put hazard warning labels on packages, provide proper shipping papers, emergency response information, and placards. These steps communicate the hazard to the shipper, the carrier, and the driver. Placards are 10 ¾ inches on each side and are diamond-shaped. Cargo tanks and other bulk packaging display the I.D. number of their contents on placards or orange panels. A placarded vehicle must have at least 4 identical placards. They are placed on the front, rear and both sides of the vehicle. Not all vehicles that carry hazardous materials need placards. The regulations about placards are given in Section 9 of this driver's manual. You can drive a vehicle carrying hazardous materials if it does not require placards. If it requires placards, you may not drive it unless you have a hazardous material endorsement on your commercial driver's license.

## ROLES IN HAZARDOUS MATERIAL TRANSPORTATION

Shipper:

- Sends products from one place to another by truck, rail, vessel, or airplane
- Uses the hazardous materials regulations to determine the product's:
  - Proper shipping name
  - Hazard class
  - Identification number
  - Packing group
  - Correct packaging
  - Correct label and markings
  - Correct placards
- Must package, mark, and label the materials; prepare shipping papers; provide emergency response information; and supply placards
- Must certify on the shipping paper that the shipment has been prepared according to the rules (unless you are pulling cargo tanks supplied by you or your employer)

Carrier:

- Takes the shipment from the shipper to its destination
- Prior to transportation, checks that the shipper correctly described, marked, labeled, and otherwise prepared the shipment for transportation
- Refuses improper shipments
- Reports accidents and incidents involving hazardous materials to the proper agencies

Driver:

- Makes sure the shipper has identified, marked, and properly labeled hazardous materials
- Refuses leaking packages and shipments
- Placards vehicle when loading, if required
- Safely transports the shipment without delay
- Follows all special rules about transporting hazardous materials
- Keeps hazardous material shipping papers and emergency response information in the proper place

# General Knowledge Practice Test #1

Want to take this practice test in an online interactive format? Check out the bonus page, which includes interactive practice questions and much more: **http://www.mometrix.com/bonus948/cdlspteall**

**1. Which of the following is a highly recommended but not required piece of emergency equipment?**
 a. Fire extinguisher
 b. Accident detail package
 c. Three reflective triangles and/or road flares

**2. In the case of tire failure, what usually prevents the vehicle from sliding back and forth like a fishtail?**
 a. Dual rear tires
 b. Hydraulic brakes
 c. Steering wheel control

**3. What will lead to the brake pedal feeling spongy or reaching the floor?**
 a. An engaged parking brake
 b. Lack of hydraulic pressure
 c. Downshifting or putting the vehicle into a lower gear

**4. What is the correct way to stop a front wheel skid?**
 a. Turn harder and brake harder.
 b. Stop turning and brake harder.
 c. Let the vehicle slow down. Stop turning and stop braking so hard.

**5. When you double your speed, it takes:**
 a. Two times as much distance to stop
 b. Four times as much distance to stop
 c. Six times as much distance to stop

**6. What is the interval in which you travel, in prime conditions, before physically applying the brakes for an oncoming hazard?**
 a. Braking distance
 b. Reaction distance
 c. Perception distance

**7. What is meant by double clutching?**
 a. Pushing down on the clutch pedal four times each time you shift gears.
 b. Shifting without using the clutch.
 c. Release the accelerator, push down on the clutch pedal and shift to neutral; then release the clutch pedal; then let the engine and gears slow down to the RPMs required for the next gear; then push in the clutch pedal and shift to the higher gear.

**8. When stab braking, at what point should you release the brakes?**
   a. Release when the wheels lock.
   b. Release every ten seconds to prevent overheating.
   c. Release when you start to skid.

**9. Hydroplaning can occur at speeds as low as:**
   a. 10 mph
   b. 20 mph
   c. 30 mph

**10. What is in hazard class 3, as defined by 49 CFR 100–185?**
   a. Flammable, nonflammable, and poisonous gases
   b. Combustible and flammable liquids
   c. Flammable solids

**11. What is something that you must do when using a fire extinguisher to fight a fire?**
   a. Stay downwind.
   b. Aim at the base of the fire.
   c. Aim at the top of the fire.

**12. When driving at night, drivers can be blinded for a short time by:**
   a. Bright light
   b. Drunk drivers
   c. Poor or confusing lighting

**13. What is the minimum tire tread requirement for all non-front tires?**
   a. $\frac{2}{32}$ inch
   b. $\frac{3}{32}$ inch
   c. $\frac{4}{32}$ inch

**14. Which of the following is true of hazardous-material fires?**
   a. Dealing with hazardous-material fires requires special training and protective gear.
   b. You should fight hazardous-material fires if no one else is around.
   c. If you suspect a cargo fire, you should open all the doors.

**15. In checking tires what are some problems that you should look for?**
   a. Too much or too little specification information on the sidewalls.
   b. Bad wear, cuts or other damage, tread separation, cut or cracked valve stems. Dual tires that come in contact, mismatched sizes, radial and bias-ply tires used together.
   c. Regrooved, recapped, or retreaded tires on the drive wheels.

**16. The function of the suspension system is:**
   a. To protect the radius (torque) rod, and reduce damage from road hazards
   b. To sustain the vehicle and its load, and keep the axles in place
   c. To help the vehicle be more stable while turning, and sustain momentum through curves

**17. When is it safe to race a train to a crossing?**
   a. Only when it's an open field and you can plainly see the train
   b. When the train is slow
   c. Never

**18. Who is responsible for preparing shipping papers, providing emergency response information, and supplying placards for hazardous material transportation?**
   a. Shipper
   b. Carrier
   c. Driver

**19. What is the minimum distance between tie downs to prevent shifting of cargo?**
   a. Every six feet.
   b. Every ten feet.
   c. Every eighteen feet.

**20. What is a problem that you can have when using your mirrors?**
   a. They never remain in the positions you have placed them.
   b. They are of no help when you are changing lanes.
   c. There are blind spots that your mirrors cannot show you.

**21. Deadly fumes can be released into the cab or roomette when damage is caused to the:**
   a. Fuel system
   b. Suspension system
   c. Exhaust system

**22. What is the proper method of swinging to make a right turn?**
   a. Button hook
   b. Jug handle
   c. Off tracking

**23. The failure of a front tire can:**
   a. Cause you to counter-steer
   b. Twist the steering wheel out of your hand
   c. Cause fishtailing

**24. What are some items that you must check especially before driving in winter weather?**
   a. CB Radio Antenna
   b. Coolant level, windshield washer antifreeze.
   c. AM-FM Radio

**25. Why do empty trucks usually require greater stopping distance than loaded trucks?**
   a. An empty truck has less traction.
   b. An empty truck has more forward momentum.
   c. An empty truck has less brakes.

**26. You can check for proper tire pressure by:**
   a. Noting mismatched tire sizes
   b. Depressing the tire with your hand
   c. Hitting your tires with a mallet

**27. When should you downshift for a curve?**
   a. Slow down to a safe speed and downshift to the proper gear before entering the curve.
   b. Slow down to a safe speed and downshift to the proper gear upon entering the curve.
   c. Slow down to a safe speed and downshift after entering the curve.

**28. Tar in the road pavement frequently rises to the surface in:**
   a. Very hot weather
   b. Mountainous terrain
   c. The night

**29. What are the three elements that make up the total stopping distance?**
   a. Speed, tire, road condition
   b. Perception, reaction, braking
   c. Control, space, momentum

**30. When you stop on the side of the road, which of the following is most likely to save your life?**
   a. Turn on your four-way emergency flashers.
   b. Place reflective triangles or flares within 10 minutes of stopping.
   c. When putting out triangles, hold them between yourself and the oncoming traffic.

**31. Accelerating, steering, shifting gears, backing, braking, and constantly checking your mirrors are all skills that you will need to understand extremely well, starting when?**
   a. Before operating your vehicle
   b. During the process of operating your vehicle
   c. After a few years of experience operating your vehicle

**32. What is the average perception time of an alert driver?**
   a. Roughly 1 second
   b. Roughly $1\frac{3}{4}$ seconds
   c. Roughly $2\frac{3}{4}$ seconds

**33. Which of the following is NOT advisable when steering to avoid a crash?**
   a. Being prepared to counter-steer
   b. Keeping both hands on the steering wheel
   c. Being sure to turn the maximum distance possible to safely clear whatever is in your way

**34. Which of the following is NOT true about crossing railroad tracks?**
   a. You cannot expect to hear the train horn until the train is close to the crossing.
   b. Double tracks require a double check.
   c. You should shift gears when crossing railroad tracks.

**35. How do you safely manage the little space you have within a driving lane?**
   a. Hug the side with the least traffic.
   b. Stay centered in your lane.
   c. Switch lanes often to maximize your space.

**36. Explosives are in what hazard class, as defined by the Hazardous Materials Regulations (HMR) found in parts 100–185 of title 49 of the Code of Federal Regulations?**
   a. Class 1
   b. Class 2
   c. Class 3

**37. What is true about downshifting before you reach a long downhill grade?**
   a. It helps prevent the brakes from overheating and losing their braking power.
   b. It puts an extra burden on the brake system.
   c. Starting on a downhill grade in low gear increases the chance of the truck picking up speed and going out of control.

**38. What can cause brakes to be weak, to apply unevenly, and to grab?**
   a. Applying too much brake pressure and accelerator at the same time
   b. Transmission in the lower gears
   c. Water in the brakes

**39. Powerful winds are more effective against:**
   a. Lighter vehicles
   b. Heavy vehicles
   c. Those entering tunnels

**40. Which of the following is NOT a characteristic of safe signaling and good communication with other drivers?**
   a. Use the low beams; high beams can irritate people in both daytime and nighttime.
   b. Use your horn frequently so that others stay aware of your presence.
   c. Whenever you are about to pass a vehicle, pedestrian, or cyclist, assume they don't see you.

**41. With your low beams on at night, about how far ahead can you see?**
   a. 250 feet
   b. 500 feet
   c. 750 feet

**42. You wish to turn right from a two-lane, two-way street to another. Your vehicle is so long that you must swing wide to make the turn. How should the turn be made?**
   a. Start turning wide before you enter the turn.
   b. You may allow your rear trailer wheels to climb over the curb.
   c. Turn wide as you complete the turn.

**43. What is the best way to use the brake pedal on a steep downhill grade?**
   a. Use a heavy pressure repeatedly.
   b. Avoid using the brakes.
   c. Shift to a lower gear before starting downgrade and use a light, steady pressure on the brake pedal.

**44. After you start the engine, air pressure should build from 50 to 90 psi within:**
   a. 3 minutes
   b. 6 minutes
   c. 10 minutes

**45. As a professional driver, if you are in a crash and not seriously hurt, you need to take three steps to prevent further damage or injury to yourself or others. Which of the following is NOT one of those three steps?**
   a. Protect the scene.
   b. Notify the authorities as soon as possible.
   c. Move any injured persons that are not able to move themselves.

**46. If your brakes become too hot while driving on a downgrade, they may start to:**
   a. Sharpen
   b. Adjust
   c. Fade

**47. Which of the following is an essential factor to consider when selecting a speed for your vehicle to drive on a grade?**
   a. Whether you are prepared to counter-steer
   b. Whether there is a law enforcement vehicle on the shoulder
   c. The total weight of your vehicle and cargo

**48. In what road condition should you slow your speed by about one-third?**
   a. Packed snow
   b. Wet road
   c. Icy road

**49. If your steering system is furnished with power steering, you should routinely:**
   a. Check it for belts with deterioration from wear and excessive tightness
   b. Check it for a complete seal on the couplings
   c. Check it for leaks, and check hoses, pumps, and fluid level

**50. Which of the following is the distance your vehicle travels from the instant your eyes recognize a threat to the moment your brain realizes it?**
   a. Braking distance
   b. Reaction distance
   c. Perception distance

# Answer Key and Explanations for Test #1

**1. B:** Highly recommended equipment for all drivers includes tire chains, equipment to assist changing tires, a record of emergency phone numbers, and an accident detail package (usually provided by employer).

**2. A:** Sometimes, failure of a rear tire will cause the vehicle to slide back and forth like a fishtail. However, dual rear tires usually prevent this.

**3. B:** A lack of appropriate pressure in the system will cause the brake pedal to feel spongy or to reach the floor.

**4. C:** Let the vehicle slow down. Stop turning and stop braking so hard.

**5. B:** When you double your speed, it takes four times as much distance to stop your vehicle, and your vehicle will have four times the destructive power in a crash.

**6. B:** The reaction distance is the interval in which you travel, in prime conditions, before physically applying the brakes for the oncoming hazard. An average driver has a reaction time between $\frac{3}{4}$ and 1 second. At 55 mph, $\frac{3}{4}$ second accounts for 61 feet traveled.

**7. C:** Release the accelerator, push down on the clutch pedal and shift to neutral; then release the clutch pedal; then let the engine and gears slow down to the RPMs required for the next gear; then push in the clutch pedal and shift to the higher gear.

**8. A:** Perform stab braking as follows: Fully apply the brakes. Release when the wheels lock. Immediately after the wheels start rolling, fully apply the brake. (It can take up to one second for the wheels to start rolling after you release the brakes. If you reapply the brakes before the wheels start rolling, the vehicle will not properly straighten out.)

**9. C:** Hydroplaning can occur at speeds as low as 30 mph if there is a substantial amount of water present.

**10. B:** Class 3 consists of combustible and flammable liquids (for example, gasoline, diesel fuel, and fuel oil).

**11. B:** Aim at the base of the fire.

**12. A:** Drivers can be blinded for a short time by bright light. It takes time to recover from this blindness. Older drivers are especially bothered by glare. Most people have been temporarily blinded by camera flash units or by the high beams of an oncoming vehicle. It can take several seconds to recover from a glare, and two seconds of glare blindness can be dangerous. A vehicle going 55 mph will travel more than half the distance of a football field during that time. Don't look directly at bright lights when driving. Look at the right side of the road. Watch the sidelines when someone coming toward you has very bright lights on.

**13. A:** You must have a tread depth of at least $\frac{4}{32}$ inch in every major groove on front tires, and at least $\frac{2}{32}$ inch on other tires. More would be better. Use a gauge to determine if you have enough tread for safe driving.

**14. A:** You might have to control minor truck fires on the road. However, unless you have the training and equipment to do so safely, don't fight hazardous-material fires. Dealing with hazardous-material fires requires special training and protective gear. When you discover a fire, call for help. You may use the fire extinguisher to keep minor truck fires from spreading to cargo before firefighters arrive. Feel trailer doors to see if they are hot before opening them. If they are hot, you may have a cargo fire and should not open the doors. Opening doors lets air in and may make the fire flare up. Without air, many fires only smolder until firefighters arrive, doing less damage. If your cargo is already on fire, it is not safe to fight the fire. Keep the shipping papers with you to give to emergency personnel as soon as they arrive. Warn other people of the danger and keep them away. If you discover a cargo leak, identify the hazardous materials leaking by using shipping papers, labels, or package location.

**15. B:** Bad wear, cuts or other damage, tread separation, cut or cracked valve stems. Dual tires that come in contact, mismatched sizes, radial and bias-ply tires used together.

**16. B:** The function of the suspension system is to sustain the vehicle and its load, and keep the axles in place; this being said, broken suspensions are very dangerous.

**17. C:** Never attempt to race a train to a crossing. It is extremely difficult to judge the speed of an approaching train.

**18. A:** The shipper must package, mark, and label the materials; prepare shipping papers; provide emergency response information; and supply placards.

**19. B:** Every ten feet.

**20. C:** There are blind spots that your mirrors cannot show you.

**21. C:** Damage to the exhaust system can potentially release deadly fumes into the cab or roomette.

**22. A:** Button hook.

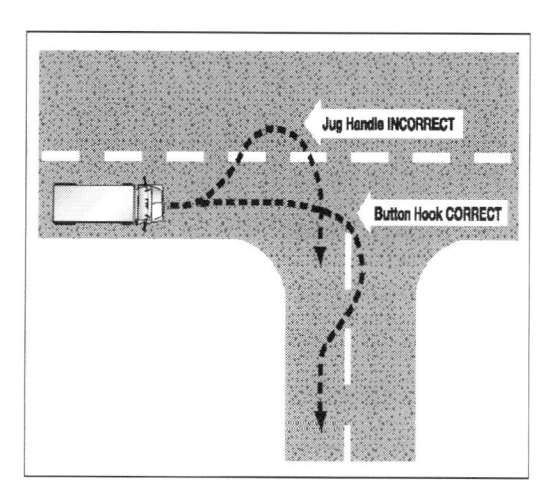

**23. B:** Grasp the steering wheel firmly. If a front tire fails, it can twist the steering wheel out of your hand. The only way to prevent this is to keep a firm grip on the steering wheel with both hands at all times.

**24. B:** Coolant level, windshield washer antifreeze.

**25. A:** An empty truck has less traction.

**26. C:** Check for proper tire pressure using an air pressure gauge or by hitting the tires with a mallet (you are feeling for bounce back from the mallet strike).

**27. A:** Slow down to a safe speed and downshift to the proper gear before entering the curve.

**28. A:** Tar in the road pavement frequently rises to the surface in very hot weather. Spots where tar "bleeds" to the surface are very slippery. Go slowly enough to prevent overheating. High speeds create more heat for tires and the engine. In desert conditions, the heat may build up to the point where it is dangerous. The heat will increase chances of tire failure or even fire, as well as engine failure.

**29. B:** Three things make up the total stopping distance: perception distance, reaction distance, and braking distance. Perception distance is the distance your vehicle travels from the instant your eyes recognize a threat to the moment your brain realizes it. The reaction distance is the interval in which you travel, in prime conditions, before physically applying the brakes for the oncoming hazard. Braking distance is the distance the vehicle will ideally travel while braking. The gross stopping range is the total minimum distance your vehicle has moved, including perception, reaction, and braking distance, until you have come to a complete stop. For an average, alert driver with a good brake, traveling at 55 mph on dry pavement, the vehicle might travel 419 feet before stopping.

**30. C:** When putting out triangles, hold them between yourself and the oncoming traffic for your own safety, increasing visibility. It could save your life.

**31. A:** To operate any vehicle safely, you must know how to control its magnitude and direction. This is especially true of CDL drivers because of the size of their vehicles. The following is a list of skills that you will need to understand extremely well before operating your vehicle: accelerating, steering, shifting gears, backing, braking, and constantly checking your mirrors. Ultimately, these skills need to be mastered, not just understood. They will ensure safe driving for you and the motorists around you.

**32. B:** The average perception time of an alert driver is roughly $1\frac{3}{4}$ seconds. When traveling at 55 mph, you will cover 142 feet in this time.

**33. C:** Do not turn any more than needed to clear whatever is in your way. The more sharply you turn, the higher the chances of a skid or rollover.

**34. C:** Do not shift gears when crossing railroad tracks.

**35. B:** Commercial vehicles take up most of their lane, so it is important to safely manage the little space you have. This is put into practice by staying centered in your lane to keep a safe clearance between you and others driving.

**36. A:** Class 1 includes six divisions: explosives (mass detonations), projection hazards, mass fire hazards, minor hazards, very insensitive, and extremely insensitive.

**37. A:** It helps prevent the brakes from overheating and losing their braking power.

**38. C:** When you drive in heavy rain or deep standing water, your brakes will get wet. Water in the brakes can cause the brakes to be weak, to apply unevenly, or to grab. This can cause lack of braking power, wheel lockups, and pulling to one side or the other. If you pull a trailer, it can also cause jackknifing. Avoid driving through deep puddles or flowing water if possible.

**39. A:** Robust winds make it difficult to stay centered in your lane. This issue occurs more with lighter vehicles and those exiting tunnels.

**40. B:** Use your horn only when needed. Otherwise, your horn may scare others.

**41. A:** With your low beams, you can see ahead about 250 feet. With your high beams, you can see ahead between 300 and 500 feet. These are approximations, of course. It will vary with each driver. You should make sure you can stop between the approximate distances by adjusting your speed accordingly.

**42. C:** Turn wide as you complete the turn.

**43. C:** Shift to a lower gear before starting downgrade and use a light, steady pressure on the brake pedal.

**44. A:** Air pressure should build from 50 to 90 psi within 3 minutes. Increasing the RPM will cause air pressure to rise to normal levels (around 120-140 psi).

**45. C:** As a professional driver, if you are in a crash and not seriously hurt, you need to take three steps to prevent further damage or injury to yourself or others: protect the scene, notify the authorities as soon as possible, and care for the injured (never move them if they are unable to move themselves).

**46. C:** You should plan ahead and obtain information about any long, steep grades along your planned route of travel. You must go slowly enough that your brakes can hold you back without getting too hot. If the brakes become too hot, they may start to "fade." This means you have to apply them harder and harder to get the same stopping power. If you continue to use the brakes hard, they can keep fading until you cannot slow down or stop at all.

**47. C:** When selecting a speed for your vehicle, you must consider all these factors: Total weight of the vehicle and cargo, length of the grade, steepness of the grade, road conditions, and weather.

**48. B:** Wet roads are dangerous and can double your stopping distance. Reduce your speed by about one-third on a wet road. For example, slow down from 55 mph to 35 mph.

**49. C:** If your steering system is furnished with power steering, check for leaks, and check hoses, pumps, and fluid level.

**50. C:** Perception distance is the distance your vehicle travels from the instant your eyes recognize a threat to the moment your brain realizes it. Certain mental and physical conditions can influence individuals' perception distances. The perception distance can also rely heavily on the visibility and the hazard itself. The average perception time of an alert driver is roughly $1\frac{3}{4}$ seconds. When traveling at 55 mph, you will cover 142 feet in this time.

# General Knowledge Practice Test #2

1. Which of the following is required on all commercial vehicles?
    a. Equipment to assist changing tires
    b. Accident detail package
    c. Spare fuses (unless your CMV has circuit breakers)

2. If a vehicle is placarded, how many identical placards must it have?
    a. 2
    b. 4
    c. 6

3. You should try to avoid backing:
    a. Whenever it's raining
    b. When you don't have a spotter
    c. Whenever possible

4. When you are on an incline and the parking brake is engaged, you should release it only:
    a. When the clutch is partly engaged
    b. Once you start the truck
    c. When you have enough power to keep from rolling back

5. What emergency equipment is required on all commercial vehicles?
    a. A record of emergency phone numbers
    b. Three reflective triangles
    c. Tire chains

6. How long does it take for the average driver to bring a heavy vehicle to a stop when driving 55 miles per hour on dry pavement?
    a. About 100 feet... about 2 seconds
    b. About 200 feet... about 4 seconds.
    c. About 300 feet... about 6 seconds.

7. Should you turn the retarder off when the road is wet, icy, or snow covered?
    a. No, because you need more braking power then.
    b. No, because the engine retarder will have no effect on traction.
    c. Yes, whenever your drive wheels have poor traction the retarder may cause a skid.

8. How do you test hydraulic brakes for their stopping action?
    a. Go about five miles per hour. Push the brake pedal firmly.
    b. With the vehicle stopped, pump the brake pedal three times. Apply firm pressure, and then hold for five seconds.
    c. With the vehicle stopped, push the brake pedal firmly, and then hold for five seconds.

9. **If you think that a tire has blown out, what should you do in stopping?**
    a. Hold the steering wheel firmly. Do not touch the brakes until the vehicle has slowed down when you can brake very gently.
    b. Hold the steering wheel firmly. Use hard braking to get off the highway as soon as possible and stop.
    c. Hold the steering wheel loosely. Use hard braking to stop.

10. **Brake fade results from excessive heat, causing:**
    a. The brakes to get out of adjustment
    b. Chemical changes in the brake lining and expansion of the brake drums
    c. The brake shoes and linings to move less to contact the drums

11. **Which of the following is NOT one of the major signs of tire failure?**
    a. You hear the loud commotion of a blowout.
    b. The vehicle thumps or vibrates.
    c. You cannot brake the vehicle properly.

12. **What is capable of reducing the clearance of a structure?**
    a. Heavy traffic
    b. Packed snow
    c. Robust winds

13. **The problems of night driving involve what three primary elements?**
    a. Braking distance, speed, and congestion density
    b. Visibility, steering, and traffic
    c. The driver, roadway, and vehicle

14. **What are three factors that accumulate the total stopping distance with hydraulic-brakes?**
    a. Brake lag distance, pedal engaging distance, rolling distance.
    b. Reaction distance, application distance, braking distance.
    c. Perception distance, reaction distance, braking distance.

15. **You can almost always avoid an object faster by:**
    a. Over-accelerating
    b. Stopping
    c. Turning

16. **Which of the following is NOT one of the four causes of skidding?**
    a. Over-braking
    b. Over-length loads
    c. Over-acceleration

17. **Step 1 of vehicle inspection entails:**
    a. Making a walk-around inspection
    b. Checking the engine compartment
    c. Reviewing the last vehicle inspection report

**18. Which of the following is the least likely to cause your vehicle to drag?**
   a. Draining channels
   b. Railroads
   c. Excess mud on the cabin

**19. What is important about the center of gravity of a load?**
   a. A high center of gravity keeps you from seeing back of your trailers.
   b. A high center of gravity means you are more likely to tip over.
   c. A high center of gravity means you may not clear certain overpasses.

**20. Why can't you count on hearing a train horn until the train is dangerously close to the crossing?**
   a. Because of weather or environmental elements
   b. Because of noise inside your vehicle
   c. Because of quiet train horns

**21. When leaving the road due to an emergency, if possible, avoid using the brakes until your speed has dropped to about:**
   a. 30 mph
   b. 20 mph
   c. 10 mph

**22. How often should you check your tires when driving in very hot weather?**
   a. Every 2 hours or every 100 miles.
   b. Every time you stop.
   c. Once each hour.

**23. If you take a curve at high speed during normal driving conditions, and your tires lose their traction, what is the most likely outcome?**
   a. The vehicle will be sent into a roll.
   b. The vehicle will hydroplane.
   c. The vehicle will skid off the road.

**24. Most people are less alert at night, especially after midnight; this is particularly true if:**
   a. You have been driving for an extended time.
   b. You are suffering from glare blindness.
   c. There are severe weather conditions.

**25. Will "fanning" your brakes, allow them to cool so that they won't overheat on a steep downgrade?**
   a. Yes, short heavy application of the brakes will prevent the brakes from overheating.
   b. No, the brake system is not affected by "fanning."
   c. No, brake drums cool very slowly and the brakes may begin to fade and have less stopping power when the pressure is not applied steadily.

**26. With a large vehicle, if you are turning left, which lane should you use if there are two left turn lanes?**
   a. Use either lane.
   b. Use the right-hand lane.
   c. Use the left-hand lane

**27. What is the predominant cause of crashes and fatalities?**
   a. Backing
   b. Visibility and traffic
   c. Driving at excessive speeds

**28. When driving a 60-foot vehicle at speeds over 40 mph, how many seconds should you leave between you and the vehicle in front of you?**
   a. 7 seconds
   b. 8 seconds
   c. 9 seconds

**29. Retarders help reduce the need for:**
   a. Brakes
   b. Power
   c. Couplings

**30. Which of the following is NOT a condition in which you would want to downshift?**
   a. After your speed has built up on a downgrade
   b. When there is a loss of hydraulic brake pressure
   c. Before entering a curve

**31. When you are stopped on the side of a curved road with an obstructed view, what are the proper intervals from your truck to place your reflective triangles?**
   a. Behind you at 10 feet, 100 feet, and 200 feet
   b. In front of you at 100 feet and behind you at 10 feet and 100 feet
   c. Behind you at 10 feet and also anywhere from 100 to 500 feet

**32. Which of the following would be a sign of brake damage?**
   a. Cracks in your drums
   b. Damage, looseness, or rust to lug nuts
   c. Missing clamps or spacers

**33. What is the major cause of most serious skids?**
   a. Turning too sharply.
   b. Locking up the wheels.
   c. Driving too fast for road conditions.

**34. What is the minimum amount of tread depth that your tires should have?**
   a. There should be at least four-thirty seconds tread depth in every major groove on the front wheels and at least two-thirty seconds inch tread on all other wheels.
   b. There should be at least one-inch tread depth in every major groove on all wheels.
   c. There should be at least four-thirty seconds inch tread depth in every large groove on all wheels.

**35. In what road condition should you slow your speed by about one-half or more?**
   a. Packed snow
   b. Wet road
   c. Icy road

**36. What plays a major role in mountain driving, slows you down on upgrades, and increases your speed on downgrades?**
   a. Velocity
   b. Gravity
   c. Fade

**37. When driving a 40-foot vehicle at speeds under 40 mph, how many seconds should you leave between you and the vehicle in front of you?**
   a. 2 seconds
   b. 4 seconds
   c. 6 seconds

**38. Free play in the steering system should not exceed:**
   a. 5 degrees
   b. 7 degrees
   c. 10 degrees

**39. Which of the following is true about planning ahead?**
   a. You must know what the traffic is doing at all times.
   b. Experienced drivers don't have to look very far ahead.
   c. You may need to discuss it with a mechanic at your company's local yard or truck stop.

**40. According to accident reports, the vehicle that trucks and buses most frequently run into is:**
   a. The one in front of them
   b. The one beside them when making a turn
   c. The one behind them

**41. Which of the following can be a type of retarder?**
   a. Shifting
   b. Electric
   c. Tire

**42. As defined by the Hazardous Materials Regulations (HMR) found in parts 100–185 of title 49 of the Code of Federal Regulations, what hazard class contains the radioactive division?**
   a. Class 6
   b. Class 7
   c. Class 8

**43. What can all retarders be activated by?**
   a. The driver
   b. Inclement weather
   c. Lightly depressing the accelerator

**44. It's a good idea to inspect your vehicle within the first 25 miles of a trip and also every:**
   a. 100 miles or 2 hours on the road
   b. 150 miles or 3 hours on the road
   c. 200 miles or 4 hours on the road

**45. What can you do to lessen the chances of having to make a sudden move to avoid hazards?**
   a. Keep your vehicle centered in your lane by watching the white line up close.
   b. Watch far enough ahead so that hazards can be anticipated.
   c. Follow the driver ahead closely and watch his brake lights.

**46. How does tire pressure affect hydroplaning?**
   a. Hydroplaning is not affected by tire pressure.
   b. Hydroplaning is more likely to occur when tire pressure is low.
   c. Hydroplaning is more likely to occur when tires are over inflated.

**47. What are some steering system defects to look for?**
   a. Missing nuts, bolts, cotter keys or other parts; bent, loose or broken parts.
   b. Steering wheel play of two degrees.
   c. Steering wheel play of five degrees.

**48. What is a good rule as to the speed you should go when driving at night?**
   a. You should keep your speed slow enough to stop within the range of your headlights.
   b. You do not have to be able to stop within the distance that you can see.
   c. You should never drive so fast as to require your high beams.

**49. Which of the following is NOT an element of safe backing?**
   a. Map the path you will follow when backing.
   b. Back fast once the area is clear.
   c. Turn on four-way flashers and sound your horn before backing.

**50. Which of the following skills will you need to understand extremely well before operating your vehicle?**
   a. Tying down
   b. Signaling
   c. Accelerating

# Answer Key and Explanations for Test #2

**1. C:** All commercial vehicles must have the following emergency equipment: fire extinguisher, spare fuses (unless your CMV has circuit breakers), and three reflective triangles.

**2. B:** Placards are $10\frac{3}{4}$ inches on each side and are diamond-shaped. Cargo tanks and other bulk packaging display the ID number of their contents on placards or orange panels. A placarded vehicle must have at least four identical placards. They are placed on the front, rear, and both sides of the vehicle. Not all vehicles that carry hazardous materials need placards. You can drive a vehicle carrying hazardous materials if it does not require placards. If it requires placards, you may not drive it unless you have a hazardous material endorsement on your commercial driver's license.

**3. C:** When operating your vehicle, you are not able to see everything behind you, which makes backing very dangerous. Try to avoid backing whenever possible.

**4. C:** Use the parking brake when on an incline to keep the vehicle in place. Release it only when you have enough power to keep from rolling back.

**5. B:** All commercial vehicles must have the following emergency equipment: fire extinguisher, spare fuses (unless your CMV has circuit breakers), and three reflective triangles.

**6. C:** About 300 feet... about 6 seconds.

**7. C:** Yes, whenever your drive wheels have poor traction the retarder may cause a skid.

**8. A:** Go about five miles per hour. Push the brake pedal firmly.

**9. A:** Hold the steering wheel firmly. Do not touch the brakes until the vehicle has slowed down when you can brake very gently.

**10. B:** Brake fade results from excessive heat, which causes expansion of the brake drums, and also causes chemical changes in the brake lining that reduce friction. As the overheated drums expand, the brake shoes and linings have to move farther to contact the drums, and the force of this contact is reduced. Continued overuse may increase brake fade until the vehicle cannot be slowed down or stopped. Brake fade is also affected by adjustment. To safely control a vehicle, every brake must do its share of the work. Brakes out of adjustment will stop doing their share before those that are in adjustment. The other brakes can then overheat and fade, and there will not be enough braking available to control the vehicle.

**11. C:** The loud commotion of a blowout is an easily recognizable sign of tire failure. If the vehicle thumps or vibrates heavily, it may be a sign that one of the tires has gone flat. If the steering feels heavy or lagging, it's probably a sign that one of the front tires has failed.

**12. B:** Repaving or packed snow is capable of reducing the clearance of a structure.

**13. C:** You are at greater risk when you drive at night. Drivers can't see hazards as quickly as in daylight, so they have less time to respond. Drivers caught by surprise are unequipped to manage a crash. The problems of night driving involve the driver, the roadway, and the vehicle.

**14. C:** Perception distance, reaction distance, braking distance.

**15. C:** Stopping is not always the safest thing to do in an emergency. When you don't have enough room to pull over, you may have to steer away from what's ahead. Remember, you can almost always turn to avoid an obstacle faster than you can stop. (However, top-heavy loads and tractors with multiple trailers may flip over.)

**16. B:** A skid happens whenever the tires lose their grip on the road. Here are the four causes:

- Braking too hard and locking up the wheels, or over-braking, as well as using the speed retarder when the road is slippery
- Turning the wheels more sharply than the vehicle can turn
- Over-accelerating
- Supplying too much power to the drive wheels, causing them to spin

Most serious skids result from driving too fast for road conditions. Drivers who adjust their driving to conditions don't over-accelerate or have to over-brake/steer from too much speed.

**17. C:** Step 1: Review the last vehicle inspection report. Drivers may be required to log a vehicle inspection report daily. The motor carrier must correct anything that hinders safety. The motor carrier must clarify on documentation whether the repairs were made or were unnecessary.

**18. C:** Draining channels can cause vehicles to drag and require special care when crossing; railroads can create the same problem when traveling across with a low underneath clearance. Don't take a chance on getting hung up halfway across.

**19. B:** A high center of gravity means you are more likely to tip over.

**20. B:** Because of noise inside your vehicle, you cannot expect to hear the train horn until the train is dangerously close to the crossing.

**21. B:** If possible, avoid using the brakes until your speed has dropped to about 20 mph. Then brake very gently to avoid skidding on a loose surface.

**22. A:** Every 2 hours or every 100 miles.

**23. C:** Drivers must adjust their speed for curves in the road. If you take a curve at high speed, the tires could lose their traction, causing you to skid off the road.

**24. A:** Fatigue (being tired) and lack of alertness are bigger problems at night. The body's need for sleep is beyond a person's control. Most people are less alert at night, especially after midnight. This is particularly true if they have been driving for an extended time. Drivers may not see hazards as soon, or react as quickly, so the probability of a crash is greater.

**25. C:** No, brake drums cool very slowly and the brakes may begin to fade and have less stopping power when the pressure is not applied steadily.

**26. B:** Use the right-hand lane.

**27. C:** Driving at excessive speeds is the predominant cause of crashes and fatalities. Properly adjust speeds to better fit weather conditions, road features (such as hills and curves), visibility, and traffic.

**28. A:** When driving a 60-foot vehicle at speeds over 40 mph, leave 7 seconds between you and the vehicle ahead. One second for each 10 feet of vehicle length, plus an additional second for safety, is $1 \times 6 + 1 = 7$ seconds. Remember that in inclement weather, these times increase greatly.

**29. A:** Retarders help slow diesel vehicles, reducing the need for using your brakes. They diminish brake wear and offer another way to slow down.

**30. A:** Shift the transmission to a low gear before starting down a grade. Do not try to downshift after your speed has already built up. You will not be able to shift into a lower gear. You may not even be able to get back into any gear, and all engine braking effect will be lost. Forcing an automatic transmission into a lower gear at high speed could damage the transmission and also lead to loss of all engine braking effect.

**31. C:** Behind you at 10 feet and also anywhere from 100 to 500 feet.

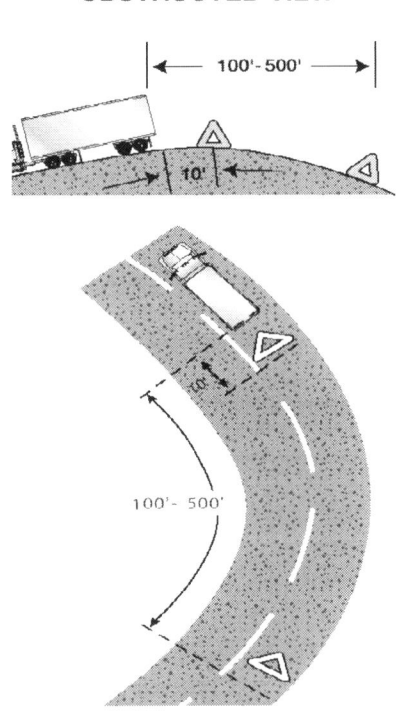

**OBSTRUCTED VIEW**

**32. A:** Look for brake drum and shoe problems on front, rear, and trailer brakes; cracks in your drums; oil, grease, or brake fluid on your brake shoes or pads; or brake shoes that are worn thin, missing, or broken.

**33. C:** Driving too fast for road conditions.

**34. A:** There should be at least four-thirty seconds tread depth in every major groove on the front wheels and at least two-thirty seconds inch tread on all other wheels.

**35. A:** On packed snow, reduce your speed by one-half or more.

**36. B:** In mountain driving, gravity plays a major role. On any upgrade, gravity slows you down. The steeper the grade, the longer the grade, or the heavier the load, the more you will have to use lower gears to climb hills or mountains. When you come down long, steep downgrades, gravity causes the speed of your vehicle to increase. You must select an appropriate safe speed, then use a low gear and proper braking techniques. You should plan ahead and obtain information about any long, steep grades along your planned route of travel.

**37. B:** When driving a 40-foot vehicle at speeds under 40 mph, leave 4 seconds between you and the vehicle ahead. One second for each 10 feet of vehicle length is $1 \times 4 = 4$ seconds. Remember that in inclement weather, these times increase greatly.

**38. C:** Free play in the steering system should not exceed 10 degrees (exactly 2 inches of leeway from the rim of a 20-inch steering wheel). Too much free play will increase difficulty in maneuvering.

**39. A:** You must know what the traffic is doing at all times from all sides of your vehicle. Experienced drivers plan ahead by looking far in front of them so they can estimate how much room they have to make any necessary moves in traffic. On the highway, most drivers look approximately one-fourth of a mile ahead. When you plan ahead, look for traffic, road conditions, sharp pavement drop-offs, and signs. Also look for slow-moving vehicles.

**40. A:** According to accident reports, the vehicle that trucks and buses most frequently run into is the one in front of them. The most common cause is following too closely.

**41. B:** These are the types of retarders: exhaust, engine, hydraulic, and electric.

**42. B:** Class 7 consists of radioactive materials (for example, uranium).

**43. A:** All retarders can be activated by the driver. The power can also be adjusted on some vehicles. When activated, retarders reduce the engine power once you take your foot off the accelerator completely. If you are pushing the accelerator, it will not reduce power. Do not use your retarders in inclement weather where slippery conditions are present, especially if the unit is empty or lightly loaded.

**44. B:** It's a good idea to inspect your vehicle within the first 25 miles of the trip and also every 150 miles or 3 hours on the road.

**45. B:** Watch far enough ahead so that hazards can be anticipated.

**46. B:** Hydroplaning is more likely to occur when tire pressure is low.

**47. A:** Missing nuts, bolts, cotter keys or other parts; bent, loose or broken parts.

**48. A:** You should keep your speed slow enough to stop within the range of your headlights.

**49. B:** Do not back fast. There is no room for error if you do. Use the lowest idler gear.

**50. C:** To operate any vehicle safely, you must know how to control its magnitude and direction. This is especially true of CDL drivers because of the size of their vehicles. The following is a list of skills that you will need to understand extremely well before operating your vehicle: accelerating, steering, shifting gears, backing, braking, and constantly checking your mirrors.

# General Knowledge Practice Test #3

**1. Which of the following is NOT helpful when driving off the road to avoid a collision?**
   a. If the shoulder is clear, stay on it until your vehicle has come to a stop.
   b. Maintain at least one set of wheels on the pavement to stay in control.
   c. Gently depress the brakes until your speed has dropped to about 20 mph.

**2. Which of the following is NOT true of signaling?**
   a. Not all vehicles' signals turn off automatically after making turns.
   b. If necessary, it is safe to signal other drivers to pass you.
   c. You should flash your brake lights to warn other drivers that you need to slow down or stop.

**3. what is the correct course of action to take if you are being tailgated?**
   a. Avoid quick changes of speed or direction.
   b. Try to reduce your following distance.
   c. Speed up, and flash your taillights on and off.

**4. Where do you place the three reflector triangles if you have to park on the side of a level highway with one-way traffic such as a divided highway?**
   a. Place them by the back of the vehicle; one within 10 feet, one within 100 feet and the other one 200 feet.
   b. Place all of them in front of the vehicle up to 500 feet.
   c. Place two in front of the vehicle at 10 feet and at 100 feet and place one on the rear of the vehicle.

**5. Which of the following is NOT advisable when being tailgated?**
   a. Sustain your velocity, since it is safer to be tailgated going slowly rather than quickly.
   b. Increase the distance between your vehicle and the one in front of you.
   c. Flash your brake lights to warn or ward off tailgaters.

**6. In making a quick turn what is a point to remember?**
   a. Do not apply the brake when you are turning.
   b. The brakes will prevent skidding in turns.
   c. Do not expect to counter-steer.

**7. When driving a 40-foot vehicle at speeds over 40 mph, how many seconds should you leave between you and the vehicle ahead of you?**
   a. 4 seconds
   b. 5 seconds
   c. 6 seconds

**8. When operating in heavy traffic, it is advisable to:**
   a. Stay in the left lane.
   b. Pass every car you can until you find an opening or lighter traffic.
   c. Match the speed of those around you.

**9. Since it is difficult to look directly at bright lights when driving, where can you look to avoid the glare of oncoming traffic?**
   a. Close your eyes momentarily.
   b. Try to look at the centerline of the highway, watching for the dotted line.
   c. Try to look at the right side of the road, watching the sidelines.

**10. You must have at least how much tread depth in every major groove of your front tires?**
   a. $\frac{2}{32}$ inch
   b. $\frac{4}{32}$ inch
   c. $\frac{6}{32}$ inch

**11. Which of the following is NOT one of the usual reasons hydraulics fail?**
   a. Loss of hydraulic pressure
   b. Failure on downgrades
   c. Overuse of stab braking

**12. What is the principal way of controlling your speed on a downgrade?**
   a. Engine braking effect
   b. Escape ramps
   c. Brakes

**13. If you are sleepy while driving, the only safe cure is to:**
   a. Slow your speed by about half or more.
   b. Get off the road and get some sleep.
   c. Stabilize your condition with proper stimulants and distractors.

**14. Where do you place the three reflector triangles if you have to park on the side of a level, straight two-lane road?**
   a. Place one within 10 feet of the rear of the vehicle, one about 100 feet to the rear and one about 100 feet from the front of the vehicle.
   b. Place one within 100 feet of the front of the vehicle, one 500 feet from the front of the vehicle and one about 100 feet from the rear of the vehicle.
   c. Place one within 10 feet from the front of the vehicle, one about 100 feet to the front and one about 500 feet to the rear of the vehicle.

**15. What is an extra element that you will need to inspect when driving a tractor trailer?**
   a. Seating
   b. Catwalk
   c. Emergency exit

**16. What does the acronym GOAL stand for?**
   a. Gear Overload and Adjustment Limits
   b. Good Observations Allow for Load
   c. Get Out And Look

**17. Which of the following can lead to other drivers turning into you?**
   a. Being blocked in when you need to change lanes
   b. Robust winds
   c. Switching lanes suddenly

**18. What are some defects to look for in the suspension system?**
   a. Spring hangers that allow movement of the axle from the proper position; cracked or broken spring hangers; spring hangers or other axle positioning parts that are cracked damaged, or missing.
   b. Oil leaks in the frame or fifth wheel assembly.
   c. Oil leaks in the brake drums.

**19. Hydroplaning is more likely to occur if:**
   a. Tire pressure is low
   b. The roadway is well drained
   c. You slow down before a curve

**20. What is the purpose of brake retarders?**
   a. To help slow down the vehicle and to reduce brake wear.
   b. To provide more traction on a slippery surface and enable a vehicle to go faster.
   c. To reduce brake wear and to reduce noise.

**21. If you must veer off the road to avoid collision, but don't have space to fully stop, which of the following is NOT helpful when merging back onto the road?**
   a. Hold the wheel tightly and turn sharply to get back on the road.
   b. Signal and gradually get back on the road.
   c. When both front tires are on the paved surface, counter-steer immediately.

**22. In what road condition should you reduce your speed to a crawl and stop driving as soon as possible?**
   a. Packed snow
   b. Wet road
   c. Icy road

**23. Who is responsible for placarding the vehicle when loading (if placards are required)?**
   a. Shipper
   b. Carrier
   c. Driver

**24. What can reflect your own headlights back into your eyes?**
   a. Other cars
   b. Fog
   c. Exhaust

**25. What is a good reason for knowing what the traffic is doing on all sides of you?**
   a. Stopping or changing lanes can take time and distance and you need to have room to make these moves safely.
   b. It is always necessary to know when you can make a U-turn.
   c. You need to eliminate all blind spots around you.

**26. When driving a 60-foot vehicle at speeds under 40 mph, how many seconds should you leave between you and the vehicle ahead of you?**
   a. 4 seconds
   b. 5 seconds
   c. 6 seconds

**27. What kind of warning signs indicate that retarders are not to be used?**
   a. Escape ramp signs
   b. No engine brake signs
   c. Wide load signs

**28. What can happen if the steering axle has an insufficient amount of weight on it?**
   a. This will make the vehicle easier to control in turns.
   b. This can make the vehicle easier to steer straight.
   c. This can make the vehicle harder to steer.

**29. In a rear-wheel braking skid, a bus or straight truck will:**
   a. Spin out
   b. Jackknife
   c. Blindside

**30. How often should cargo inspections be made?**
   a. After every break during driving.
   b. Once each hour.
   c. Every 25 miles.

**31. When you are stopped on the side of a two-way road or undivided highway, what are the proper intervals from your truck to place your reflective triangles?**
   a. Behind you at 10 feet, 100 feet, and 200 feet
   b. In front of you at 100 feet and behind you at 10 feet and 100 feet
   c. Behind you at 10 feet and also anywhere from 100 to 500 feet

**32. When inspecting your suspension system, you should check for:**
   a. Cracked or broken spring supporters
   b. Loose, broken, or missing mufflers, vents, pipeage, and vertical branches
   c. Missing bolts, nuts, cotter pins, or any other parts on the steering box

**33. You can check for ice on the road by:**
   a. Finding a shaded spot or bridge and noting any loss in grip
   b. Looking at the edges of the roadway
   c. Reaching outside the window and feeling the mirror or antenna

**34. Which of the following is NOT an element of controlled braking?**
   a. Applying the brakes without locking the wheels
   b. Jamming on the brakes
   c. Performing small steering movements

**35. What should you do immediately once you realize you've gotten hung up on a railroad crossing?**
   a. Call 911
   b. Call a towing service
   c. Call your company dispatcher

**36. What are two factors in knowing when to shift?**
   a. Using transmission speed and clutch stroke.
   b. Using engine speed and road speed.
   c. Using road speed and "feel" of the road.

**37. What can cause the driving wheels to skid on slippery surfaces?**
   a. Tie rods
   b. Pushing in the clutch
   c. Engine brake or speed retarder

**38. You are driving a vehicle with a light load. Traffic is moving at 35 miles per hour in a 55 mile per hour zone. What is most likely the safest speed for your vehicle in this situation?**
   a. 55 miles per hour
   b. 35 miles per hour
   c. 45 miles per hour

**39. For the last step of your inspection, you:**
   a. Start the engine and inspect the inside of the cab.
   b. Make a walk-around inspection.
   c. Start the engine and check the brake system.

**40. You are driving on a two-lane road when an oncoming driver drifts into your lane and is heading straight for you. What is one action to take?**
   a. Braking while veering to the right when possible.
   b. Quickly turn to the left.
   c. Speed up to maneuver around the oncoming vehicle.

**41. Most serious skids result from:**
   a. Driving too fast for road conditions
   b. Braking too hard and locking up the wheels
   c. Turning the wheels more sharply than the vehicle can turn

**42. How do you test hydraulic brakes for a leak?**
   a. With the vehicle under way at a low speed, apply firm pressure, stopping the vehicle as quickly as possible.
   b. With the vehicle stopped, push down the brake pedal and do not release for at least five seconds.
   c. With the vehicle stopped, pump the brake pedal three times. Apply firm pressure, and then hold for five seconds.

**43. If carrying high-risk cargo, make sure you have:**
   a. Proper documents and placards
   b. Load locks
   c. Wheel chocks

**44. To follow the trailer during your backing:**
   a. Turn in the direction the trailer is going.
   b. Rotate the steering wheel in the direction that you want the back of your trailer to go.
   c. Turn the steering wheel in the opposite direction of where you want the back of your trailer to go.

**45. The regulations that tell shippers how to package hazardous materials safely, and tell drivers how to load, transport, and unload the materials, are called:**
   a. Containment rules
   b. Handling guidelines
   c. Risk regulations

**46. Who is responsible for reporting accidents and incidents involving hazardous materials to the proper agencies?**
   a. Shipper
   b. Carrier
   c. Driver

**47. Should you always be looking into the distance ahead?**
   a. Yes, You should be prepared for all problems ahead.
   b. No, you should shift your attention vertically and horizontally.
   c. Yes, by concentrating on the vehicle directly ahead you will be prepared for all emergencies.

**48. What can cause the vehicle to slide back and forth like a fishtail?**
   a. Failure of a rear tire
   b. Failure of a front tire
   c. Failure of the hydraulic brakes

**49. Once you've begun to hydroplane, you can regain control by:**
   a. Engaging the retarders and steering away from the water or sludge
   b. Releasing the accelerator and pushing in the clutch
   c. Gently braking

**50. Which of the following is NOT a type of retarder?**
   a. Exhaust
   b. Hydraulic
   c. Suspension

# Answer Key and Explanations for Test #3

**1. C:** In some emergencies, you may have to drive off the road. It may be less risky than facing a collision with another vehicle. The majority of shoulders are strong enough to support the weight of a large vehicle and therefore offer an available escape route. Here are some guidelines, if you leave the road: If possible, avoid using the brakes until your speed has dropped to about 20 mph. Then brake very gently to avoid skidding on a loose surface. Maintain one set of wheels on the pavement to stay in control. If the shoulder is clear, stay on it until your vehicle has come to a stop. Signal and check your mirrors before pulling back onto the road.

**2. B:** Do not signal other drivers to pass you. They cannot see around you and it could lead to an accident.

**3. A:** Avoid quick changes of speed or direction.

**4. A:** Place them by the back of the vehicle; one within 10 feet, one within 100 feet and the other one 200 feet.

**5. C:** When being tailgated, refrain from attempting tricks such as flashing brake lights to ward off tailgaters.

**6. A:** Do not apply the brake when you are turning.

**7. B:** When driving a 40-foot vehicle at speeds over 40 mph, leave 5 seconds between you and the vehicle ahead. One second for each 10 feet of vehicle length, plus an additional second for safety, is $1 \times 4 + 1 = 5$ seconds. Remember that in inclement weather, these times increase greatly.

**8. C:** When operating in heavy traffic, it is advisable to match your speed with the speed of others. It is an unnecessary risk to drive over the designated speed limit in the hope of saving time. This increases the chances of a wreck with every car you pass and increases mental stress, which in turn leads to fatigue. Going with the flow of traffic is safer and easier.

**9. C:** Try to look at the right side of the road, watching the sidelines.

**10. B:** Enough tread is especially important in winter conditions. You must have a tread depth of at least $\frac{4}{32}$ inch in every major groove of your front tires. More would be better. Use a gauge to determine if you have enough tread for safe driving.

**11. C:** When brakes are properly cared for, they rarely falter. Hydraulics usually fail because of a loss of hydraulic pressure or failure on downgrades.

**12. A:** You must use the braking effect of the engine as the principal way of controlling your speed. The braking effect of the engine is greatest when it is near the governed RPMs and the transmission is in the lower gears. Save your brakes so you will be able to slow or stop as required by road and traffic conditions. Know where the escape ramps are located on your route, and use them if you lose your brakes.

**13. B:** If you are sleepy, the only safe cure is to get off the road and get some sleep. If you don't, you risk your life and the lives of others.

**14. A:** Place one within 10 feet of the rear of the vehicle, one about 100 feet to the rear and one about 100 feet from the front of the vehicle.

**15. B:** If you are driving a tractor trailer, also check the catwalk, as well as all parts of the coupling system (fifth wheel lower plate, etc.). You will not be able to see the lower plate if the vehicle is hooked up. Make sure the crank handle to your landing gear is secure and your gear is lifted all the way.

**16. C:** Map the path you will follow when backing. **Get out and look** (GOAL) is very important when backing, during your road test, and in everyday driving.

**17. C:** Switching lanes suddenly can lead to other drivers turning into you.

**18. A:** Spring hangers that allow movement of the axle from the proper position; cracked or broken spring hangers; spring hangers or other axle positioning parts that are cracked damaged, or missing.

**19. A:** Hydroplaning is more likely to occur if tire pressure is low, or the tread is worn. (The grooves in a tire carry away the water; if they aren't deep, they don't work well.)

**20. A:** To help slow down the vehicle and to reduce brake wear.

**21. B:** If you are forced to return to the road before you can stop, use the following procedure: Hold the wheel tightly and turn sharply to get back on the road safely. Don't try to gradually get back on the road. If you do, your tires might grab unexpectedly, and you could lose control. When both front tires are on the paved surface, counter-steer immediately. The two turns should be made as a cohesive "steer-counter-steer" move.

**22. C:** If the road is icy, reduce your speed to a crawl. Stop driving as soon as possible.

**23. C:** The driver placards the vehicle when loading, if required.

**24. B:** Fog reflects light and can reflect your own headlights back into your eyes. Use only your low beams. Look for road edge markings to guide you. Even light fog reduces your ability to see and judge distances. If possible, pull off the road and wait until the fog has lifted.

**25. A:** Stopping or changing lanes can take time and distance and you need to have room to make these moves safely.

**26. C:** When driving a 60-foot vehicle at speeds under 40 mph, leave 6 seconds between you and the vehicle ahead. One second for each 10 feet of vehicle length is $1 \times 6 = 6$ seconds. Remember that in inclement weather, these times increase greatly.

**27. B:** Because retarders can be loud, some city ordinances do not allow their use within city limits. You should see signs saying "No Engine Brakes" or something similar.

**28. C:** This can make the vehicle harder to steer.

**29. A:** Rear-wheel braking skids occur when the rear drive wheels lock. Because locked wheels have less traction than rolling wheels, the rear wheels usually slide sideways in an attempt to "catch up" with the front wheels. In a bus or straight truck, the vehicle will slide sideways in a "spinout."

**30. A:** After every break during driving.

**31. B:** In front of you at 100 feet and behind you at 10 feet and 100 feet.

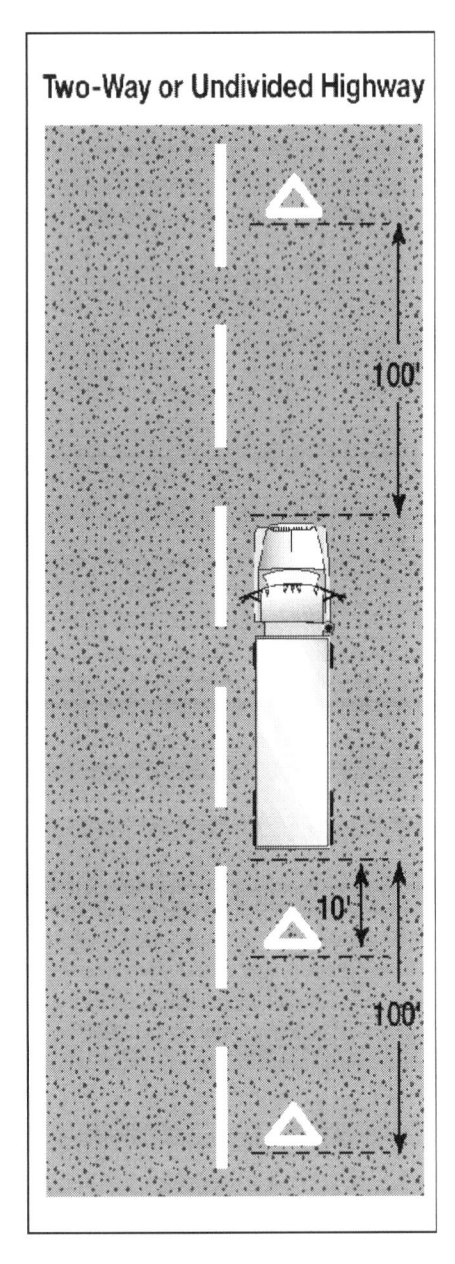

**32. A:** Look for front, rear, and trailer suspension defects, including cracked or broken spring supporters.

**33. C:** Check for ice on the road by reaching outside the window and feeling the mirror, antenna, or mirror support. If these are icy, then so is the road.

**34. B:** Apply the brakes without locking the wheels, and maintain command. Perform small steering movements while in this state. If you need to make a larger steering adjustment, or if the wheels lock, then release the brakes. Reapply the brakes at the earliest opportunity. You never want to lose control while braking. It is important not to panic. Refrain from jamming on the brakes. Emergency braking does not mean slamming them with all your strength. That would cause a lockup and a skid. If this occurs, you will be unable to control the vehicle.

**35. A:** Vehicles that have low ground clearance, such as drop frame trailers and car carriers, can hang up on railroad crossings with steep approaches. If you get hung up on a railroad crossing, call 911 immediately so that the scheduled trains can be notified to stop.

**36. B:** Using engine speed and road speed.

**37. C:** Adjust turning and braking to conditions. Make turns as gently as possible. Do not brake any harder than necessary, and don't use the engine brake or speed retarder. (They can cause the driving wheels to skid on slippery surfaces.)

**38. B:** 35 miles per hour

**39. C:** Start the engine and check the brake system.

**40. A:** Braking while veering to the right when possible.

**41. A:** Most serious skids result from driving too fast for road conditions. Drivers who adjust their driving to conditions don't over-accelerate or have to over-brake/steer from too much speed.

**42. C:** With the vehicle stopped, pump the brake pedal three times. Apply firm pressure, and then hold for five seconds.

**43. A:** Make sure your truck is not overloaded for its rating/permits. Be sure that the cargo is level and fasten in before departure. Also, if you are using load locks, make sure they are in place before transport. If carrying high-risk cargo, make sure you have all proper documents and placards for the load.

**44. A:** To follow the trailer during your backing, you need to turn in the direction the trailer is going. This will straighten the position of your truck relative to the trailer.

**45. A:** Transporting hazardous materials can be risky. The regulations are intended to protect you, those around you, and the environment. They tell shippers how to package the materials safely, and they tell drivers how to load, transport, and unload the material. These are called "containment rules."

**46. B:** The carrier reports accidents and incidents involving hazardous materials to the proper agencies.

**47. B:** No, you should shift your attention vertically and horizontally.

**48. A:** Sometimes, failure of a rear tire will cause the vehicle to slide back and forth like a fishtail. However, dual rear tires usually prevent this.

**49. B:** In poor weather conditions, water or sludge gathers on the road, and can cause vehicles to hydroplane. Hydroplaning can be described as water skiing—the tires lose their ability to properly grip the road, having no traction. This may make braking or steering uncontrollable. You can regain control by releasing the accelerator and pushing in the clutch. This will slow your vehicle and let the wheels turn freely. When hydroplaning, do not attempt to slow down by braking. If the drive wheels start to skid, push in the clutch to let them turn freely.

**50. C:** These are the types of retarders: exhaust, engine, hydraulic, and electric.

# General Knowledge Practice Test #4

**1. Emergency steering and what other maneuver are two sides of the same coin?**
   a. Counter-steering
   b. Mountain driving
   c. Offtracking

**2. Must you show your logbook to officers?**
   a. Yes.
   b. No.
   c. Only after they have read you your rights.

**3. Black ice is formed when:**
   a. There is a thin enough layer of ice that you can see the road through it
   b. There are contaminants or oil mixed with the ice
   c. Extreme weather or driving conditions cause dense compaction of snow

**4. Which of the following is NOT true when dealing with a hazardous leak?**
   a. Many people injure themselves by touching hazardous materials.
   b. You can safely identify the material, or find the source of a leak, by smell.
   c. If hazardous materials are spilling from your vehicle, you should not move it any more than safety requires.

**5. What should you do if your vehicle hydroplanes?**
   a. Let up on the clutch.
   b. Release the accelerator and push in the clutch.
   c. Push down on the accelerator releasing the clutch.

**6. How far ahead should you look while driving?**
   a. 100 feet
   b. Four seconds
   c. 12 to 15 seconds

**7. What is one reason that you can never assure that you're safe by reading the heights posted at bridges and overpasses?**
   a. Repaving or packed snow may have decreased the clearances since the heights were posted.
   b. The weight of a cargo van can change its height with an empty van being lighter or lower.
   c. Some roads can cause your vehicle to tilt.

**8. Which of the following is NOT an element of the walk-around inspection?**
   a. Check all mirrors
   b. Check door latches
   c. Check tank straps for wear

**9. What is the most common method used by those learning to shift gears?**
   a. Double clutch method
   b. Inspection method
   c. Shift restriction method

**10. In a drive-wheel skid, a vehicle towing a trailer will:**
   a. Spin out
   b. Jackknife
   c. Blindside

**11. How many times more distance does it take to stop whenever you double your speed?**
   a. Twice as much distance.
   b. Three times as much distance.
   c. Four times as much distance.

**12. If you hear the loud bang of a blowout, what should you do?**
   a. Brake gently until the vehicle has slowed down.
   b. Always assume it was one of your tires, and use your mirrors to check.
   c. Assume the noise is from another vehicle if yours does not have any immediate issues or adverse effects on your driving.

**13. When driving how much space should you try to keep in front of you?**
   a. One second for each 15 feet of your vehicle length at speeds below 40 miles per hour.
   b. Over 40 miles per hour at least one second for each 10 feet of your vehicle length plus one extra second.
   c. With a forty-foot vehicle leave 5 seconds between you and the vehicle ahead when going below 40 miles per hour.

**14. When inspecting the flue system, you should check for:**
   a. Loose, broken, or missing mounting brackets, clamps, bolts, or nuts
   b. Oil, grease, or brake fluid on your shoes or pads
   c. Radius rod, U-bolts, or spring supporters that are cracked, damaged, or missing

**15. To prohibit others from passing you while mid-turn:**
   a. Reach the middle of the intersection prior to beginning the pivot.
   b. Keep the rear of the vehicle in close proximity to the curb.
   c. Back up to allow traffic room to pass you before attempting the turn.

**16. Drivers who have trouble staying in their lane or maintaining speed, or who stop without reason, are likely:**
   a. Using power steering
   b. Experiencing low visibility
   c. Under the influence of alcohol or drugs

**17. Why is having plenty of driving space essential to being a safe driver?**
   a. Space gives other, faster drivers room to safely pass you.
   b. Space helps vehicles around you to know of your intentions.
   c. Space gives you time to think and take action.

**18. What are some things to do when you are backing your vehicle?**
   a. First, look at your path. Second, back slowly. Third, back, straight back.
   b. Insist on having a helper to guide you.
   c. Back and turn from the right whenever possible.

**19. You are always required to yield the right-of-way to:**
   a. Trains
   b. Traffic to your left
   c. Trucks larger than your own

**20. What is the minimum amount of tie downs that you should have?**
   a. Two
   b. Four
   c. Six

**21. What is one way of knowing when you have the right engine speed and road speed to shift gears?**
   a. When the engine is lugging.
   b. By shifting whenever you notice heavy smoke coming from the exhaust stack.
   c. Using the sound of the engine to know the appropriate time to shift.

**22. What could cause your vehicle to whip?**
   a. A lack of tire chains
   b. Sharp motion applied to the steering wheel
   c. Backing

**23. How would you control your steering when backing with a trailer?**
   a. Always turn in the direction the trailer is already going.
   b. Rotate the steering wheel in the direction that you want the back of your trailer to go.
   c. Turn the steering wheel in the opposite direction of where you want the back of your trailer to go.

**24. Which of the following should you check while inspecting the engine compartment?**
   a. Parking brake
   b. Oil level
   c. Controls (for loose movement, jamming up or sticking, damage, or improper setting)

**25. To steer your vehicles when backing without a trailer:**
   a. Turn the steering wheel in the opposite direction of where you want the back of your vehicle to go.
   b. Rotate the steering wheel in the direction that you want the back of your vehicle to go.
   c. Adjust your steering wheel minimally, and pull up and realign your truck often.

**26. The only way you may know if one of your dual tires goes out is by:**
   a. Getting out and looking
   b. The steering wheel getting twisted out of your hands
   c. The steering feeling heavy or lagging

**27. In emergencies you may be able to miss an obstacle more quickly than you can stop. What is a characteristic of heavy vehicles when they are turned quickly?**
   a. Top-heavy vehicles and tractors with multiple trailers cannot be turned quickly.
   b. Top-heavy vehicles and tractors with multiple trailers will unhook when turned quickly.
   c. Top-heavy vehicles and tractors with multiple trailers may flip over when turned quickly.

**28. On a yearly basis, how many drivers avoid injury by using escape ramps?**
   a. Dozens
   b. Hundreds
   c. Thousands

**29. Downshifting, pumping the brakes, and using the parking brake are all options when experiencing:**
   a. Hydroplaning
   b. Brake failure on a downgrade
   c. Loss of hydraulic pressure

**30. What is the number one cause of roadway fatalities in work zones?**
   a. Speeding
   b. Distracted driving
   c. DUI

**31. Neglecting to put your vehicle into the right gear while driving will result in:**
   a. Ease of stopping/shorter stopping time
   b. Less control
   c. Damage to the coupling

**32. In relation to your truck, what space is compact when carrying cargo and usually forgotten about?**
   a. Space below
   b. Space behind
   c. Space overhead

**33. Which of the following is the distance the vehicle will travel, in ideal conditions, while braking?**
   a. Braking distance
   b. Reaction distance
   c. Perception distance

**34. If you take a curve at high speed during normal driving conditions, and your tires keep their grip, what is the most likely outcome?**
   a. The vehicle will be sent into a roll.
   b. The vehicle will hydroplane.
   c. The vehicle will skid off the road.

**35. Ice will remain longer when:**
   a. It starts to rain.
   b. It's black ice.
   c. It's on shady parts of the road.

**36. What are some hazards that are frequently seen on the highway?**
   a. Workers, children, inattentive drivers, hurrying drivers, impaired drivers, suicides.
   b. Work zones, accidents.
   c. Road edge drop-offs, crashed airplanes, disabled vehicles.

**37. As a driver for what are you responsible regarding your cargo?**
   a. Inspecting your cargo, knowing that your cargo is securely tied down or covered, recognizing overloads and poorly balanced loads.
   b. Inspecting your cargo and keeping rainwater from getting under the pallets.
   c. Shifting your cargo at state lines and sliding your fifth wheel.

**38. In holding a steering wheel what is the proper way to place your hands?**
   a. Loosely with at least one hand on the wheel.
   b. One hand at the top of the wheel and one hand at the bottom of the wheel. In terms of the clock your hands should be at six o'clock and twelve o'clock.
   c. Firmly with both hands and your hands should be on opposite sides of the wheel. In terms of the clock, your hands should be at three o'clock and nine o'clock.

**39. Which of the following do you check by pumping the pedal 3 times, followed by applying firm pressure to the pedal and holding steady for 5 seconds, and finally ensuring the pedal is motionless?**
   a. Hydraulic brakes
   b. Parking brakes
   c. Air brakes

**40. The brakes lock up more readily when the trailer is:**
   a. Empty
   b. Full
   c. Old

**41. Which of the following can you utilize to check the traffic around you and issues on your own vehicle?**
   a. Retarders
   b. Signals
   c. Mirrors

**42. Which of the following does NOT reduce the clearance of a structure?**
   a. Repaving
   b. Packed snow
   c. Heavy load

**43. When you are stopped on the side of a one-way road or divided highway, what are the proper intervals from your truck to place your reflective triangles?**
   a. Behind you at 10 feet, 100 feet, and 200 feet
   b. In front of you at 100 feet and behind you at 10 feet and 100 feet
   c. Behind you at 10 feet and also anywhere from 100 to 500 feet

**44. What is controlled braking?**
   a. Brake so that your wheels will stop rolling and bring the vehicle to a quick stop.
   b. Apply your brakes fully and do not release them.
   c. Applying a lot of pressure to the brakes without locking the wheels.

**45. Which of the following is NOT advisable during a tire failure?**
   a. Grasp the steering wheel firmly.
   b. Brake until the vehicle slows down.
   c. After you've come to a stop, get out and check all the tires.

**46. What is the purpose of blocking and bracing?**
   a. To keep cargo from sliding, falling and getting out of balance.
   b. To keep containers from getting dirty.
   c. To support the trailer structure.

**47. In the case of brake failure while on a downgrade, what is the best option?**
   a. A side road that flattens out or turns uphill
   b. An open field
   c. An escape ramp

**48. When driving in very hot weather, you should inspect your tires every:**
   a. Two hours or 100 miles
   b. Four hours or 200 miles
   c. Six hours or 300 miles

**49. When can you drive a vehicle carrying hazardous materials if you do NOT have a hazardous material endorsement on your CDL?**
   a. Never
   b. If the vehicle does not require placards
   c. After filling out and signing a driver's report

**50. Which of the following is a required piece of emergency equipment for all commercial vehicles?**
   a. Emergency Response Guide (ERG)
   b. Spare windshield wiper blades
   c. Fire extinguisher

# Answer Key and Explanations for Test #4

**1. A:** When steering to avoid crashing, be prepared to "counter-steer" (turn the wheel back in the other direction) once you've passed whatever was blocking your path. Think of emergency steering and counter-steering as two parts of one driving action.

**2. A:** Yes.

**3. A:** Black ice is formed when the ice is a thin enough layer that you can see the road through it, creating the illusion that the pavement is wet. Be conscious of this in freezing temperatures.

**4. B:** Do not touch any leaking material—many people injure themselves by touching hazardous materials. Do not try to identify the material or find the source of a leak by smell. Toxic gases can destroy your sense of smell and can injure or kill you even if they don't smell. Never eat, drink, or smoke around a leak or spill. If hazardous materials are spilling from your vehicle, do not move it any more than safety requires. You may move off the road and away from places where people gather, if doing so serves safety. Only move your vehicle if you can do so without danger to yourself or others.

**5. B:** Release the accelerator and push in the clutch.

**6. C:** 12 to 15 seconds

**7. A:** Repaving or packed snow may have decreased the clearances since the heights were posted.

**8. A:** Checking the mirrors would be part of step 3, when you start the engine and inspect the inside of the cab.

**9. A:** Double clutching is the most common method used by those learning to shift gears. It is commonly used in truck-driving schools. This is the standard process:

- Remove your foot from the accelerator. Push in the clutch and shift into neutral.
- Release the clutch.
- Let the engine slow down the RPMs required for the next gear (usually 1,000 RPMs slower, but this can vary from truck to truck).
- Push in the clutch and shift to the higher gear.
- Let off the clutch and push the accelerator as you would on takeoff.

**10. B:** With vehicles towing trailers, a drive-wheel skid can let the trailer push the towing vehicle sideways, causing a sudden jackknife.

**11. C:** Four times as much distance.

**12. B:** You may hear a loud bang that often accompanies a blowout. However, you may mistake the noise for another vehicle, as yours will not have an immediate effect on your driving. It is best to always assume it was one of yours and to use your mirrors to check.

**13. B:** Over 40 miles per hour at least one second for each 10 feet of your vehicle length plus one extra second.

**14. A:** Flue system defects include: loose, broken, or missing exhaust mufflers, vents, pipeage, and vertical branches; system parts rubbing against elements of the fuel system, tires, or other mobile accessories of the vehicle; loose, broken, or missing mounting brackets, clamps, bolts, or nuts; and any leaking parts of the exhaust system.

**15. B:** If you are unable to complete a right turn without hitting another automobile, then swing as you make the turn. To prohibit others from passing you while mid-turn, keep the rear of the vehicle in close proximity to the curb.

**16. C:** Drunk drivers and drivers under the influence of drugs are a hazard to themselves and to you. Be especially alert around the closing times for bars and taverns. Watch for drivers who have trouble staying in their lane or maintaining speed, stop without reason, or show other signs of being under the influence of alcohol or drugs.

**17. C:** To be a safe driver, make sure your vehicle has plenty of space. This is because, if something goes wrong, space gives you time to think and to take action. This is why you need to manage space. While this is true for all drivers, it is especially important for drivers of large vehicles. Large vehicles take up more space, so they require more space for stopping and turning.

**18. A:** First, look at your path. Second, back slowly. Third, back, straight back.

**19. A:** You are required to yield the right-of-way to trains. If there is more than one track, make sure all tracks are clear before crossing. Many railroad-highway crossings also have gates with flashing red lights and bells. Stop when the lights begin to flash and before the gate lowers across the road lane. Remain stopped until the gates go up and the lights have stopped flashing. Proceed when it is safe. Never attempt to race a train to a crossing. It is extremely difficult to judge the speed of an approaching train.

**20. A:** Two.

**21. C:** Using the sound of the engine to know the appropriate time to shift.

**22. B:** Place both hands on the steering wheel. They should be on opposite sides of the steering wheel. Avoid sharp motions to the steering wheel; this could cause your vehicle to whip due to its length.

**23. C:** When backing with a trailer, you need to turn the steering wheel in the opposite direction of where you want the back of your trailer to go.

**24. B:** Check the engine compartment for: oil level, status of the hoses, coolant level in the radiator, fluid level and the state of the hoses concerning power steering, windshield washer fluid, battery connections, battery security and fluid level, automatic transmission fluid level (engine must be running), belts for deterioration from wear and excessive tightness, split or tattered electrical insulation wiring, and leaks in the engine compartment of: fuel, coolant, oil, power steering fluid, hydraulic fluid, and battery fluid.

**25. B:** When backing vehicles without trailers, rotate the steering wheel in the direction that you want the back of your vehicle to go.

**26. A:** After you've come to a stop, get out and check all the tires. Do this even if the vehicle seems to be handling right. If one of your dual tires goes out, the only way you may know it is by getting out and looking at it.

**27. C:** Top-heavy vehicles and tractors with multiple trailers may flip over when turned quickly.

**28. B:** Every year, hundreds of drivers avoid injury by using escape ramps. Some escape ramps use soft gravel that resists the motion of the vehicle and brings it to a stop. Others turn uphill, using the hill to stop the vehicle and soft gravel to hold it in place.

**29. C:** Lacking the appropriate pressure in the system will lead the brake pedal to feel spongy or to reach the floor. In this event, do the following: Downshift, or put the vehicle into a lower gear, to help slow the vehicle. Pump the brakes; sometimes this will cause the pedal to generate enough hydraulic pressure to stop the vehicle. Use the parking brake. The parking brake is separate, so it will still properly function. Be aware of an escape route—an open field, side street, or escape ramp. Turning uphill is a good way to slow and stop the vehicle, but make sure the vehicle does not start rolling backward after you stop. Also, putting the vehicle in a low gear, applying the parking brake, and rolling into an obstacle are all ways to stop.

**30. A:** The number one cause of fatalities in work zones on the roadway is speeding. Be aware of your speedometer and surroundings when going through road construction. Decrease your speed in the event of adverse weather or road conditions (even more so if the workers are on the roadway). Not only could this save the lives of the workers, but tickets for speeding in work zones are typically double the amount of a normal ticket. It pays to slow down.

**31. B:** Correct shifting of gears is vital. Failure to put your vehicle into the right gear while driving will mean less control, and you may have a more difficult time stopping.

**32. A:** The space under the vehicle is compact when carrying cargo and usually forgotten about. This is an issue when traveling along a dirt road or unpacked yards because the chances of getting hung up are increased.

**33. A:** Braking distance is the distance the vehicle will travel, in ideal conditions, while braking. For example, with a good brake, reaching a complete stop from 55 mph on dry pavement takes approximately 216 feet.

**34. A:** Drivers must adjust their speed for curves in the road. If you take a curve at high speed, the tires could keep their grip, sending the vehicle into a roll.

**35. C:** Ice will remain on shady parts of the road after it has melted in other areas.

**36. B:** Work zones, accidents.

**37. A:** Inspecting your cargo, knowing that your cargo is securely tied down or covered, recognizing overloads and poorly balanced loads.

**38. C:** Firmly with both hands and your hands should be on opposite sides of the wheel. In terms of the clock, your hands should be at three o'clock and nine o'clock.

**39. A:** Start the engine and check the brake system. If driving with hydraulic brakes, pump the pedal 3 times. Apply firm pressure to the pedal and hold steady for 5 seconds. The pedal should be motionless. If movement occurs, there may be problems, such as a leak. This must be fixed immediately.

**40. A:** The brakes are designed to control the maximum weight of the unit; therefore, the brakes lock up more readily when the trailer is empty or lightly loaded. This can cause skidding and loss of control.

**41. C:** Use your mirrors to check the traffic around you, and to check your vehicle for any problems (flat tires, fire, problems with cargo straps, etc.). Using your mirrors is especially vital when turning, changing lanes, or merging. Do not lose focus on the road ahead. Use your mirrors to check your tires. If you are carrying open cargo, check the mirrors to see that all of your straps or chains are still secure. Also, look for a flapping or bulging tarp.

**42. C:** Repaving or packed snow is capable of reducing the clearance of a structure. Weight is a factor that affects the height of a vehicle. A full load is shorter than an empty one; therefore, even if you can clear a structure with cargo, it doesn't mean you can with an empty bed.

**43. A:** Behind you at 10 feet, 100 feet, and 200 feet.

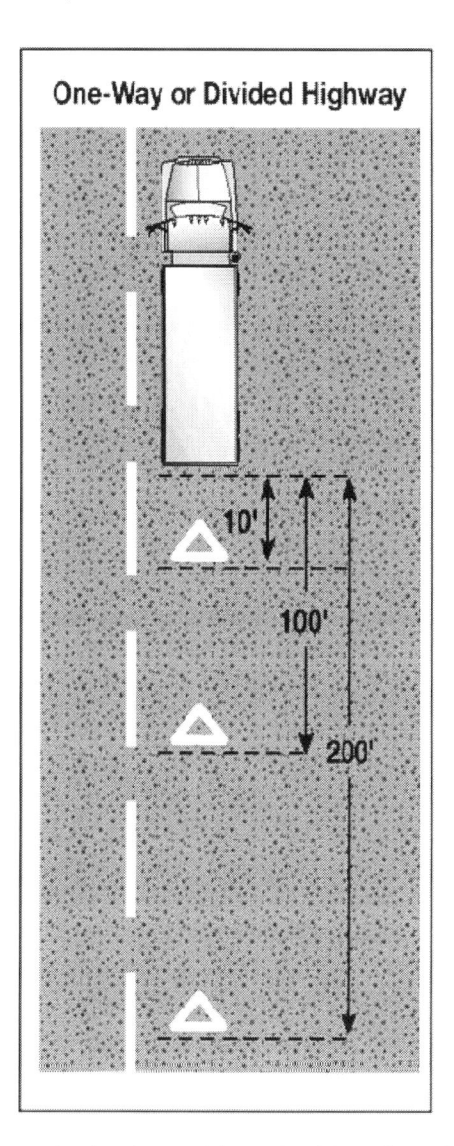

**44. C:** Applying a lot of pressure to the brakes without locking the wheels.

**45. B:** Keep off the brake. It's natural to want to halt in an emergency, but braking when a tire has failed could cause you to lose control. Unless you're about to run into something, stay off the brake until the vehicle has slowed down. Then brake very gently, pull off the road, and stop.

**46. A:** To keep cargo from sliding, falling and getting out of balance.

**47. C:** Once the brakes have failed, find something outside the truck to stop the movement. The best option for this is an escape ramp. If there is one available, there will be signs letting you know where each location is. Ramps can be found a few miles away from a downgrade.

**48. A:** Check the tire mounting and air pressure. Inspect the tires every two hours or every 100 miles when driving in very hot weather. Air pressure increases with temperature. Do not let air out, or the pressure will be too low when the tires cool off. If a tire is too hot to touch, remain stopped until the tire cools off. Otherwise, the tire may blow out or catch fire.

**49. B:** Not all vehicles that carry hazardous materials need placards. You can drive a vehicle carrying hazardous materials if it does not require placards. If it requires placards, you may not drive it unless you have a hazardous material endorsement on your commercial driver's license.

**50. C:** All commercial vehicles must have the following emergency equipment: fire extinguisher, spare fuses (unless your CMV has circuit breakers), and three reflective triangles.

# Air Brakes Endorsement

## Air Brakes

Air brakes use compressed air to make the brakes work. They are a good and safe way of stopping large and heavy vehicles, but the brakes must be well maintained and used properly. When we discuss air brakes, we are actually discussing three different braking systems. They are:

- The service brake system applies and releases the brakes when you use the brake pedal during normal driving.
- The parking brake system applies and releases the parking brakes when you use the parking brake control. There are parking brakes for the truck and the trailer. When connected to a trailer, always set both brakes when parking.
- The emergency brake system uses parts of the service and parking brake systems to stop the vehicle in a brake system failure.

## Air Brake System Parts

**Air compressor**: The air compressor pumps air into the air storage tanks (reservoirs). It is connected to the engine through gears or a v-belt. The compressor may be air cooled or may be cooled by the engine cooling system. It may have its own oil supply or be lubricated by engine oil. If the compressor has its own oil supply, check the oil level before driving.

**Air compressor governor**: The governor controls when the air compressor will pump air into the air storage tanks. When air tank pressure rises to the "cut-out" level (around 125 pounds per-square-inch or "psi"), the governor stops the compressor from pumping air. When the tank pressure falls to the "cut-in" pressure (around 100 psi), the governor allows the compressor to start pumping again.

**Air storage tanks**: Air storage tanks are used to hold compressed air. The number and size of air tanks varies among vehicles. The tanks will hold enough air to allow the brakes to be used several times, even if the compressor stops working.

**Air tank drains**: Compressed air usually has some water and some compressor oil in it, which is bad for the air brake system. For example, the water can freeze in cold weather and cause brake failure. The water and oil tend to collect in the bottom of the air tank. Be sure that you drain the air tanks completely. Each air tank is equipped with a drain valve in the bottom. There are two types:

- Manual—Manually operated by turning a quarter turn or by pulling a cable. You must drain the tanks yourself at the end of each day of driving.
- Automatic—The water and oil are automatically expelled. These tanks may be equipped for manual draining as well. Automatic air tanks are available with electric heating devices, which help prevent freezing of the automatic drain in cold weather.

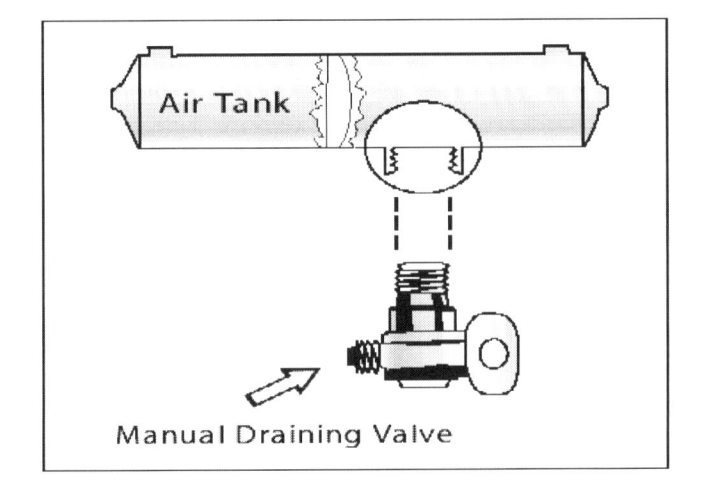

**Alcohol evaporator**: Some air brake systems have an alcohol evaporator to put alcohol into the air system. This helps to reduce the risk of ice in air brake valves and other parts during cold weather. Ice inside the system can make the brakes stop working. Check the alcohol container and fill up as necessary, every day during cold weather. Daily air tank drainage is still needed to get rid of water and oil. (Unless the system has automatic drain valves.)

**Safety valve**: A safety relief valve is installed in the first tank the air compressor pumps air to. The safety valve protects the tank and the rest of the system from too much pressure. The valve is usually set to open at 150 psi. If the safety valve releases air, something is wrong. Have the fault fixed by a mechanic.

**The brake pedal**: You put on the brakes by pushing down the brake pedal. (It is also called the foot valve or treadle valve.) Pushing the pedal down harder applies more air pressure. Letting up on the brake pedal reduces the air pressure and releases the brakes. Releasing the brakes lets some compressed air go out of the system, so the air pressure in the tanks is reduced. It must be made up by the air compressor. Pressing and releasing the pedal unnecessarily can let air out faster than the compressor can replace it. If the pressure gets too low, the brakes won't work.

**Foundation brakes**: Foundation brakes are used at each wheel. The most common type is the s-cam drum brake.

**Brake drums, shoes, and linings**: Brake drums are located on each end of the vehicle's axles. The wheels are bolted to the drums. The braking mechanism is inside the drum. To stop, the brake shoes and linings are pushed against the inside of the drum. This causes friction, which slows the vehicle (and creates heat). The heat a drum can take without damage depends on how hard and how long the brakes are used. Too much heat can make the brakes stop working.

**DRUM BRAKE**

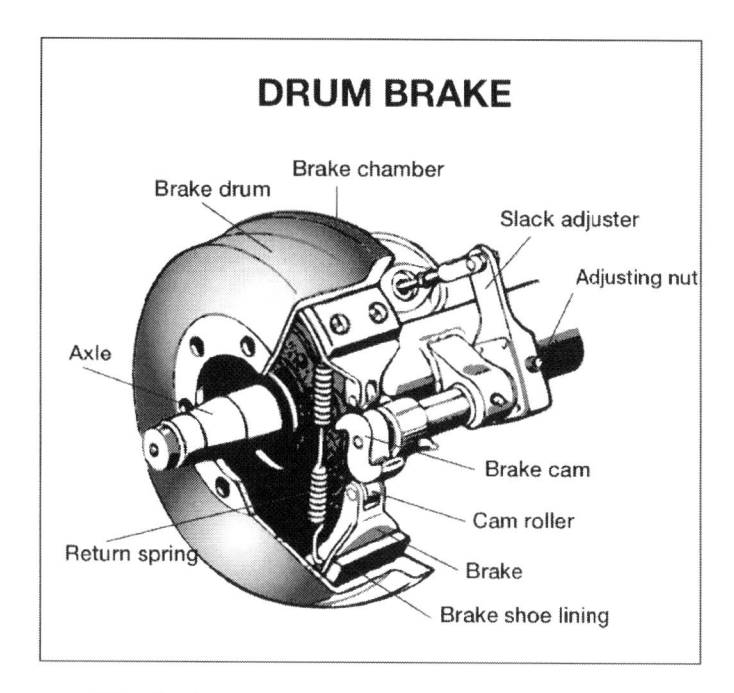

- Brake drum
- Brake chamber
- Slack adjuster
- Adjusting nut
- Axle
- Brake cam
- Cam roller
- Return spring
- Brake
- Brake shoe lining

**Supply pressure gauges**: All vehicles with air brakes have a pressure gauge connected to the air tank. If the vehicle has a dual air brake system, there will be a gauge for each half of the system. (Or a single gauge with two needles.) Dual systems will be discussed later. These gauges tell you how much pressure is in the air tanks.

**Application pressure gauge**: This gauge shows you how much air pressure is being applied to the brakes. (This gauge is not on all vehicles.) Increasing application pressure to hold the same speed means the brakes are fading. You should slow down and use a lower gear. The need for increased pressure can also be caused by brakes out of adjustment, air leaks, or mechanical problems.

**Low air pressure warning**: A low air pressure warning signal is required on vehicles with air brakes. A warning signal you can see must come on before the air pressure in the tanks falls below 60 psi. (Or one half the compressor governor cut out pressure on older vehicles.) The warning is usually a red light. A buzzer may also come on.

**Stop light switch**: Drivers behind you must be warned when you put your brakes on. The air brake system does this with an electric switch that works by air pressure. The switch turns on the brake lights when you put on the air brakes.

**Front brake limiting valve**: Some older vehicles (made before 1975) have a front brake limiting valve and a control in the cab. The control is usually marked "normal" and "slippery." When you put the control in the "slippery" position, the limiting valve cuts the "normal" air pressure to the front brakes by half. Limiting valves were used to reduce the chance of the front wheels skidding on slippery surfaces. However, they actually reduce the stopping power of the vehicle. Front wheel braking is good under all conditions. Tests have shown front wheel skids from braking are not likely even on ice. Make sure the control is in the "Normal" position to have normal stopping power. Many vehicles have automatic front wheel limiting valves. They reduce the air to the front brakes except when the brakes are put on very hard (60 psi or more application pressure). These valves cannot be controlled by the driver.

**Spring brakes**: Many vehicles have automatic front wheel limiting valves. They reduce the air to the front brakes except when the brakes are put on very hard (60 psi or more application pressure).

These valves cannot be controlled by the driver. Tractor and straight truck spring brakes will activate fully when air pressure drops to a range between 20 to 45 psi (typically 20 to 30 psi). Do not wait for the brakes to come on automatically. When the low air pressure warning light and buzzer first come on, bring the vehicle to a safe stop right away, while you still have control of the brakes. The braking power of spring brakes depends on the brakes being in adjustment. If the brakes are not adjusted properly, neither the regular brakes nor the emergency/parking brakes will work right.

**Parking brake controls**: In newer vehicles with air brakes, you put on the parking brakes using a diamond-shaped, yellow, push-pull control knob. You pull the knob out to put the parking brakes (spring brakes) on, and push it in to release them. On older vehicles, the parking brakes may be controlled by a lever. Use the parking brakes whenever you park.

Never push the brake pedal down when the spring brakes are on. If you do, the brakes could be damaged by the combined forces of the springs and the air pressure. Many brake systems are designed in a way that will not allow this to happen. However, not all systems are set up that way, and those that are may not always work.

**Modulating control valves**: In some vehicles a control handle on the dash board may be used to apply the spring brakes gradually. This is called a modulating valve. It is spring-loaded so you have a feel for the braking action. The more you move the control lever, the harder the spring brakes come on. They work this way so you can control the spring brakes if the service brakes fail. When parking a vehicle with a modulating control valve, move the lever as far as it will go and hold it in place with the locking device.

**Dual parking control valves**: When main air pressure is lost, the spring brakes come on. Some vehicles, such as buses, have a separate air tank which can be used to release the spring brakes. This is so you can move the vehicle in an emergency. One of the valves is a push-pull type and is used to put on the spring brakes for parking. The other valve is spring loaded in the "out" position. When you push the control in, air from the separate air tank releases the spring brakes so you can move. When you release the button, the spring brakes come on again. There is only enough air in the separate tank to do this a few times. Therefore, plan carefully when moving. Otherwise, you may be stopped in a dangerous location when the separate air supply runs out. Use the parking brakes whenever you park.

**Anti-Lock Braking Systems (ABS)**: Truck tractors with air brakes built on or after March 1, 1997, and other air brakes vehicles, (trucks, buses, trailers, and converter dollies) built on or after March 1, 1998, are required to be equipped with antilock brakes. Many commercial vehicles built before these dates have been voluntarily equipped with ABS. Check the certification label for the date of manufacture to determine if your vehicle is equipped with ABS. ABS is a computerized system that keeps your wheels from locking up during hard brake applications. Vehicles with ABS have yellow malfunction lamps to tell you if something isn't working. Tractors, trucks, and buses will have yellow ABS malfunction lamps on the instrument panel. Trailers will have yellow ABS malfunction lamps on the left side, either on the front or rear corner. Dollies manufactured on or after March 1, 1998 are required to have a lamp on the left side.

On newer vehicles, the malfunction lamp comes on at start-up for a bulb check, and then goes out quickly. On older systems, the lamp could stay on until you are driving over five mph. If the lamp stays on after the bulb check, or goes on once you are underway, you may have lost ABS control at one or more wheels. In the case of towed units manufactured before it was required by the Department of Transportation, it may be difficult to tell if the unit is equipped with ABS. Look under the vehicle for the electronic control unit (ECU) and wheel speed sensor wires coming from the back of the brakes. ABS is an addition to your normal brakes. It does not decrease or increase your normal braking capability. ABS only activates when wheels are about to lock up. ABS does not necessarily shorten your stopping distance, but it does help you keep the vehicle under control during hard braking.

## Dual Air Brake Systems

Most heavy-duty vehicles use dual air brake systems for safety. A dual air brake system has two separate air brake systems, which use a single set of brake controls. Each system has its own air tanks, hoses, lines, etc. One system typically operates the regular brakes on the rear axle or axles. The other system operates the regular brakes on the front axle (and possibly one rear axle). Both systems supply air to the trailer (if there is one). The first system is called the "primary" system. The other is called the "secondary" system. Before driving a vehicle with a dual air system, allow time for the air compressor to build up a minimum of 100 psi pressure in both the primary and secondary systems. Watch the primary and secondary air pressure gauges (or needles, if the system has two needles in one gauge). Pay attention to the low air pressure warning light and buzzer. The warning light and buzzer should shut off when air pressure in both systems rises to a value set by the manufacturer. This value must be greater than 60 psi. The warning light and buzzer should come on before the air pressure drops below 60 psi in either system. If this happens while driving, you should stop right away and safely park the vehicle. If one air system is very low on pressure, either the front or the rear brakes will not be operating fully. This means it will take you longer to stop. Bring the vehicle to a safe stop, and have the air brakes system fixed.

## Inspecting Air Brake Systems

There are more things to inspect on a vehicle with air brakes than one without them:

- Engine compartment check
  - Check the air compressor drive belt if the compressor is belt driven. Check the condition and tightness of the belt.
- Walk-around inspection
  - Check the manual slack adjusters on the S-Cam brakes.
  - Park on level ground and chock the wheels.
  - Turn off the parking brakes so you can move the slack adjusters.
  - Use gloves and pull hard on each slack adjuster that you can reach.
  - If a slack adjuster moves more than about one inch where the push rod attaches to it, it probably needs adjustment.
  - Adjust it or have it adjusted. Vehicles with too much brake slack can be hard to stop. Out-of-adjustment brakes are the most common problem found in roadside inspections.
  - Check the brake drums (or discs), linings and hoses.
  - Brake drums or discs cannot have cracks longer than half the width of the friction area.
  - Linings (friction material) cannot be loose, soaked with oil or grease. They cannot be dangerously thin.
  - Mechanical parts must be in place and should not be broken or missing.
  - Check the air hoses connected to the brake chambers to make sure they are not cut or worn due to rubbing.

- Check the air brake system.
  - Checking the air brake system is different from the hydraulic brake check shown in Section 1: General Knowledge.
    - Test the low-pressure warning signal.
    - Shut off the engine when you have enough air pressure so that the low-pressure warning signal is off.
    - Turn on the electrical power and step on and off the brake pedal to reduce air tank pressure.
    - The low air pressure warning signal must come on before the pressure drops to less than 60 psi in the air tank (or tank with the lowest air pressure in dual air systems).
    - If the warning signal doesn't work, you could lose air pressure without knowing it. This could cause sudden emergency braking. In dual systems, the stopping distance will be increased. Only limited braking can be done before the spring brakes come on.
  - Be sure that spring brakes come on automatically.
    - Chock the wheels, release the parking brakes when you have enough air pressure and shut off the engine.
    - Step on and off the brake pedal to reduce the air tank pressure.
    - The parking brake knob should pop out when the air pressure falls to the manufacturer's specification (usually 20-40 psi). This causes the spring brakes to come on.
    - Check the rate of air pressure build-up.
    - When the engine is at operating RPM (check the manufacturer's specifications to determine the correct operating RPM), the pressure should build from 85 to 100 psi within 45 seconds in dual air systems.
    - If the vehicle has larger than minimum air tanks, the buildup time can be longer. Check the manufacturer's specifications.
    - In single air systems (built before 1975), pressure typically builds from 50 to 90 psi within 3 minutes with the engine at an idle speed of 600-900 RPM.
    - If air pressure does not build fast enough, your pressure may drop too low during driving. This will require an emergency stop. Don't drive until you get the problem fixed.
  - Test the air leakage rate.
    - When the air system is fully charged (120-125 psi), turn off the engine, release the service brake and time the air pressure drop. The loss rate should be less than 2 psi in one minute for single vehicles. It should be less than 3 psi in one minute for combination vehicles.
    - Apply 90 psi or more with the brake pedal. After the initial pressure drop, if air pressure falls more than 3 psi in one minute for single vehicles (4 psi for combination vehicles), the air loss rate is too high.
    - Check for air leaks and fix them before driving or you could lose your brakes while driving.

- o Check the air compressor governor cut-in and cut-out pressures.
    - ❖ Air compressor pumping should start at about 100 psi and stop at about 125 psi. Check the manufacturer's specifications.
    - ❖ Run the engine at a fast idle. The air governor should cut out the air compressor at the manufacturer's specified pressure. The air pressure shown by your gauge(s) will stop rising.
    - ❖ With the engine idling, step on and off the brake to reduce the air tank pressure. The compressor should cut in at the manufacturer's specified cut-in pressure. The pressure should begin to rise.
    - ❖ If the air governor does not work as described above, it may need to be fixed. A governor that does not work right may not keep enough air pressure for safe driving.
- o Test the parking brake. Stop the vehicle, put on the parking brake, and gently pull against it in a low gear to test that the parking brake will hold.
- o Test the service brakes.
    - ❖ Wait for normal air pressure to build, release the parking brake, move the vehicle forward slowly (about 5 mph) and apply the brakes firmly using the brake pedal.
    - ❖ Watch to see if the vehicle pulls to one side, feels unusual or stops slowly.
    - ❖ This test can show you problems which you would not know about until you used the brakes on the road.

## Using Air Brakes

### Normal Stops

Push the brake pedal down. Control the pressure so the vehicle comes to a smooth, safe stop. If you have a manual transmission, don't push the clutch in until the engine rpm is down close to idle. When stopped, select a starting gear.

### Braking with Anti-Lock Brakes

When you brake hard on slippery surfaces in a vehicle without ABS, your wheels may lock up. When your steering wheels lock up, you lose steering control. When your other wheels lock up, you may skid, jackknife, or even spin the vehicle. ABS helps you avoid wheel lock up. The computer senses impending lockup, reduces the braking pressure to a safe level, and you maintain control. You may or may not be able to stop faster with ABS, but you should be able to steer around an obstacle while braking, and avoid skids caused by over braking. Having ABS on only the tractor, only the trailer, or even on only one axle, still gives you more control over the vehicle during braking. Brake normally. When only the tractor has ABS, you should be able to maintain steering control, and there is less chance of jackknifing. But, keep your eye on the trailer and let up on the brakes (if you can safely do so) if it begins to swing out. When only the trailer has ABS, the trailer is less likely to swing out, but if you lose steering control or start a tractor jackknife, let up on the brakes (if you can safely do so) until you gain control. When you drive a tractor-trailer combination with ABS, you should brake as you always have. In other words:

- Use only the braking force necessary to stop safely and stay in control.
- Brake the same way, regardless of whether you have ABS on the tractor, the trailer, or both.
- As you slow down, monitor your tractor and trailer and back off the brakes (if it is safe to do so) to stay in control.

There is only one exception to this procedure, if you always drive a straight truck or combination with working ABS on all axles, in an emergency stop, you can fully apply the brakes. Without ABS, you still have normal brake functions. Drive and brake as you always have. Remember, if your ABS malfunctions, you still have regular brakes. Drive normally, but get the system serviced soon.

## BRAKING ON DOWNGRADES

The use of brakes on a long and/or steep downgrade is only a supplement to the braking effect of the engine. Once the vehicle is in the proper low gear, the following is the proper braking technique:

- Apply the brakes just hard enough to feel a definite slowdown.
- When your speed has been reduced to approximately five mph below your "safe" speed, release the brakes. (This application should last for about three seconds.)
- When your speed has increased to your "safe" speed, repeat steps 1 and 2.

For example, if your "safe" speed is 40 mph, you would not apply the brakes until your speed reaches 40 mph. You now apply the brakes hard enough to gradually reduce your speed to 35 mph and then release the brakes. Repeat this as often as necessary until you have reached the end of the downgrade.

## STOPPING DISTANCE

Air brakes increase your stopping distance. Hydraulic brakes (used on cars and light/medium trucks) work instantly. Air brakes take half a second or more for the air to flow through the lines to the brakes. Due to this, vehicles with air brakes require more stopping distance than vehicles with other types of brakes. The total stopping distance for vehicles with air brake systems is made up of four different factors:

- Perception distance: the distance your vehicle travels from the time your eyes see a hazard until your brain recognizes it
- Reaction distance: the distance your vehicle travels from the time your brain tells your foot to move from the accelerator until the time your foot pushes the brake
- Brake lag distance: the distance your vehicle travels from the time your foot pushes the air brake until the brake takes hold
- Braking distance: the distance your vehicle travels between the time the brakes take hold and the vehicle stops

By adding these distances together, you will get your total stopping distance. The air brake lag distance at 55 mph on dry pavement adds about 32 feet. So at 55 mph for an average driver under good traction and brake conditions, the total stopping distance is over 450 feet.

## BRAKE FADING OR FAILURE

Brakes are designed so brake shoes or pads rub against the brake drum or disks to slow the vehicle. Braking creates heat, but brakes are designed to take a lot of heat. However, brakes can fade or fail from excessive heat caused by using them too much and not relying on the engine braking effect. Excessive use of the service brakes causes overheating and leads to brake fade. Excessive heat in the brakes causes chemical changes in the lining which reduces friction and causes the brake drums to expand. As the overheated drums expand, the brake shoes and linings have to move farther to contact the drums, and the force of this contact is reduced. Continued overuse may increase brake fade until the vehicle cannot be slowed down or stopped. Brake fade is also affected by adjustment. To safely control a vehicle, every brake must do its share of the work. Brakes out of adjustment will stop doing their share before those that are in adjustment. The other brakes can then overheat and fade, and there will not be enough braking available to control the vehicle(s). Brakes can get out of adjustment quickly, especially when they are hot. Therefore, check brake adjustment often.

## Low Air Pressure

If the low air pressure warning comes on, stop and safely park your vehicle as soon as possible. There might be an air leak in the system. Controlled braking is possible only while enough air remains in the air tanks. The spring brakes will come on when the air pressure drops into the range of 20-45 psi. A heavily loaded vehicle will take a long distance to stop because the spring brakes do not work on all axles. Lightly loaded vehicles or vehicles on slippery roads may skid out of control when the spring brakes come on. It is much safer to stop while there is enough air in the tanks to use the foot brakes.

## Parking Brakes

Any time you park, use the parking brakes, except as noted below. Pull the parking brake control knob out to apply the parking brakes, push it in to release. The control will be a yellow, diamond-shaped knob labeled "parking brakes" on newer vehicles. On older vehicles, it may be a round blue knob or some other shape (including a lever that swings from side to side or up and down). Don't use the parking brakes if the brakes are very hot (from just having come down a steep grade), or if the brakes are very wet in freezing temperatures. If they are used while they are very hot, they can be damaged by the heat. If they are used in freezing temperatures when the brakes are very wet, they can freeze so the vehicle cannot move. Use wheel chocks on a level surface to hold the vehicle. Let hot brakes cool before using the parking brakes. If the brakes are wet, use the brakes lightly while driving in a low gear to heat and dry them. If your vehicle does not have automatic air tank drains, drain your air tanks at the end of each working day to remove moisture and oil. Otherwise, the brakes could fail. Never leave your vehicle unattended without applying the parking brakes or chocking the wheels. The vehicle could roll, causing injury and damage.

# Air Brakes Endorsement Practice Test #1

**1. The antilock braking system (ABS) only activates when:**
   a. You tap the brakes.
   b. You are in a skid.
   c. Your wheels are about to lock up.

**2. In dual air systems, when the engine is at operating RPM, the air pressure should build from 85 to 100 psi within how many seconds?**
   a. Within 30 seconds
   b. Within 45 seconds
   c. Within 60 seconds

**3. What are two other names for the brake pedal?**
   a. It can be called the foot valve or the relay valve.
   b. It can be called the foot valve or treadle valve.
   c. It can be called the relay valve or air compressor valve.

**4. How do you test that the parking brake will hold?**
   a. When stopped, engage the parking brake, and ensure the parking brake knob pops out.
   b. Stop the vehicle, put on the parking brake, and gently pull against it in a low gear.
   c. Wait for normal air pressure to build, move the vehicle forward slowly, and apply the brakes firmly.

**5. No automatic tank drains - when should you drain the air tanks?**
   a. Once a week.
   b. Once a month.
   c. Every day.

**6. What truck tractors with air brakes are required to be equipped with antilock brakes?**
   a. Those built on or after March 1, 1997
   b. Those built on or after March 1, 2001
   c. Those built on or after March 1, 2003

**7. Byproducts of the air compression process, like water and compressor oil, tend to collect in the bottom of the:**
   a. Air compressor
   b. Air compressor governor
   c. Air storage tanks

**8. Which of the following are located on each end of the vehicle's axles, with the wheels bolted to them?**
   a. Linings
   b. Drums
   c. Shoes

**9. How many different braking systems are included in air brakes?**
   a. 2
   b. 3
   c. 4

**10. Perception distance is the distance your vehicle travels:**
   a. From the time your foot pushes the air brake until the brake takes hold
   b. From the time your brain tells your foot to move from the accelerator until the time your foot pushes the brake
   c. From the time your eyes see a hazard until your brain recognizes it

**11. How often should you check the alcohol evaporator in cold weather?**
   a. Check the alcohol container and fill up as necessary once each week.
   b. Check the alcohol container once each fall before cold weather starts.
   c. Check the alcohol container and fill up as necessary every day.

**12. If the air pressure drops and the spring brakes come on, what vehicle is most likely to skid out of control?**
   a. A lightly loaded vehicle
   b. A vehicle with a heavy load
   c. A vehicle in average traction and brake conditions

**13. When making a normal stop when should you push in the clutch?**
   a. Experienced drivers do not use the clutch.
   b. Do not push in the clutch until there is vibration.
   c. Do not push the clutch in until the engine R.P.M.'s are down close to idle.

**14. What should you do before checking free play in manual slack adjusters?**
   a. Park in a secure location and remove all wheel chocks.
   b. Park on level ground so that the wheels will not have to be choked.
   c. Park on level ground and chock the wheels and release parking brakes.

**15. The cracks in brake drums or discs cannot be longer than:**
   a. Half the width of the friction area
   b. One-third the width of the friction area
   c. One-quarter the width of the friction area

**16. What should you look for in checking an air compressor belt?**
   a. Check for belts that are the wrong color.
   b. Check for belts that are not made of rubber.
   c. Check belts for excessive wear and cracks and tightness.

**17. What are the three types of low air pressure warning devices?**
   a. A siren . . . or a horn . . . or 4-way flashers.
   b. A red light . . . or a buzzer . . . or a wigwag.
   c. An air horn . . . or an amber light . . . or a whistle.

18. Brakes can get out of adjustment quickly, especially when they are:
    a. Old
    b. Heavy
    c. Hot

19. On S-Cam brakes what happens to the air when you push the brake pedal?
    a. Air pressure forces out the push rod and moves the slack adjuster.
    b. Air pressure works only with wedge brakes and not with S-Cam brakes.
    c. Air pressure is converted into hydraulic pressure.

20. What are the three braking systems?
    a. The parking brake and emergency brake and thermal system
    b. The service brake and parking brake and emergency system.
    c. The service brake and emergency and the inverse system.

21. What is stab braking?
    a. Putting the brakes on hard without locking the wheels or turning
    b. Pressing the brake pedal hard and releasing brakes when wheels lock up.
    c. Applying a constant pressure to the brakes.

22. In normal driving parking and emergency brakes are usually held back by?
    a. Electric relay switches.
    b. Wheel chocks.
    c. Air pressure.

23. Before driving a vehicle with a dual air system, allow time for the air compressor to build up a minimum of:
    a. 100 psi pressure in both the primary and secondary systems
    b. 75 psi pressure in the primary system and 50 psi in the secondary system
    c. 125 psi pressure in both the primary and secondary systems

24. If you are driving a straight truck or combination with working ABS on all axles, in an emergency stop, you can:
    a. Fully apply the brakes.
    b. Apply the brakes just hard enough to feel a definite slowdown.
    c. Only use the braking force necessary to stop safely and stay in control.

25. What does the air compressor governor control?
    a. It controls emergency warning systems.
    b. It controls when the compressor will pump air into the air storage tanks.
    c. It controls how the compressor will pump air into the air lines.

# Answer Key and Explanations for Test #1

**1. C:** ABS is an addition to your normal brakes. It does not decrease or increase your normal braking capability. ABS only activates when wheels are about to lock up. ABS does not necessarily shorten your stopping distance, but it does help you keep the vehicle under control during hard braking.

**2. B:** When the engine is at operating RPM (check the manufacturer's specifications to determine the correct operating RPM), the pressure should build from 85 to 100 psi within 45 seconds in dual air systems.

**3. B**: It can be called the foot valve or treadle valve.

**4. B:** To test the parking brake: Stop the vehicle, put on the parking brake, and gently pull against it in a low gear to test that the parking brake will hold.

**5. C**: Every day.

**6. A:** Truck tractors with air brakes must be equipped with antilock brakes if they were built on or after March 1, 1997. Other air-brake vehicles (trucks, buses, trailers, and converter dollies) must be equipped with antilock brakes if they were built on or after March 1, 1998.

**7. C:** Compressed air usually has some water and some compressor oil in it, which is bad for the air brake system. For example, the water can freeze in cold weather and cause brake failure. The water and oil tend to collect in the bottom of the air tank. Be sure that you drain the air tanks completely. Each air tank is equipped with a drain valve in the bottom.

**8. B:** Brake drums are located on each end of the vehicle's axles. The wheels are bolted to the drums. The braking mechanism is inside the drum.

**9. B:** When we discuss air brakes, we are actually discussing three different braking systems: the service brake system, parking brake system, and emergency brake system.

**10. C:** Perception distance is the distance your vehicle travels from the time your eyes see a hazard until your brain recognizes it.

**11. C**: Check the alcohol container and fill up as necessary every day.

**12. A:** Controlled braking is possible only while enough air remains in the air tanks. The spring brakes will come on when the air pressure drops into the range of 20-45 psi. A heavily loaded vehicle will take a long distance to stop because the spring brakes do not work on all axles. Lightly loaded vehicles or vehicles on slippery roads may skid out of control when the spring brakes come on. It is much safer to stop while there is enough air in the tanks to use the foot brakes.

**13. C**: Do not push the clutch in until the engine R.P.M.'s are down close to idle.

**14. C**: Park on level ground and chock the wheels and release parking brakes.

**15. A:** Brake drums or discs cannot have cracks longer than half the width of the friction area.

**16. C**: Check belts for excessive wear and cracks and tightness.

**17. B**: A red light . . . or a buzzer . . . or a wigwag.

**18. C:** Brakes can get out of adjustment quickly, especially when they are hot. Therefore, check brake adjustment often.

**19. A**: Air pressure forces out the push rod and moves the slack adjuster.

**20. B**: The service brake and parking brake and emergency system.

**21. B**: Pressing the brake pedal hard and releasing brakes when wheels lock up.

**22. C**: Air pressure.

**23. A:** Before driving a vehicle with a dual air system, allow time for the air compressor to build up a minimum of 100 psi pressure in both the primary and secondary systems. Watch the primary and secondary air pressure gauges (or needles, if the system has two needles in one gauge). Pay attention to the low air pressure warning light and buzzer. The warning light and buzzer should shut off when air pressure in both systems rises to a value set by the manufacturer.

**24. A:** If you always drive a straight truck or combination with working ABS on all axles, in an emergency stop, you can fully apply the brakes.

**25. B**: It controls when the compressor will pump air into the air storage tanks.

# Air Brakes Endorsement Practice Test #2

1. If the air compressor begins to leak what keeps air in the tanks?
   a. The slack adjusters.
   b. The alcohol evaporator.
   c. The one-way check valve.

2. As compared to vehicles with other kinds of brakes, the total stopping distance for vehicles with air brake systems is:
   a. Lessened
   b. The same
   c. Increased

3. What kind of warning signal is required on vehicles with air brakes?
   a. A high air pressure warning signal.
   b. A low air pressure warning signal.
   c. A changing air pressure warning signal.

4. When making a very quick stop you should brake so that you?
   a. Can turn quickly to get out the way of hazards.
   b. Skid to maximize stopping distance.
   c. Stay in a straight line and can steer.

5. Safety valves on air compressor tanks are generally set to open at what psi?
   a. 125 psi
   b. 150 psi
   c. 175 psi

6. What is another name for controlled braking?
   a. Steady braking.
   b. Hard braking.
   c. Squeeze braking.

7. Where are foundation brakes found?
   a. At each wheel.
   b. On every other axle.
   c. On the drive wheels only.

8. The effectiveness of the spring brakes depends on the adjustment of?
   a. Emergency brakes.
   b. Service brakes.
   c. Front wheel brakes.

9. Combination vehicle: brakes released. The maximum air released?
   a. One pound per square inch.
   b. Less than two pounds per square inch.
   c. Less than three pounds per square inch.

**10. In regard to air brakes, which of the following systems applies and releases the brakes when you use the brake pedal during normal driving?**
   a. Service brake system
   b. Parking brake system
   c. Emergency brake system

**11. How do you test the service brakes?**
   a. Stop the vehicle, firmly press the brake pedal, and then gently press the accelerator at the same time.
   b. While in motion, alternate between using the retarders and the service brakes.
   c. Wait for normal air pressure to build, release the parking brake, move the vehicle forward slowly, and then apply the brakes firmly.

**12. The emergency brake utilizes parts of what systems to stop the vehicle in a brake system failure?**
   a. Truck brake system and dual air brake system
   b. Hydraulic brake system and trailer brake system
   c. Service brake system and parking brake system

**13. If oil and water collect in the air tanks what can happen to the brakes?**
   a. The brakes can fail.
   b. Brake linings will automatically slip loose
   c. The brakes will work better.

**14. Reaction distance is the distance your vehicle travels:**
   a. From the time the brakes take hold to the time the vehicle stops
   b. From the time your brain tells your foot to move from the accelerator until the time your foot pushes the brake
   c. From the time your eyes see a hazard until your brain recognizes it

**15. What vehicles with air brakes other than truck tractors (for example, trucks, buses, trailers, and converter dollies) are required to be equipped with antilock brakes?**
   a. Those built on or after March 1, 1992
   b. Those built on or after March 1, 1998
   c. Those built on or after March 1, 2004

**16. After applying brakes fully, maximum air loss in one minute - single vehicles?**
   a. Two pounds per square inch.
   b. Three pounds per square inch.
   c. Four pounds per square inch.

**17. What gauge shows you how much air pressure is being applied to the brakes?**
   a. Air pressure gauge
   b. Supply pressure gauge
   c. Application pressure gauge

**18. What does the air compressor do?**
   a. Pumps air into the air storage tanks.
   b. Keeps the tires inflated to proper pressure
   c. Comes on only if you have to make an emergency stop.

**19. Which of the following is characterized by a control handle on the dashboard used to apply the spring brakes gradually?**
   a. Front brake limiting valve
   b. Modulating control valve
   c. Dual parking control valve

**20. For combination vehicles, when the air system is fully charged, the engine is turned off, and the service brakes are released, the air loss rate should be how many psi in one minute?**
   a. Less than 1 psi
   b. Less than 2 psi
   c. Less than 3 psi

**21. Almost anytime you park, you should use the parking brakes. Which of the following is an exception to that rule?**
   a. When the brakes are very hot
   b. If the brakes are wet in warm weather
   c. Whenever the brakes are extremely old

**22. A slack adjuster probably needs adjustment if it moves (where the push rod attaches to it) more than about:**
   a. $\frac{1}{2}$ inch
   b. 1 inch
   c. $1\frac{3}{4}$ inches

**23. At what time can you push the brake pedal down when the spring brakes are already engaged?**
   a. Anytime
   b. Occasionally
   c. Never

**24. Where are brake shoes and linings located?**
   a. Directly beneath the foot valve.
   b. Inside each brake drum
   c. On the outside of certain brake drums.

**25. At 55 mph on dry pavement, the air brake lag distance adds about:**
   a. 26 feet
   b. 32 feet
   c. 44 feet

# Answer Key and Explanations for Test #2

**1. C**: The one-way check valve.

**2. C**: Air brakes increase your stopping distance. Hydraulic brakes (used on cars and light/medium trucks) work instantly. Air brakes take half a second or more for the air to flow through the lines to the brakes. Due to this, vehicles with air brakes require more stopping distance than vehicles with other types of brakes.

**3. B**: A low air pressure warning signal.

**4. C**: Stay in a straight line and can steer.

**5. B**: A safety relief valve is installed in the first tank the air compressor pumps air to. The safety valve protects the tank and the rest of the system from building too much pressure. The valve is usually set to open at 150 psi. If the safety valve releases air, something is wrong. Have the fault fixed by a mechanic.

**6. C**: Squeeze braking.

**7. A**: At each wheel.

**8. B**: Service brakes.

**9. C**: Less than three pounds per square inch.

**10. A**: The service brake system applies and releases the brakes when you use the brake pedal during normal driving.

**11. C**: To test the service brakes: Wait for normal air pressure to build, release the parking brake, move the vehicle forward slowly (about 5 mph), and apply the brakes firmly using the brake pedal. Watch to see if the vehicle pulls to one side, feels unusual, or stops slowly. This test can show you problems that you would not know about until you used the brakes on the road.

**12. C**: The emergency brake system uses parts of the service and parking brake systems to stop the vehicle in a brake system failure.

**13. A**: The brakes can fail.

**14. B**: Reaction distance is the distance your vehicle travels from the time your brain tells your foot to move from the accelerator until the time your foot pushes the brake.

**15. B**: Truck tractors with air brakes must be equipped with antilock brakes if they were built on or after March 1, 1997. Other air-brake vehicles (trucks, buses, trailers, and converter dollies) must be equipped with antilock brakes if they were built on or after March 1, 1998.

**16. B**: Three pounds per square inch.

**17. C**: The application pressure gauge shows you how much air pressure is being applied to the brakes. (This gauge is not on all vehicles.) When there is an increase in the application pressure required to hold the same speed, it means the brakes are fading. You should slow down and use a lower gear. The need for increased pressure can also be caused by brakes being out of adjustment, air leaks, or mechanical problems.

**18. A**: Pumps air into the air storage tanks.

**19. B:** In some vehicles, a control handle on the dashboard may be used to apply the spring brakes gradually. This is called a modulating valve. It is spring-loaded so you have a feel for the braking action. The more you move the control lever, the harder the spring brakes come on. They work this way so you can control the spring brakes if the service brakes fail. When parking a vehicle with a modulating control valve, move the lever as far as it will go and hold it in place with the locking device.

**20. C:** When the air system is fully charged (120-125 psi), turn off the engine, release the service brake, and time the air pressure drop. The loss rate should be less than 2 psi in one minute for single vehicles. It should be less than 3 psi in one minute for combination vehicles.

**21. A:** Don't use the parking brakes if the brakes are very hot (from just having come down a steep grade), or if the brakes are very wet in freezing temperatures. If they are used while they are very hot, they can be damaged by the heat. If they are used in freezing temperatures when the brakes are very wet, they can freeze, and the vehicle cannot move. Use wheel chocks on a level surface to hold the vehicle. Let hot brakes cool before using the parking brakes. If the brakes are wet, use the brakes lightly while driving in a low gear to heat and dry them.

**22. B:** When inspecting the air brake system, turn off the parking brakes so you can move the slack adjusters. Use gloves and pull hard on each slack adjuster that you can reach. If a slack adjuster moves more than about 1 inch where the push rod attaches to it, it probably needs adjustment. Adjust it or have it adjusted. Vehicles with too much brake slack can be hard to stop. Out-of-adjustment brakes are the most common problem found in roadside inspections.

**23. C:** Never push the brake pedal down when the spring brakes are on. If you do, the brakes could be damaged by the combined forces of the springs and the air pressure. Many brake systems are designed in a way that does not allow this. However, not all systems are set up that way, and those that are may not always work.

**24. B**: Inside each brake drum.

**25. B:** By adding together perception distance, reaction distance, brake lag distance, and braking distance, you will get your total stopping distance. The air brake lag distance at 55 mph on dry pavement adds about 32 feet. So at 55 mph, for an average driver under good traction and brake conditions, the total stopping distance is over 450 feet.

# Air Brakes Endorsement Practice Test #3

1. What is used to make the brakes work?
    a. Compressed Oxygen.
    b. Compressed Nitrogen.
    c. Compressed air.

2. What is a dual air brake system?
    a. Two separate air brake systems with a single set of brake controls.
    b. One air brake system with two sets of brake controls.
    c. Two separate air brake systems with two sets of brake controls.

3. With the engine at an idle speed of 600-900 RPM, single air systems built before 1975 typically build pressure from 50 to 90 psi within:
    a. 1 minute
    b. 2 minutes
    c. 3 minutes

4. What is used to turn on the stop lights in an air brakes system?
    a. An electric switch that works by air pressure
    b. A computer.
    c. A motion sensor in the wheels.

5. The parking brake knob should pop out when the air pressure falls to the manufacturer's specification, which is usually:
    a. 20-40 psi
    b. 50-70 psi
    c. 80-100 psi

6. When braking on a downgrade, when should you release the brakes?
    a. When your speed has been reduced to approximately 2 mph below your "safe" speed
    b. When your speed has been reduced to approximately 5 mph below your "safe" speed
    c. When your speed has been reduced to approximately 10 mph below your "safe" speed

7. Which of the following is NOT advisable when performing normal stops with air brakes?
    a. Control the pressure so the vehicle comes to a smooth, safe stop.
    b. If you have a manual transmission, push the clutch in right after braking.
    c. When stopped, select a starting gear.

8. Braking distance is the distance your vehicle travels:
    a. From the time the brakes take hold until the vehicle stops
    b. From the time your foot pushes the air brake until the brake takes hold
    c. From the time your brain tells your foot to move from the accelerator until the time your foot pushes the brake

**9. As compared to having no antilock braking systems, having ABS on only the tractor, on only the trailer, or on only one axle, gives you:**
   a. Less control over the vehicle during braking
   b. The same amount of control over the vehicle during braking
   c. More control over the vehicle during braking

**10. Single vehicle: brakes released. Maximum air leakage in one minute?**
   a. One pound per square inch.
   b. Less than two pounds per square inch.
   c. Less than three pounds per square inch.

**11. In tractors and straight trucks, what will activate fully when air pressure drops to a range between 20 and 45 psi?**
   a. Electronic control unit (ECU)
   b. Cam roller
   c. Spring brakes

**12. What is a purpose of an alcohol evaporator?**
   a. It takes alcohol from the air system.
   b. It reduces risk of ice in brake valves and other parts in cold weather.
   c. It is designed to save fuel in warm weather.

**13. Suppose you are testing the low-pressure warning signal. To be functioning properly, the signal must come on before the pressure drops below what psi in the air tank?**
   a. 20
   b. 40
   c. 60

**14. What do air brakes use to make the brakes work?**
   a. A mixture of air and hydraulic fluid
   b. Liquid oxygen
   c. Compressed air

**15. After applying brakes fully max. air loss in one minute - combination vehicles?**
   a. Two pounds per square inch.
   b. Three pounds per square inch.
   c. Four pounds per square inch.

**16. What are the two types of air tank drains?**
   a. Manually operated... Emergency.
   b. Automatic... Emergency.
   c. Manually operated... Automatic.

**17. How much compressed air must the storage tanks hold?**
   a. At least one hundred and twenty pounds of air.
   b. A maximum of one atmosphere.
   c. Enough air to allow brakes to be used when the air compressor stops working.

**18. When should the air governor cut out the air compressor?**
   a. At about the manufacturer specified air pressure.
   b. At about ten pounds per square inch.
   c. At about one hundred and ten pounds per square inch.

**19. What happens when a brake lining is pushed against the inside of the drum?**
   a. The brakes will always squeal.
   b. This causes friction which slows the vehicle and creates heat.
   c. This causes heat which automatically causes the brakes to lock up.

**20. Which of the following is associated with older vehicles made before 1975?**
   a. Front brake limiting valve
   b. Modulating control valve
   c. Dual parking control valve

**21. Why do some buses have a separate air tank to release spring brakes?**
   a. So you can move the vehicle in an emergency.
   b. To simplify servicing the air brake system.
   c. So that the brakes will release quicker.

**22. Where will you find the drain valve for each air tank?**
   a. In the bottom of the tank.
   b. At the top of the tank.
   c. It is usually found above the tank.

**23. For single vehicles, when the air system is fully charged, the engine is turned off, and the service brakes are released, the air loss rate should be how many psi in one minute?**
   a. Less than 2 psi
   b. Less than 3 psi
   c. Less than 4 psi

**24. Which of the following was used in an effort to reduce the chance of the front wheels skidding on slippery surfaces, but actually reduces the stopping power of the vehicle?**
   a. Front brake limiting valve
   b. Modulating control valve
   c. Dual parking control valve

**25. Which of the following is responsible for keeping the air storage tanks within the correct pressure range?**
   a. Air compressor governor
   b. Alcohol evaporator
   c. Air tank drains

# Answer Key and Explanations for Test #3

**1. C**: Compressed air.

**2. A**: Two separate air brake systems with a single set of brake controls.

**3. C**: In single air systems built before 1975, pressure typically builds from 50 to 90 psi within 3 minutes with the engine at an idle speed of 600-900 RPM.

**4. A**: An electric switch that works by air pressure

**5. A:** The parking brake knob should pop out when the air pressure falls to the manufacturer's specification (usually 20-40 psi). This causes the spring brakes to come on.

**6. B:** The use of brakes on a long and/or steep downgrade is only a supplement to the braking effect of the engine. Once the vehicle is in the proper low gear, the proper braking technique is: Apply the brakes just hard enough to feel a definite slowdown. When your speed has been reduced to approximately 5 mph below your "safe" speed, release the brakes. (This application should last for about 3 seconds.) When your speed has increased to your "safe" speed, repeat steps one and two.

**7. B:** When using air brakes for normal stops: Push the brake pedal down. Control the pressure so the vehicle comes to a smooth, safe stop. If you have a manual transmission, don't push the clutch in until the engine rpm is down close to idle. When stopped, select a starting gear.

**8. A:** Braking distance is the distance your vehicle travels from the time the brakes take hold until the vehicle stops.

**9. C:** Having ABS on only the tractor, on only the trailer, or even on only one axle, still gives you more control over the vehicle during braking. Brake normally. When only the tractor has ABS, you should be able to maintain steering control, and there is less chance of jackknifing. But keep your eye on the trailer and let up on the brakes (if you can safely do so) if it begins to swing out. When only the trailer has ABS, the trailer is less likely to swing out, but if you lose steering control or start a tractor jackknife, let up on the brakes (if you can safely do so) until you gain control. When you drive a tractor-trailer combination with ABS, you should brake as you always have.

**10. B**: Less than two pounds per square inch.

**11. C:** Tractor and straight truck spring brakes will activate fully when air pressure drops to a range between 20 and 45 psi (typically 20 to 30 psi). Do not wait for the brakes to come on automatically. When the low air pressure warning light and buzzer first come on, bring the vehicle to a safe stop right away, while you still have control of the brakes.

**12. B**: It reduces risk of ice in brake valves and other parts in cold weather.

**13. C:** The low air pressure warning signal must come on before the pressure drops below 60 psi in the air tank (or the tank with the lowest air pressure, in dual air systems).

**14. C:** Air brakes use compressed air to make the brakes work. They are a good and safe way of stopping large and heavy vehicles, but the brakes must be well maintained and used properly.

**15. C**: Four pounds per square inch.

**16. C**: Manually operated... Automatic.

**17. C**: Enough air to allow brakes to be used when the air compressor stops working.

**18. A**: At about the manufacturer specified air pressure.

**19. B**: This causes friction which slows the vehicle and creates heat.

**20. A:** Some older vehicles (made before 1975) have a front brake limiting valve and a control in the cab. The control is usually marked "normal" and "slippery." When you put the control in the "slippery" position, the limiting valve cuts the "normal" air pressure to the front brakes by half. Limiting valves were meant to reduce the chance of the front wheels skidding on slippery surfaces. However, they actually reduce the stopping power of the vehicle. Front wheel braking is good under all conditions. Tests have shown front wheel skids from braking are not likely even on ice. Make sure the control is in the "normal" position to have normal stopping power.

**21. A**: So you can move the vehicle in an emergency.

**22. A**: In the bottom of the tank.

**23. A:** When the air system is fully charged (120-125 psi), turn off the engine, release the service brake, and time the air pressure drop. The loss rate should be less than 2 psi in one minute for single vehicles. It should be less than 3 psi in one minute for combination vehicles.

**24. A:** Some older vehicles (made before 1975) have a front brake limiting valve and a control in the cab. The control is usually marked "normal" and "slippery." When you put the control in the "slippery" position, the limiting valve cuts the "normal" air pressure to the front brakes by half. Limiting valves were meant to reduce the chance of the front wheels skidding on slippery surfaces. However, they actually reduce the stopping power of the vehicle. Front wheel braking is good under all conditions. Tests have shown front wheel skids from braking are not likely even on ice. Make sure the control is in the "normal" position to have normal stopping power.

**25. A:** The governor controls when the air compressor will pump air into the air storage tanks. When air tank pressure rises to the "cut-out" level (around 125 pounds per square inch, or psi), the governor stops the compressor from pumping air. When the tank pressure falls to the "cut-in" pressure (around 100 psi), the governor allows the compressor to start pumping again.

# Cargo and Transport Vehicles Endorsement

This section covers hauling cargo safely. You must first understand basic cargo safety rules to get a CDL. Cargo that is loaded poorly, or that is not secured, is a danger to yourself and others. Loose cargo can:

- Fall from the vehicle and cause a crash
- Hurt or kill you if you stop quickly or crash
- Make it difficult for you to steer the vehicle

Additionally, loose cargo can be damaged by sliding back and forth and can damage the vehicle. You may load and secure the cargo yourself, or someone else may load and secure it. In either case, you must:

- Inspect the cargo, unless it is a sealed load or the manner of handling makes inspection impractical
- Recognize overloads and poorly balanced weight
- Ensure that the cargo is properly secured

If you plan to carry hazardous materials that will require placards on your vehicle, you must have a hazardous materials endorsement. You must also be at least 21 years of age.

## Definitions of Weight

> Gross vehicle weight (GVW: The total weight of a single vehicle plus the cargo.
> Gross combination weight (GCW): The total weight of a powered unit (tractor) plus the trailer or trailers plus the cargo.
> Gross vehicle weight rating (GVWR): The maximum GVW specified by the manufacturer for a single vehicle plus the cargo (maximum scale weight).
> Axle weight: The weight transferred to the ground by an axle or set of axles.

## Legal Weight Limits

You must keep weights within legal limits. States have maximums for GVWs, GCWs, and axle weights. Often, maximum axle weights are set by a bridge formula. A bridge formula permits less maximum axle weight for axles that are closer together. This is to prevent overloading bridges and roadways.

## Overloading Affects Safety

Overloading can have bad effects on steering, braking, and speed control. Overloaded trucks have to go very slowly on upgrades. Worse, they may gain too much speed on downgrades. Stopping distance increases. Brakes can fail when forced to work too hard. During bad weather or in mountains, it may not be safe to operate at legal maximum weights. Take this into account before driving.

## Don't Be Top Heavy

The height of the vehicle's center of gravity is very important for safe handling. A high center of gravity (cargo piled up high or heavy cargo on top) means you are more likely to tip over. It is most dangerous in curves, or if you have to swerve to avoid a hazard. It is very important to distribute the cargo so it is as low as possible. Put the heaviest parts of the cargo under the lightest parts.

## Balance the Weight

Poor weight balance can make vehicle handling unsafe. Too much weight on the steering axle can cause hard steering. It can damage the steering axle and tires. Under-loaded front axles (caused by shifting weight too far to the rear) can make the steering axle weight too light to steer safely. Too little weight on the driving axles can cause poor traction. The drive wheels may spin easily. During bad weather, the truck may not be able to keep going. Weight that is loaded so there is a high center of gravity causes greater chance of rollover. On flat bed vehicles, there is also a greater chance that the load will shift to the side or fall off.

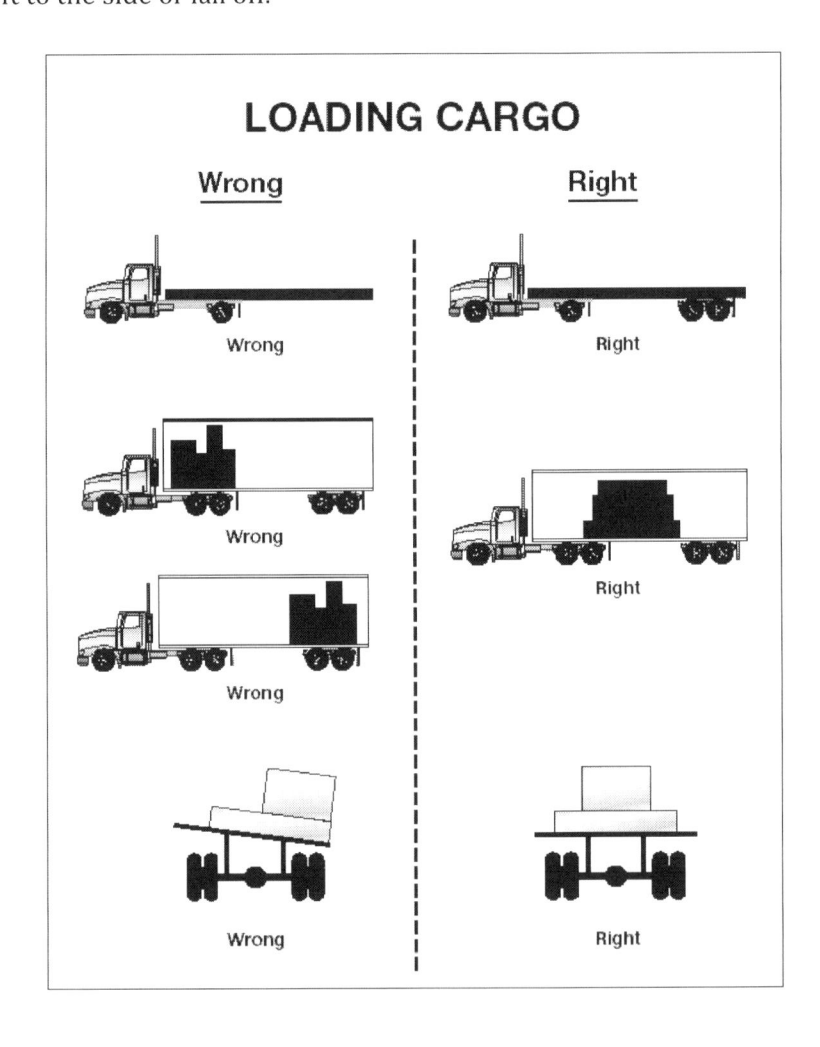

**LOADING CARGO**

Wrong | Right

## Securing Cargo
### Blocking
Blocking is used in the front, back, and/or sides of a piece of cargo to keep it from sliding. Blocking is shaped to fit snugly against cargo. It is secured to the cargo deck to prevent cargo movement.

### Bracing
Bracing is also used to prevent movement of cargo. Bracing goes from the upper part of the cargo to the floor and/or walls of the cargo compartment.

### Cargo Tie Downs
On flatbed trailers or trailers without sides, cargo must be secured to keep it from shifting or falling off. In closed vans, tie downs can also be important to prevent cargo shifting that may affect the handling of the vehicle. Tiedowns must be of the proper type and proper strength. Federal regulations require the aggregate working load limit of any securement system used to secure an article or group of articles against movement must be at least one-half times the weight of the article or group of articles. Proper tie down equipment must be used, including ropes, straps, chains, and tensioning devices (winches, ratchets, clinching components). Tiedowns must be attached to the vehicle correctly (hooks, bolts, rails, rings). Cargo should have at least one tie down for each ten feet of cargo. Make sure you have enough tie downs to meet this need. No matter how small the cargo, it should have at least two tie downs.

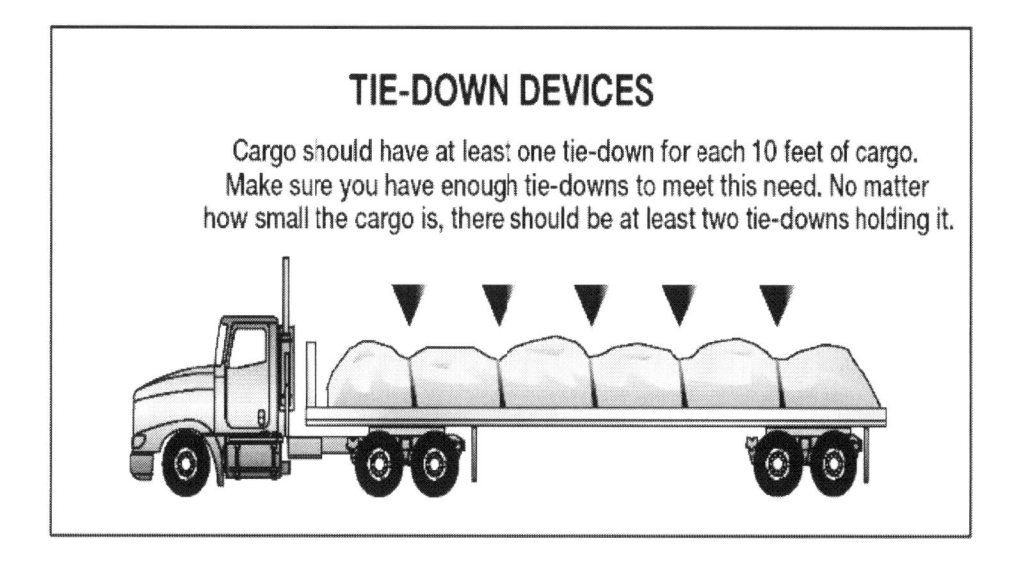

**TIE-DOWN DEVICES**

Cargo should have at least one tie-down for each 10 feet of cargo. Make sure you have enough tie-downs to meet this need. No matter how small the cargo is, there should be at least two tie-downs holding it.

If you are carrying a load that includes heavy pieces of metal, you need to be aware of the special requirements for securing them. The requirements will vary based on the particulars of the load.

### Header Boards
The front-end header boards, also called headache racks, are designed to prevent your cargo from breaking through into the cab in case of a sudden stop or collision. Always verify that this structure is in good condition before driving. If it does not prevent the cargo from moving forward toward the cab, it is not in a condition to be driven.

## Covering Cargo

There are two basic reasons for covering cargo:

- To protect people from spilled cargo
- To protect the cargo from weather

Spill protection is a safety requirement in many states. Be familiar with the laws in the states you drive in. You should look at your cargo covers in the mirrors from time to time while driving. A flapping cover can tear loose, uncovering the cargo, and possibly block your view or someone else's.

## Sealed and Containerized Loads

Containerized loads generally are used when freight is carried part way by rail or ship. Delivery by truck occurs at the beginning and/or end of the journey. Some containers have their own tie down devices or locks that attach directly to a special frame. Others have to be loaded onto flatbed trailers. They must be properly secured just like any other cargo. You cannot inspect sealed loads, but you should check that you don't exceed gross weight and axle weight limits.

## Other Cargo
### Hanging Meat

Hanging meat (suspended beef, pork, lamb) in a refrigerated truck can be a very unstable load with a high center of gravity. Particular caution is needed on sharp curves such as off ramps and on ramps. Go slowly.

### Livestock

Livestock can move around in a trailer, causing unsafe handling. With less than a full load, use false bulkheads to keep livestock bunched together. Even when bunched, special care is necessary because livestock can lean on curves. This shifts the center of gravity and makes rollover more likely.

### Over-Length, Over-Width and Overweight Loads

Over-length, over-width and overweight loads require special transit permits. Driving is usually limited to certain times. Special equipment may be necessary such as "wide load" signs, flashing lights, flags, etc. Such loads may require a police escort or pilot vehicles bearing warning signs or flashing lights. These special loads require special driving care. Check with each state you plan to travel through for specific requirements.

### Dry Bulk Tanks

Dry bulk tanks require special care because they have a high center of gravity, and the load can shift. Be extremely cautious (slow and careful) going around curves and making sharp turns.

# Tank Vehicles Endorsement

A tank endorsement is required for certain vehicles that transport liquids or gases. The liquid or gas does not have to be a hazardous material. A tank endorsement is required if your vehicle needs a Class A or B CDL and you want to haul a liquid or liquid gas in a permanently mounted cargo tank rated at 119 gallons or more or a portable tank rated at 1,000 gallons or more. A tank endorsement is also required for Class C vehicles when the vehicle is used to transport hazardous materials in liquid or gas form in the above described rated tanks. Before loading, unloading, or driving a tanker, inspect the vehicle. This makes sure that the vehicle is safe to carry the liquid or gas and is safe to drive.

## INSPECTING TANK VEHICLES

Tank vehicles have special items that you need to check. Tank vehicles come in many types and sizes. You need to check the vehicle's operator manual to make sure you know how to inspect your tank vehicle. On all tank vehicles, the most important item to check for is leaks. Check under and around the vehicle for signs of any leaking. Don't carry liquids or gases in a leaking tank. To do so is a crime. You will be cited and prevented from driving further. You may also be liable for the cleanup of any spill. In general, check the following:

- Check the tank's body or shell for dents or leaks.
- Check the intake, discharge, and cut-off valves. Make sure the valves are in the correct position before loading, unloading, or moving the vehicle.
- Check pipes, connections, and hoses for leaks, especially around joints.
- Check manhole covers and vents. Make sure the covers have gaskets and they close correctly. Keep the vents clear so they work correctly.
- Check special purpose equipment. If your vehicle has any one of the following equipment, make sure it works:
  - Vapor recovery kits
  - Grounding and bonding cables
  - Emergency shut-off systems
  - Built-in fire extinguisher

Never drive a tank vehicle with open valves or manhole covers. Check the emergency equipment required for your vehicle. Find out what equipment you are required to carry and make sure you have it and know how it works.

## DRIVING TANK VEHICLES

Hauling liquids in tanks requires special skills. When driving a tank vehicle, always bear in mind the following concerns:

- **Tank vehicles have a high center of gravity**. High center of gravity means that much of the load's weight is carried high up off the road. This makes the vehicle top-heavy and easy to roll over. Liquid tankers are especially easy to roll over. Tests have shown that tankers can turn over at the speed limits posted for curves. Take highway curves and on ramp/off ramp curves well below the posted speeds.

- **Watch out for liquid surge**. Liquid surge results from movement of the liquid in partially filled tanks. This movement can have bad effects on handling. For example, when coming to a stop, the liquid will surge back and forth. When the wave hits the end of the tank, it tends to push the truck in the direction the wave is moving. If the truck is on a slippery surface such as ice, the wave can shove a stopped truck out into an intersection. The driver of a liquid tanker must be very familiar with the handling of the vehicle.
- **Bulkheads**. Some liquid tanks are divided into several smaller tanks by bulkheads. When loading and unloading the smaller tanks, the driver must pay attention to weight distribution. Don't put too much weight on the front or rear of the vehicle.
- **Baffled tanks**. Baffled liquid tanks have bulkheads in them with holes that let the liquid flow through. The baffles help to control the forward and backward liquid surge. Side-to-side surge can still occur. This can cause a roll over.
- **Unbaffled tanks**. Unbaffled liquid tankers (sometimes called smooth-bore tanks) have nothing inside to slow down the flow of the liquid. Therefore, forward-and-back surge is very strong. Unbaffled tanks are usually those that transport food products such as milk. (Sanitation regulations forbid the use of baffles because of the difficulty in cleaning the inside of the tank.) Be extremely cautious (slow and careful) in driving smooth bore tanks, especially when starting and stopping.
- **Outage**. Never load a cargo tank totally full. Liquids expand as they warm. This is called outage. You must leave room for the liquid to expand. Different liquids expand by different amounts and require different amounts of outage. You must know the outage requirement for the liquids that you haul.
- **How much to load?** A full tank of dense liquid, such as some acids, may exceed legal weight limits. Therefore, you may often only partially fill tanks with heavy liquids. The amount of liquid that you can load into a tank depends on:
    - Amount that the liquid will expand in transit
    - Weight of the liquid
    - Legal weight limits

Always fasten your safety belt when you drive.

## SAFE DRIVING RULES

The following are rules for safe driving:

- **Drive smoothly**. Because of the high center of gravity and the surge of the liquid, you must start, slow down, and stop very smoothly. Also, make smooth turns and lane changes.
- **Use controlled or stab braking**. If you must stop quickly to avoid a crash, use controlled or stab braking. Also, remember that if you steer quickly while braking, your vehicle may roll over.
- **Slow down before curves**. Slow down before curves, then accelerate slightly through the curve. The posted speed for a curve may be too fast for a tank vehicle.
- **Maintain a safe stopping distance between you and the vehicle ahead**. Keep in mind how much space you need to stop your vehicle. Remember that wet roads double the normal stopping distance. Empty tank vehicles may take longer to stop than full ones.
- **Skids**. Don't over steer, over accelerate, or over brake. If you do, your vehicle may skid. On tank trailers, if your drive wheels or trailer wheels begin to skid, your vehicle may jackknife. When any vehicle starts to skid, you must take action to restore traction to the wheels.

# Cargo and Tank Endorsement Practice Test #1

**1. What is the most important thing to check for when inspecting tank vehicles?**
   a. Vapor
   b. Shell
   c. Leaks

**2. Which of the following is NOT true about basic cargo safety?**
   a. Loose cargo can hurt or kill you if you stop quickly or crash.
   b. Overloading does not affect your safety while driving.
   c. You must inspect the cargo, unless it is a sealed load or the manner of handling makes inspection impractical.

**3. If transporting flammable cargo over a railroad track you may shift gears?**
   a. When the sound of your engine tells you it is time to shift gears
   b. When your tachometer shows 1100 RPM or higher
   c. Do not shift gears when crossing over railroad tracks.

**4. Which of the following is NOT a determining factor for the amount of liquid that you can load into a tank?**
   a. Weight of the liquid
   b. Amount that the liquid will expand in transit
   c. Spill prevention

**5. A tank endorsement is required for:**
   a. Vehicles with a Class A or B CDL requirement and a permanently mounted cargo tank rated at up to 100 gallons
   b. Vehicles with a Class A or B CDL requirement and a portable tank rated at 1,000 gallons or more
   c. Class C vehicles used to transport solid hazardous materials

**6. What is overturn protection?**
   a. Guards to protect fittings and valves in case of a rollover
   b. Weight reducers that will cause the trailer to ride lower
   c. Guards that keep a tractor from turning too sharply and breaking air lines

**7. How is a bulkhead different from a baffle?**
   a. Bulkheads are larger than baffles.
   b. Bulkheads are liquid-tight and baffles have holes in them.
   c. Bulkheads are placed vertically while baffles are horizontal.

**8. Often, maximum axle weights are set by:**
   a. A bridge formula
   b. An interlocking formula
   c. An axle formula

9. Which of the following is shaped to fit snugly against cargo and is secured to the cargo deck?
    a. Blocking
    b. Bracing
    c. Tie-downs

10. Are smooth bore tankers different to drive than tankers with tank baffles?
    a. No, except that smooth bore tanks usually transport food products.
    b. Yes, forward and back surge is strong in smooth bore tankers.
    c. No, but tanks with bulkheads or baffles are harder to keep clean.

11. Which of the following is a crime?
    a. Carrying liquids or gases in a leaking tank
    b. Skipping the cargo inspection when the load is sealed
    c. Driving with a weight over your GVWR

12. Which of these helps determine the amount of liquid you can load in a tank?
    a. The size of the opening in the dome lid
    b. The amount that the liquid might expand in transit
    c. The maximum speed at which you will be driving

13. A 'tank vehicle' includes?
    a. Portable tanks having a capacity of 100 gallons or more
    b. Dry bulk tank vehicles
    c. Transit mix trucks and cement mixers

14. What are two problems especially important to tanker operation?
    a. A high center of gravity and the liquid surge of the cargo transported
    b. A low center of gravity and leakage from tanks
    c. The tendency of milk to spoil and driver inability to see into the tank

15. Gross vehicle weight rating (GVWR) refers to:
    a. The maximum GVW specified by the manufacturer for a single vehicle plus the cargo (maximum scale weight)
    b. The total weight of a powered unit (tractor), the trailer or trailers, and the cargo
    c. The total weight of a single vehicle and the cargo

16. Baffles offer little resistance to?
    a. Front-to-back surge
    b. Back-to-front surge
    c. Side-to-side surge

17. A 'tank vehicle' includes any portable tank having a liquid capacity of?
    a. 100 gallons or more
    b. 500 gallons or more
    c. 1,000 gallons or more

**18. In what direction does liquid surge cause a vehicle to move?**
   a. Forward and much faster
   b. Backward and much slower
   c. It will tend to move the vehicle in the direction that the liquid moves.

**19. Gross vehicle weight (GVW) refers to:**
   a. The total weight of a powered unit (tractor), the trailer or trailers, and the cargo
   b. The total weight of a single vehicle and the cargo
   c. The weight transferred to the ground by an axle or set of axles

**20. What is another name for header boards?**
   a. Heading mount
   b. Headache rack
   c. Top panel

# Answer Key and Explanations for Test #1

**1. C:** Tank vehicles have special items that you need to check. Tank vehicles come in many types and sizes. You need to check the vehicle's operator manual to make sure you know how to inspect your tank vehicle. On all tank vehicles, the most important item to check for is leaks. Check under and around the vehicle for signs of any leaking. Don't carry liquids or gases in a leaking tank. To do so is a crime. You will be cited and prevented from driving further. You may also be liable for the cleanup of any spill.

**2. B:** Overloading can have bad effects on steering, braking, and speed control. Overloaded trucks have to go very slowly on upgrades. Worse, they may gain too much speed on downgrades. Stopping distance increases. Brakes can fail when forced to work too hard. During bad weather or on mountains, it may not be safe to operate at legal maximum weights.

**3. C**: Do not shift gears when crossing over railroad tracks.

**4. C:** A full tank of dense liquid (certain acids, for example) may exceed legal weight limits. Therefore, you may often only partially fill tanks with heavy liquids. The amount of liquid that you can load into a tank depends on the amount that the liquid will expand in transit, the weight of the liquid, and legal weight limits.

**5. B:** A tank endorsement is required for certain vehicles that transport liquids or gases. The liquid or gas does not have to be a hazardous material. A tank endorsement is required if your vehicle needs a Class A or B CDL and you want to haul a liquid or gas in a permanently mounted cargo tank rated at 119 gallons or more, or a portable tank rated at 1,000 gallons or more. A tank endorsement is also required for Class C vehicles when the vehicle is used to transport hazardous materials in liquid or gas form in the rated tanks described above. Before loading, unloading, or driving a tanker, inspect the vehicle. This makes sure that the vehicle is safe to carry the liquid or gas and is safe to drive.

**6. A**: Guards to protect fittings and valves in case of a rollover

**7. B**: Bulkheads are liquid-tight and baffles have holes in them.

**8. A:** You must keep weights within legal limits. States have maximums for GVWs, GCWs, and axle weights. Often, maximum axle weights are set by a bridge formula. A bridge formula permits less maximum axle weight for axles that are closer together. This is to prevent overloading bridges and roadways.

**9. A:** Blocking is used in the front, back, and/or sides of a piece of cargo to keep it from sliding. Blocking is shaped to fit snugly against cargo. It is secured to the cargo deck to prevent cargo movement.

**10. B**: Yes, forward and back surge is strong in smooth bore tankers.

**11. A:** Don't carry liquids or gases in a leaking tank. To do so is a crime. You will be cited and prevented from driving further. You may also be liable for the cleanup of any spill.

**12. B**: The amount that the liquid might expand in transit

**13. C**: Transit mix trucks and cement mixers

**14. A**: A high center of gravity and the liquid surge of the cargo transported

**15. A:** Gross vehicle weight rating (GVWR) is the maximum GVW specified by the manufacturer for a single vehicle plus the cargo (maximum scale weight).

**16. C**: Side-to-side surge

**17. C**: 1,000 gallons or more

**18. C**: It will tend to move the vehicle in the direction that the liquid moves.

**19. B:** Gross vehicle weight (GVW) is the total weight of a single vehicle plus the cargo.

**20. B:** The front-end header boards, also called headache racks, are designed to prevent your cargo from breaking through into the cab in case of a sudden stop or collision. Always verify that this structure is in good condition before driving. If it does not prevent the cargo from moving forward toward the cab, it is not in a condition to be driven.

# Cargo and Tank Endorsement Practice Test #2

**1. How soon can you remove placards when you unload flammables from a tanker?**
   a. After you have completed unloading, but before you drive away
   b. Before you start to unload or during the unloading
   c. After the tank has been cleaned or another commodity has been loaded

**2. Which of the following is NOT one of the two basic reasons for covering cargo?**
   a. To protect people from spilled cargo
   b. To protect the roadway from loose materials/debris
   c. To protect the cargo from weather

**3. What is a dome cover?**
   a. A cover to protect an opening where a tank is filled
   b. A cover to protect a drain on the bottom of the tank
   c. An extra cover to protect the cab in case of a rollover

**4. A vehicle with empty tanks may?**
   a. Be stopped more quickly with the emergency brakes
   b. Require a greater stopping distance than a loaded tanker
   c. Have better traction at all times than does a loaded tanker

**5. Which of the following will make it more likely for you to tip over?**
   a. Cargo tie-downs
   b. High center of gravity
   c. Aggregate working load

**6. Why is the danger of liquid surge more when a tank is less than full?**
   a. Liquid has more room to move in a partially-filled tank.
   b. The air pressure is greater inside a partially-filled tank.
   c. Many semi trailer tanks are slanted so that the lower end is at the back.

**7. On tank trailers, if your drive wheels or trailer wheels begin to skid, your vehicle may:**
   a. Overheat
   b. Jackknife
   c. Surge

**8. Unbaffled liquid tankers are sometimes also called:**
   a. Liquid surge tanks
   b. Smooth-bore tanks
   c. Dairy tanks

**9. When are containerized loads generally used?**
   a. When freight is carried part of the way by rail or ship
   b. When materials are particularly hazardous or fragile
   c. When severe weather or driving conditions are expected

**10. You should be cautious while hauling hanging meat loads and dry bulk tanks because they both:**
   a. Tend to lower the center of gravity
   b. Necessitate a pilot vehicle
   c. Have a high center of gravity

**11. On which of the following is there a greater chance that the load will shift to the side or fall off?**
   a. Tank vehicles
   b. Containerized loads
   c. Flat-bed vehicles

**12. Never drive a tank vehicle with:**
   a. Open manhole covers
   b. Grounding and bonding cables
   c. A high center of gravity

**13. One of these helps determine the amount of liquid you can load in a tank.**
   a. The legal weight and load limits of your vehicle
   b. The wheelbase between your front and second axles
   c. The number of pumps that can be used to load your tank

**14. What is a reason for filling a tank only partially?**
   a. The shipper ordered a small quantity.
   b. The shipment was too light in weight.
   c. The tank had a hole that leaked liquid.

**15. Why should you find out the 'Outage' for the liquids you are transporting?**
   a. Different liquids expand by different amounts.
   b. You cannot operate a tank if the electrical system is not working.
   c. A liquid that has frozen is no longer considered to be a liquid.

**16. When you load a tank that has bulkheads, it is most important to check?**
   a. The size of the hose connections
   b. The size of the bulkheads
   c. Weight distribution of the commodity being loaded

**17. Under-loaded driving axles are more likely to:**
   a. Cause the drive wheels to spin easily
   b. Cause hard steering
   c. Pull against heavy cargo

**18. What can liquid surge do to the handling of a tank vehicle?**
   a. Surge improves your ability to turn corners tighter.
   b. Surge may move the vehicle in the direction the liquid moves in the tank.
   c. Surge causes tank contamination.

**19. As compared to a smooth bore tank, a tank with bulkheads or baffles?**
   a. Will have less front-to-back surge
   b. Will have less side-to-side surge
   c. There will be no difference.

**20. Which of the following is positioned from the upper part of the cargo to the floor and/or walls of the cargo compartment?**
   a. Blocking
   b. Headache rack
   c. Bracing

# Answer Key and Explanations for Test #2

**1. C**: After the tank has been cleaned or another commodity has been loaded

**2. B:** There are two basic reasons for covering cargo: to protect people from spilled cargo, and to protect the cargo from weather.

**3. A**: A cover to protect an opening where a tank is filled

**4. B**: Require a greater stopping distance than a loaded tanker

**5. B:** The height of the vehicle's center of gravity is very important for safe handling. A high center of gravity (cargo piled up high, or heavy cargo on top) means you are more likely to tip over. It is most dangerous in curves, or if you have to swerve to avoid a hazard. It is very important to distribute the cargo so it is as low as possible. Put the heaviest parts of the cargo under the lightest parts.

**6. A**: Liquid has more room to move in a partially-filled tank.

**7. B:** Don't over-steer, over-accelerate, or-over brake. If you do, your vehicle may skid. On tank trailers, if your drive wheels or trailer wheels begin to skid, your vehicle may jackknife. When any vehicle starts to skid, you must take action to restore traction to the wheels.

**8. B:** Unbaffled liquid tankers (sometimes called smooth-bore tanks) have nothing inside to slow down the flow of the liquid. Therefore, forward-and-back surge is very strong. Unbaffled tanks are usually those that transport food products such as milk. (Sanitation regulations forbid the use of baffles because of the difficulty in cleaning the inside of the tank.) Be extremely cautious (slow and careful) in driving smooth-bore tanks, especially when starting and stopping.

**9. A:** Containerized loads are generally used when freight is carried part of the way by rail or ship. Delivery by truck occurs at the beginning and/or end of the journey. Some containers have their own tie-down devices or locks that attach directly to a special frame. Others have to be loaded onto flatbed trailers. They must be properly secured, just like any other cargo. You cannot inspect sealed loads, but you should check that you don't exceed gross weight and axle weight limits.

**10. C:** Hanging meat (suspended beef, pork, lamb) in a refrigerated truck can be a very unstable load with a high center of gravity. Particular caution is needed on sharp curves such as off ramps and on ramps. Dry bulk tanks require special care because they also have a high center of gravity, and the load can shift. Be extremely cautious (slow and careful) going around curves and making sharp turns.

**11. C:** Poor weight balance can make vehicle handling unsafe. Weight that is loaded so there is a high center of gravity causes greater chance of rollover. On flat-bed vehicles, there is also a greater chance that the load will shift to the side or fall off.

**12. A:** Never drive a tank vehicle with open valves or manhole covers.

**13. A**: The legal weight and load limits of your vehicle

**14. A**: The shipper ordered a small quantity.

**15. A**: Different liquids expand by different amounts.

**16. C**: Weight distribution of the commodity being loaded

**17. A:** Too little weight on the driving axles can cause poor traction. The drive wheels may spin easily. During bad weather, the truck may not be able to keep going.

**18. B**: Surge may move the vehicle in the direction the liquid moves in the tank.

**19. A**: Will have less front-to-back surge

**20. C:** Bracing is used to prevent movement of cargo. Bracing goes from the upper part of the cargo to the floor and/or walls of the cargo compartment.

# Cargo and Tank Endorsement Practice Test #3

1. **Gross combination weight (GCW) refers to:**
   a. The total weight of a powered unit (tractor), the trailer or trailers, and the cargo
   b. The total weight of a single vehicle and the cargo
   c. The weight transferred to the ground by an axle or set of axles

2. **What is a tank compartment?**
   a. A tank for storing hoses and couplings
   b. A liquid-tight division of a tank
   c. A wall with many openings

3. **Why are unbaffled tanks used to transport food products?**
   a. Sanitation regulations often forbid the use of baffles.
   b. Food products are lighter than gasoline and require less support.
   c. The baffles cause syrups to congeal.

4. **Which is true about the emergency steering of tankers?**
   a. Do not apply the brakes when making a quick turn.
   b. Counter-steering is easy with a loaded tanker.
   c. Never try to stop a tanker without turning.

5. **When loading a tanker, you must consider weight distribution because?**
   a. You do not want to put too much weight on the front or on the rear.
   b. Computers will not check this for you.
   c. Tanks cannot be bent or strained.

6. **Which of the following is most likely to shift while in transport?**
   a. Dry bulk tanks and livestock
   b. Over-length and over-width cargo
   c. Hanging meat and containerized loads

7. **Why is the stopping of a tank vehicle on a slippery surface extra hazardous?**
   a. Liquid surge will tend to shove the vehicle ahead.
   b. A vehicle on a slippery surface can become stuck more easily.
   c. The wave of the liquid inside the tank may hit the rear of the tank.

8. **While driving a tank vehicle, if you must stop quickly to avoid a crash, how should you brake?**
   a. A combination of spring and rear-wheel braking
   b. Engine braking
   c. Controlled or stab braking

**9. With tank vehicles 'Outage' means?**
   a. An electrical failure when the engine is shut off
   b. Sparks that fly up from the pavement when touched by a ground wire
   c. Space that must be left in a cargo tank for liquids to expand

**10. What is designed to prevent your cargo from breaking through into the cab in case of a sudden stop or collision?**
   a. Cargo tie-downs
   b. Bracers
   c. Header boards

**11. The side-to-side surge of liquid in a tank can cause a vehicle to?**
   a. Stop instantly
   b. Bend at the fifth wheel connection
   c. Roll over

**12. Which of the following is NOT necessarily true if you plan to carry hazardous materials that will require placards on your vehicle?**
   a. You must be at least 21 years of age.
   b. You must have a hazardous materials endorsement.
   c. You must supply the placards.

**13. The amount that a liquid can expand in transit can be affected by?**
   a. The grade that is being pulled
   b. The suddenness with which the brakes are applied
   c. The temperature of the load

**14. Do the speed limits posted for on-ramps and off-ramps apply to tankers?**
   a. Yes, all limits are set with tankers in mind.
   b. No, tankers are exempt.
   c. Not necessarily

**15. Which of the following is NOT true regarding tank vehicles?**
   a. Bulkhead tanks have nothing inside to slow down the flow of the liquid.
   b. Tank vehicles have a high center of gravity.
   c. Liquid surge results from movement of the liquid in partially filled tanks.

**16. Under-loaded front axles are more likely to:**
   a. Cause the drive wheels to spin easily
   b. Lighten the steering axle and make it hard to steer
   c. Produce a rollover

**17. Which is a factor that determines the amount of liquid you can load in a tank?**
   a. The failure of molasses to flow properly in cold weather
   b. The height of the tractor
   c. The weight of the liquid

**18. Which of the following is a combination of the maximum GVW specified by the manufacturer for a single vehicle, and the cargo (maximum scale weight)?**
- a. Gross combination weight (GCW)
- b. Gross vehicle weight rating (GVWR)
- c. Axle weight

**19. A bridge formula permits less maximum axle weight for axles that are:**
- a. Closer together
- b. Farther apart
- c. Unbalanced

**20. When securing a load on a flatbed trailer, at minimum there should be one tie down for every:**
- a. Five feet of cargo
- b. Ten feet of cargo
- c. Fifteen feet of cargo

# Answer Key and Explanations for Test #3

**1. A:** Gross combination weight (GCW) is the total weight of a powered unit (tractor), the trailer or trailers, and the cargo.

**2. B:** A liquid-tight division of a tank

**3. A:** Sanitation regulations often forbid the use of baffles.

**4. A:** Do not apply the brakes when making a quick turn.

**5. A:** You do not want to put too much weight on the front or on the rear.

**6. A:** Dry bulk tanks require special care because they have a high center of gravity, and the load can shift. Livestock can move around in a trailer, causing unsafe handling. With less than a full load, use false bulkheads to keep livestock bunched together. Even then, special care is necessary because livestock can lean on curves. This shifts the center of gravity and makes rollover more likely.

**7. A:** Liquid surge will tend to shove the vehicle ahead.

**8. C:** If you must stop quickly to avoid a crash, use controlled or stab braking. Also, remember that if you steer quickly while braking, your vehicle may roll over.

**9. C:** Space that must be left in a cargo tank for liquids to expand

**10. C:** The front-end header boards, also called headache racks, are designed to prevent your cargo from breaking through into the cab in case of a sudden stop or collision. Always verify that this structure is in good condition before driving. If it does not prevent the cargo from moving forward toward the cab, it is not in a condition to be driven.

**11. C:** Roll over

**12. C:** If you plan to carry hazardous materials that will require placards on your vehicle, you must have a hazardous materials endorsement. You must also be at least 21 years of age. Part of the shipper's role (not the driver's) is to package, mark, and label the materials, prepare shipping papers, provide emergency response information, and supply placards.

**13. C:** The temperature of the load

**14. C:** Not necessarily

**15. A:** Some liquid tanks are divided into several smaller tanks by bulkheads. When loading and unloading the smaller tanks, the driver must pay attention to weight distribution. Don't put too much weight on the front or rear of the vehicle.

**16. B:** Under-loaded front axles (caused by shifting weight too far to the rear) can make the steering axle weight too light to steer safely.

**17. C:** The weight of the liquid.

**18. B:** Gross vehicle weight rating (GVWR) is the maximum GVW specified by the manufacturer for a single vehicle plus the cargo (maximum scale weight).

**19. A:** You must keep weights within legal limits. States have maximums for GVWs, GCWs, and axle weights. Often, maximum axle weights are set by a bridge formula. A bridge formula permits less maximum axle weight for axles that are closer together. This is to prevent overloading bridges and roadways.

**20. B:** Cargo should have at least one tie down for each ten feet of cargo. Make sure you have enough tie downs to meet this need. No matter how small the cargo, it should have at least two tie downs.

# Combination Vehicles (Doubles and Triples) Endorsement

## TRAILER HAND VALVE

The trailer hand valve (also called the trolley valve or Johnson bar) works the trailer brakes. The trailer hand valve should be used only to test the trailer brakes. Do not use it in driving because of the danger of making the trailer skid. The foot brake sends air to all of the brakes on the vehicle (including the trailer(s)). There is much less danger of causing a skid or jackknife when using just the foot brake. Never use the hand valve for parking because all the air might leak out unlocking the brakes (in trailers that don't have spring brakes). Always use the parking brakes when parking. If the trailer does not have spring brakes, use wheel chocks to keep the trailer from moving.

## TRACTOR PROTECTION VALVE

The tractor protection valve keeps air in the tractor or truck brake system should the trailer break away or develop a bad leak. The tractor protection valve is controlled by the "trailer air supply" control valve in the cab. The control valve allows you to open and shut the tractor protection valve. The tractor protection valve will close automatically if air pressure is low (in the range of 20-45 psi). When the tractor protection valve closes, it stops any air from going out of the tractor. It also lets the air out of the trailer emergency line. This causes the trailer emergency brakes to come on, with possible loss of control. (Emergency brakes are covered later.)

## TRAILER AIR SUPPLY CONTROL

The trailer air supply control on newer vehicles is a red eight-sided knob, which you use to control the tractor protection valve. You push it in to supply the trailer with air, and pull it out to shut the air off and put on the trailer emergency brakes. The valve will pop out (thus closing the tractor protection valve) when the air pressure drops into the range of 20-45 psi. Tractor protection valve controls or "emergency" valves on older vehicles may not operate automatically. There may be a lever rather than a knob. The "normal" position is used for pulling a trailer. The "emergency" position is used to shut the air off and put on the trailer emergency brakes.

## TRAILER AIR LINES

Every combination vehicle has two air lines, the service line and the emergency line. They run between each vehicle (tractor to trailer, trailer to dolly, dolly to second trailer, etc.)

### SERVICE AIR LINE

The service line (also called the control line or signal line) carries air, which is controlled by the foot brake or the trailer hand brake. Depending on how hard you press the foot brake or hand valve, the pressure in the service line will similarly change. The service line is connected to relay valves. These valves allow the trailer brakes to be applied more quickly than would otherwise be possible.

### EMERGENCY AIR LINE

The emergency line (also called the supply line) has two purposes. First, it supplies air to the trailer air tanks. Second, the emergency line controls the emergency brakes on combination vehicles. Loss of air pressure in the emergency line causes the trailer emergency brakes to come on. The pressure loss could be caused by a trailer breaking loose, thus tearing apart the emergency air hose. Or it could be caused by a hose, metal tubing, or other part breaking, letting the air out. When the emergency line loses pressure, it also causes the tractor protection valve to close (the air supply knob will pop out). Emergency lines are often coded with the color red (red hose, red couplers, or other parts) to keep from getting them mixed up with the blue service line.

## Hose Couplers or Glad Hands

Glad hands are coupling devices used to connect the service and emergency air lines from the truck or tractor to the trailer. The couplers have a rubber seal, which prevents air from escaping. Clean the couplers and rubber seals before a connection is made. When connecting the glad hands, press the two seals together with the couplers at a 90-degree angle to each other. A turn of the glad hand attached to the hose will join and lock the couplers. It helps if you moisten the rubber seals. When coupling, make sure to couple the proper glad hands together. To help avoid mistakes, colors are sometimes used. Blue is used for the service lines and red for the emergency (supply) lines. Sometimes, metal tags are attached to the lines with the words "service" and "emergency" stamped on them.

If you do cross the air lines, supply air will be sent to the service line instead of going to charge the trailer air tanks. Air will not be available to release the trailer spring brakes (parking brakes). If the spring brakes don't release when you push the trailer air supply control, check the air line connections. Older trailers do not have spring brakes. If the air supply in the trailer air tank has leaked away there will be no emergency brakes, and the trailer wheels will turn freely. If you crossed the air lines, you could drive away but you wouldn't have trailer brakes. This would be very dangerous. Always test the trailer brakes before driving with the hand valve or by pulling the air supply (tractor protection valve) control. Pull gently against them in a low gear to make sure the brakes work.

Some vehicles have "dead end" or dummy couplers to which the hoses may be attached when they are not in use. This will prevent water and dirt from getting into the coupler and the air lines. Use the dummy couplers when the air lines are not connected to a trailer. If there are no dummy couplers, the glad hands can sometimes be locked together (depending on the couplings). It is very important to keep the air supply clean.

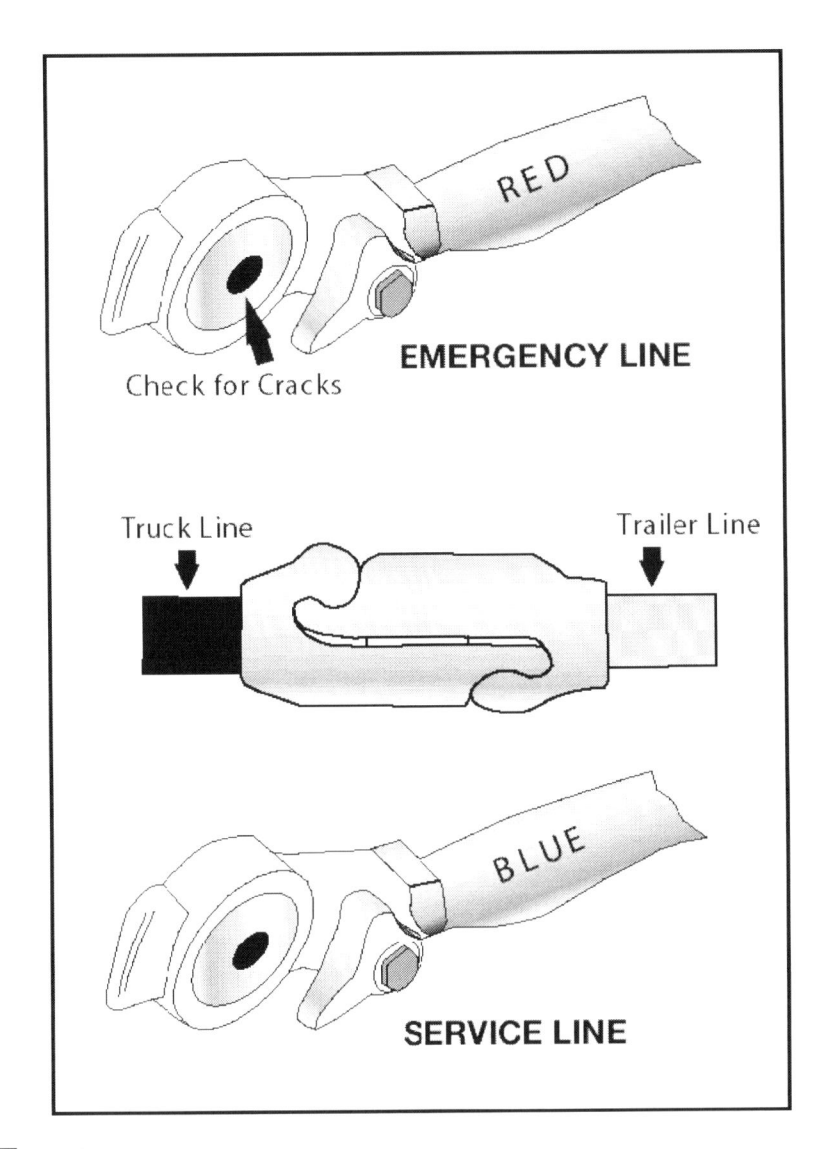

## Trailer Air Tanks

Each trailer and converter dolly have one or more air tanks. They are filled by the emergency (supply) line from the tractor. They provide the air pressure used to operate trailer brakes. Air pressure is sent from the air tanks to the brakes by relay valves. The pressure in the service line tells how much pressure the relay valves should send to the trailer brakes. The pressure in the service line is controlled by the brake pedal (and the trailer hand brake). It is important that you don't let water and oil build up in the air tanks. If you do, the brakes may not work correctly. Each tank has a drain valve on it and you should drain each tank every day. If your tanks have automatic drains, they will keep most moisture out. But you should still open the drains to make sure.

## Shut-Off Valves

Shut-off valves (also called cut-out cocks) are used in the service and supply air lines at the back of trailers used to tow other trailers. These valves permit closing the air lines off when another trailer is not being towed. You must check that all shut-off valves are in the open position except the ones at the back of the last trailer, which must be closed.

## TRAILER SERVICE, PARKING, AND EMERGENCY BRAKES

New trailers have spring brakes just like trucks and truck tractors. Converter dollies and trailers built before 1975 are not required to have spring brakes. Trailers that do not have spring brakes have emergency brakes which work from the air stored in the trailer air tank. The emergency brakes come on whenever air pressure in the emergency line is lost. These trailers do not have a parking brake. The emergency brakes come on whenever the air supply knob is pulled out or the trailer is disconnected. But the brakes will not hold if there is not sufficient air pressure in the trailer air tank. Eventually, the air will leak away and there will be no brake. Therefore, always use wheel chocks when you park trailers without spring brakes. A major leak in the emergency line will cause the tractor protection valve to close and the trailer emergency brakes to come on. You may not notice a leak in the service line until you put the brakes on. Then, the air loss from the leak will lower the air tank pressure quickly. If it goes low enough, the trailer emergency brakes will come on.

# Inspecting Combination Vehicles

## COUPLING SYSTEM AND LANDING GEAR

Check the fifth wheel (lower):

- Securely mounted to frame
- No missing or damaged parts
- Make sure there is enough grease (if the trailer is not hooked up)
- No visible space between the upper and lower fifth wheel
- Locking jaws around the shank, **not** the head of the kingpin
- Release arm properly seated and safety latch/lock engaged

Check the fifth wheel (upper):

- Glide plate securely mounted to trailer frame
- Kingpin not damaged

Check the sliding fifth wheel:

- Slide not damaged or parts missing
- Properly greased
- All locking pins present and locked in place
- If air powered, no air leaks
- Check that the fifth wheel is not so far forward that the tractor frame will hit the landing gear, or that the cab will hit the trailer, during turns

Check the air and electric lines to the trailer:

- Electrical cord firmly plugged in and secured
- Air lines properly connected to glad hands, no air leaks, properly secured with enough slack for turns
- All lines free from damage

Check the landing gear:

- Fully raised, no missing parts, not bent or otherwise damaged
- Crank handle in place and secured
- If power operated, no air or hydraulic leaks

## DOUBLES AND TRIPLES

Inspect the double and triple trailers:

- Shut-off valves (at rear of trailers, in service and emergency lines):
    - Rear of front trailer—OPEN
    - Rear of last trailer—CLOSED
    - Converter dolly air tank drain valve—CLOSED
- Be sure air lines are supported and glad hands are properly connected.
- If spare tire is carried on converter gear (dolly), make sure it's secured.
- Be sure pintle-eye of dolly is in place in pintle hook of trailer(s).
- Make sure pintle hook is latched.
- Safety chains should be secured to trailer(s).
- Be sure light cords are firmly in sockets on trailers.

## AIR BRAKES

Make these checks in addition to the pre-trip checks that you make for your air brakes. The following section explains how to check air brakes on combination vehicles. Check the airbrakes on a double or triple trailer the same way you check them for any combination vehicle.

- Check that air flows to all trailers:
    - Use the tractor parking brake and/or chock the wheels to hold the vehicle.
    - Wait for air pressure to reach normal, then push in the red "trailer air supply" knob. This will supply air to the emergency (supply) lines.
    - Use the trailer handbrake to provide air to the service line.
    - Go to the rear of the rig. Open the emergency line shut-off valve at the rear of the last trailer. You should hear air escaping, showing the entire system is charged.
    - Close the emergency line valve.
    - Open the service line valve to check that service pressure goes through all the trailers (this test assumes that the trailer handbrake or the service brake pedal is on), and then close the valve. If you do NOT hear air escaping from both lines, check that the shut-off valves on the trailers and dollies are in the OPEN position. You MUST have air all the way to the back for all the brakes to work.

- Test tractor protection valve:
    - Charge the trailer air brake system (build up normal air pressure and push the "air supply" knob in).
    - Shut the engine off.
    - Step on and off the brake pedal several times to reduce the air pressure in the tanks.
    - The trailer air supply control (also called the tractor protection valve control) should pop out (or go from "normal" to "emergency" position) when the air pressure falls into the pressure range specified by the manufacturer. (Usually in the 20-45 psi range.)
    - If the tractor protection valve doesn't work right, an air hose or trailer brake leak could drain all the air from the tractor. This would cause the emergency brakes to come on, with possible loss of control.

- Test the trailer emergency brakes:
    - Charge the trailer air brake system and check that the trailer rolls freely.
    - Then stop and pull out the trailer air supply control (also called tractor protection valve control or trailer emergency valve) or place it in the "emergency" position.
    - Pull gently on the trailer with the tractor to check that the trailer emergency brakes are on.
- Test the trailer service brakes:
    - Check for normal air pressure, release the parking brakes, move the vehicle forward slowly, and apply trailer brakes with the hand control (trolley valve), if so equipped. You should feel the brakes come on.

*Note:* The trailer brakes should be tested with the hand valve, but in normal operation, the trailer brakes are controlled with the foot pedal. The foot pedal applies air to the service brakes at all wheels.

# Coupling and Uncoupling Combination Vehicles

## COUPLING AND UNCOUPLING

Coupling and uncoupling is basic to the safe operation of combination vehicles. Wrong coupling and uncoupling can be dangerous. The makes and models of rigs are different, so learn the details of coupling and uncoupling for the trucks that you will operate.

## COUPLING TRACTOR AND SEMI-TRAILER

Inspect the fifth wheel:

- Check for damaged/missing parts.
- Check to see that mounting to the tractor is secure. Make sure there are no cracks in the frame.
- Be sure that the fifth wheel plate is greased. Failure to keep the fifth wheel plate greased could cause steering problems because of friction between the tractor and trailer.
- Check if fifth wheel is in the proper position for coupling:
    - The wheel should be tilted down toward the rear of the tractor.
    - The jaws should be open.
    - The safety unlocking handle should be in the automatic lock position.
- If you have a sliding fifth wheel, make sure it is locked.
- Make sure that the trailer kingpin is not bent or broken.

Inspect the area and chock the wheels:

- Make sure the area around the vehicle is clear.
- Make sure the trailer wheels are chocked or the spring brakes are on.
- Make sure any cargo is secured so that it will not move while the tractor is being coupled to the trailer.

Position the tractor:

- Put the tractor directly in front of the trailer. Never back under the trailer at an angle. This could cause the trailer to move sideways and break the landing gear.
- Check position, using outside mirrors, looking down both sides of the trailer.

Back slowly:

- Back until the fifth wheel just touches the trailer.
- Don't hit the trailer.

Secure the tractor:

- Put on the parking brake.
- Put the transmission in neutral.

Check the trailer height:

- The trailer should be low enough that it is raised slightly by the tractor when the tractor is backed under it. Raise or lower the trailer as needed. (If the trailer is too low, the tractor may strike and damage the trailer nose; if the trailer is too high, it may not couple correctly.)
- Check that the kingpin and fifth wheel are aligned.

Connect the air lines to the trailer:

- Check the glad hand seals and connect the tractor emergency air line to the trailer emergency glad hand.
- Check the glad hand seals and connect the tractor service air line to the trailer service glad hand.
- Make sure the air lines are safely supported so that they won't be crushed or caught while you back the tractor under the trailer.

Supply air to the trailer:

- From cab, push in the "air supply" knob or move the tractor protection valve control from the "emergency" to the "normal" position to supply air to the trailer brake system.
- Wait until the air pressure is normal.
- Check brake system for crossed air lines:
  - Shut engine off so you can hear the brakes.
  - Apply and release the trailer brakes and listen for the sound of the trailer brakes being applied and released. You should hear the brakes move when applied and air escape when the brakes are released.
  - Check the air brake system pressure gauge for signs of major air loss.
- When you are sure trailer brakes are working, start the engine.
- Make sure the air pressure is up to normal.

Lock the trailer brakes:

- Pull out the trailer air supply knob or move the tractor protection valve from normal to emergency.

Back under the trailer:

- Use the lowest reverse gear.
- Back the tractor slowly under the trailer to avoid hitting the kingpin too hard.
- Stop when the kingpin is locked into the fifth wheel.

Check the connection for security:

- Raise the trailer landing gear slightly off the ground.
- Pull the tractor gently forward while the trailer brakes are locked to be sure that the trailer is locked onto the tractor.
- Secure the vehicle.
- Put the transmission in neutral.
- Put on the parking brakes.
- Shut off the engine and take the key with you so someone else won't move the truck while you are under it.

Inspect the coupling:

- Use a flashlight if necessary.
- Make sure that there is no space between the upper and lower fifth wheel. If there is space, something is wrong. The kingpin may be on top of closed fifth wheel jaws, which would allow the trailer to come loose very easily.
- Go under the trailer and look into the back of the fifth wheel. Make sure the fifth wheel jaws have closed around the shank of the kingpin. Refer to the diagram:

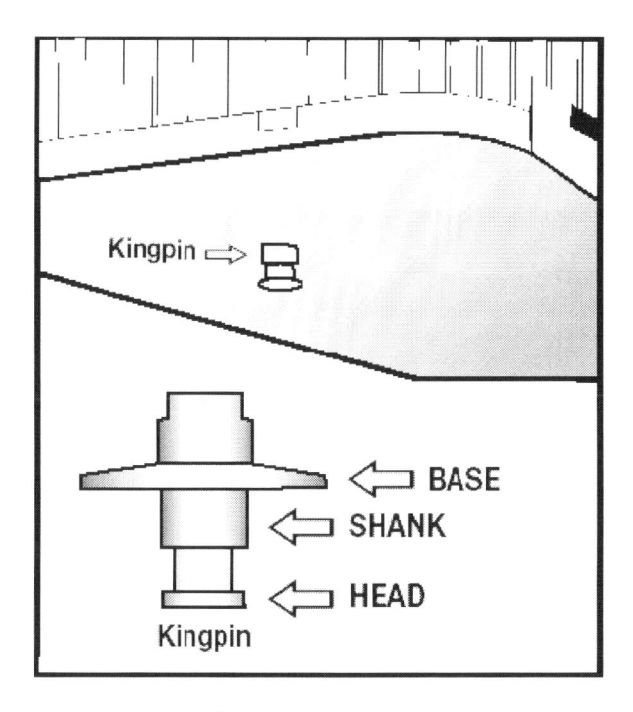

- Check that the locking lever is in the lock position.
- Check that the safety latch is in the position over the locking lever. On some fifth wheels, the catch must be put in place by hand.
- If the coupling isn't right, don't drive the coupled unit. Get it fixed.

Connect the electrical cord and check the air lines:

- Plug the electrical cord into the trailer and fasten the safety catch.
- Check the air and electrical lines for signs of damage.
- Make sure the air and electrical lines will not hit any moving parts of the vehicle.

Raise the front trailer supports (landing gear):

- Use low gear range to begin raising the landing gear. Once free of weight, switch to the high gear range.
- Raise the landing gear all the way up. Never drive with the landing gear part of the way up. It could catch on railroad tracks or other things.
- After raising the landing gear, secure the crank handle.
- When the full weight of the trailer is resting on the tractor:
  - Check for enough clearance between the rear of the tractor frame and the landing gear. When the tractor turns sharply, it must not hit the landing gear.
  - Check that there is enough clearance between the top of the tractor tires and the nose of the trailer.

When finished, remove the trailer wheel chocks and store them in a safe place.

## UNCOUPLING TRACTOR AND SEMI-TRAILER

Position the rig:

- Make sure the surface of the parking area can support the weight of the trailer.
- Line up the tractor with the trailer. Pulling out at an angle can damage the landing gear.

Ease the pressure on the locking jaws:

- Shut off the trailer air supply to lock the trailer brakes.
- Ease pressure on the fifth wheel locking jaws by backing up gently. This will help you release the fifth wheel locking lever.
- Put the parking brakes on while the tractor is pushing against the kingpin. This will hold the rig with pressure off the locking jaws.

Chock the trailer wheels:

- Chock the trailer wheels if the trailer doesn't have spring brakes or if you aren't sure. The air could leak out of the trailer air tank and release the emergency brakes. Without chocks, the trailer could move.

Lower the landing gear:

- If the trailer is empty, lower the landing gear until it makes firm contact with the ground.
- If the trailer is loaded, turn the crank in low gear a few extra turns after the landing gear makes firm contact with the ground. This will lift some weight off the tractor. This makes it easier to unlatch the fifth wheel. It also makes it easier to couple next time.

Disconnect the air lines and electrical cable:

- Disconnect the air lines from the trailer. Connect the glad hands to the dummy couplers at the back of the cab or couple them together.
- Hang the electrical cable with the plug down to prevent moisture from entering it.
- Make sure the lines are supported so they won't be damaged while driving the tractor.

Unlock the fifth wheel:

- Raise the release handle lock.
- Pull the release handle to the open position.
- Keep your feet and legs clear of the rear tractor wheels to avoid serious injury in case the vehicle moves.

Pull the tractor partly clear of the trailer:

- Pull the tractor forward until the fifth wheel comes out from under the trailer.
- Stop with the tractor frame under the trailer. This prevents the trailer from falling to the ground if the landing gear collapses or sinks.

Secure the tractor:

- Apply the parking brake.
- Place the transmission in neutral.

Inspect the trailer supports:

- Make sure the ground is supporting the trailer.
- Make sure the landing gear is not damaged.

Pull the tractor clear of the trailer.

- Release the parking brakes.
- Check the area and drive the tractor forward until it clears the trailer.

## COUPLING TWIN TRAILERS

Secure the second (rear) trailer:

- If the second trailer doesn't have spring brakes, drive the tractor close to the trailer.
- Connect the emergency line and charge the trailer air tank.
- Disconnect the emergency line.
- If the slack adjusters are set correctly, this will set the trailer emergency brakes.
- If you aren't sure about the trailer brakes, chock the wheels.

Couple the tractor and first semi-trailer:

- Follow the steps for coupling tractor and semi-trailer on the preceding pages.

    *CAUTION: The semi-trailer with the heaviest load should be immediately behind the tractor. The lighter trailer should be in the rear.*

(A converter gear or dolly is a coupling device with one or two axles and a fifth wheel. It is used to couple a semi-trailer to the rear of a tractor-trailer combination, forming twin trailers.)

Position the converter dolly in front of the second (rear) trailer:

- Release the dolly brakes by opening the dolly air tank petcock. If the dolly has spring brakes, use the dolly parking brake control.
- If it isn't too far, wheel the dolly into position by hand. Line it up with the kingpin.
- Otherwise, use the tractor and first semi-trailer to pick up the converter dolly:
    - Position the combination (tractor and first semi-trailer) as close as possible to the converter dolly.
    - Move the dolly to the rear of the first semi-trailer and couple it to the trailer.
    - Lock the pintle hook.
    - Secure the dolly support in the raised position.
    - Pull the dolly into position as close as possible to the nose of the second semi-trailer.
    - Lower the dolly support.
    - Unhook the dolly from the first trailer.
    - Wheel the dolly into position in front of the second trailer in line with the kingpin.

Connect the converter dolly to the front trailer:

- Back the first semi-trailer into position in front of the dolly tongue.
- Hook the dolly to the front trailer:
    - Lock the pintle hook.
    - Secure the converter gear support in the raised position.
- Be sure that the trailer brakes are locked or that the wheels are chocked.
- Make sure the trailer height is correct. It must be slightly lower than the center of the fifth wheel so that the trailer is raised slightly when the dolly is pushed under it.
- Back the converter dolly under the rear trailer.
- Raise the landing gear slightly off the ground to prevent damage if the trailer moves.
- Test the coupling by pulling against the pin of the rear semi-trailer.
- Make a visual check of the coupling:
    - Make sure that there is no space between the upper and lower fifth wheel. If there is, something is wrong.
    - Make sure the fifth wheel jaws have closed around the shank of the kingpin.
- Connect the safety chains, air hoses and light cords.
- Close the converter dolly air tank petcock and shut-off valves at the rear of the second trailer. The service and emergency line shut-off valve at the rear of the second trailer should be closed.
- Open the shut-off valves located in the rear of the first trailer and on the dolly.
- Raise the landing gear.
- Charge the trailers' air supply:
    - Push in the trailer air supply knob.
    - Check for air at the rear of the second trailer by opening the emergency line shut-off valve.
    - If there is no air pressure there, something is wrong and the brakes won't work.

## UNCOUPLING TWIN TRAILERS

Uncouple the rear trailer:

- Park the rig in a straight line on firm level ground.
- Apply the parking brakes so that the rig won't move.
- Chock the wheels on the second trailer if it doesn't have spring brakes.
- Lower the landing gear of the second trailer enough to remove some weight from the dolly.
- Close the air shut-off valve at the rear of the first trailer and on the dolly.
- Disconnect all dolly air and electric lines and secure them.
- Release the dolly brakes.
- Release the converter dolly fifth wheel latch.
- Slowly pull the tractor, first trailer and dolly forward to pull the dolly from under the second trailer.

Uncouple the converter dolly:

- Lower the dolly landing gear.
- Disconnect the safety chains.
- Apply the converter gear spring brakes or administer wheel chocks.
- Release the pintle hook on the first trailer.
- Carefully pull away until you are clear of the dolly.

    *CAUTION: Never unlock the pintle hook with the dolly still under the rear trailer. The dolly tow bar could fly up. This could cause injury and would make it very difficult to re-couple.*

## COUPLING AND UNCOUPLING TRIPLE TRAILERS

Couple the second and third trailers:

- Couple the tractor to the second (middle) and third (rear) trailers using the steps outlined on the preceding pages for coupling doubles.
- Uncouple the tractor and pull away from the second and third trailers.

Couple the tractor and first trailer to the second and third trailers:

- Couple the tractor to the first (front) trailer using the steps outlined on the preceding pages.
- Move the converter dolly into position and attach the first trailer to the second trailer using the steps outlined for coupling doubles. The coupling is now finished.

Uncouple the triple rig:

- Uncouple the third (rear) trailer using the steps previously outlined for uncoupling the rear trailer and the convertor dolly in a double rig.
- Then uncouple the second trailer and second convertor dolly in the same way.

# Driving Combination Vehicles

## Rollovers

More than half of truck driver deaths in crashes are the result of truck rollovers. When more cargo is piled up in a truck, the "center of gravity" moves higher up from the road. The truck becomes easier to turn over. Fully loaded rigs are ten times more likely to roll over in a crash than empty rigs. The following two things will help you prevent rollover:

- Keep the cargo as close to the ground as possible, and drive slowly around turns. Keeping cargo low is even more important in combination vehicles than in straight trucks. Also, keep the load centered on your rig. If the load is to one side so it makes a trailer lean, a rollover is more likely. Make sure your cargo is centered and spread out as much as possible.
- Rollovers happen when you turn too fast. Drive slowly around corners, on ramps, and off ramps. Avoid quick lane changes, especially when fully loaded.

## Rearward Amplification and the Crack-the-Whip Effect

"Rearward amplification" causes the crack-the-whip effect. See the chart below for the eight types of combination vehicles and the rearward amplification each has in a quick lane change. Rigs with the least crack-the-whip effect are shown at the top and those with the most, at the bottom. Rearward amplification of 2.0 in the chart means that the rear trailer is twice as likely to turn over as the tractor. You can see that triples have a rearward amplification of 3.5. This means you can roll the last trailer of triples 3.5 times as easily as a five-axle tractor.

### INFLUENCE OF COMBINATION TYPE ON REARWARD AMPLIFICATION

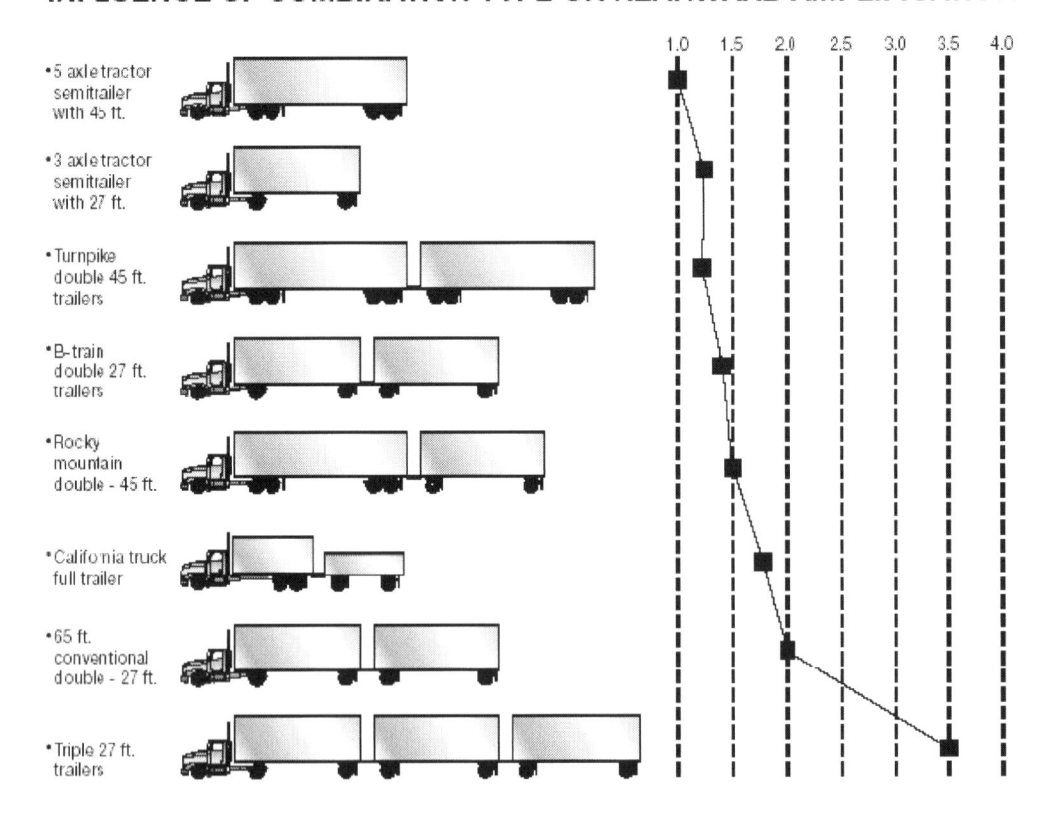

## STEERING

Steer gently and smoothly when you are pulling trailers. If you make a sudden movement with your steering wheel, your trailer could tip over. Follow far enough behind other vehicles (at least 1 second for each 10 feet of your vehicle length, plus another second if going over 40 mph). Look far enough down the road to avoid being surprised and having to make a sudden lane change. At night, drive slowly enough to see obstacles with your headlights before it is too late to change lanes or stop gently. Slow down to a safe speed before going into a turn.

## BRAKING

Control your speed whether fully loaded or empty. Large combination vehicles take longer to stop when they are empty than when they are fully loaded. When lightly loaded, the very stiff suspension springs and strong brakes give poor traction and make it very easy to lock up the wheels. Your trailer can swing out and strike other vehicles. Your tractor can jackknife very quickly. You also must be very careful about driving "bobtail" tractors (tractors without semi-trailers). Tests have shown that bobtails can be very hard to stop smoothly. It takes them longer to stop than a tractor-semitrailer loaded to maximum gross weight. In any combination rig, allow lots of following distance and look far ahead, so you can brake early. Don't be caught by surprise and have to make a "panic" stop.

## RAILROAD-HIGHWAY CROSSINGS

Railroad-highway crossings can also cause problems, particularly when pulling trailers with low underneath clearance. These trailers can get stuck on raised crossings:

- Low slung units (lowboy, car carrier, moving van, possum-belly livestock trailer).
- Single-axle tractor pulling a long trailer with its landing gear set to accommodate a tandem-axle tractor.

If for any reason you get stuck on the tracks, get out of the vehicle and away from the tracks. Check signposts or signal housing at the crossing for emergency notification information. Call 911 or another emergency number. Give the location of the crossing using all identifiable landmarks, especially the DOT number, if posted.

## PREVENTING SKIDS

When the wheels of a trailer lock up, the trailer will tend to swing around. This is more likely to happen when the trailer is empty or lightly loaded. This type of jackknife is often called a "trailer jackknife." The procedure for stopping a trailer skid is:

- Recognize the skid. The earliest and best way to recognize that the trailer has started to skid is by seeing it in your mirrors. Any time you apply the brakes hard, check the mirrors to make sure the trailer is staying where it should be. Once the trailer swings out of your lane, it's very difficult to prevent a jackknife.
- Stop using the brake. Release the brakes to get traction back. Do not use the trailer hand brake (if you have one) to "straighten out the rig." This is the wrong thing to do since the brakes on the trailer wheels caused the skid in the first place. Once the trailer wheels grip the road again, the trailer will start to follow the tractor and straighten out.

## OFFTRACKING

When a vehicle goes around a corner, the rear wheels follow a different path than the front wheels. This is called "offtracking" or "cheating." The figure below shows how offtracking causes the path followed by a tractor to be wider than the rig itself. Longer vehicles will offtrack more. The rear wheels of the powered unit (truck or tractor) will offtrack some, and the rear wheels of the trailer will offtrack even more. If there is more than one trailer, the rear wheels of the last trailer will offtrack the most.

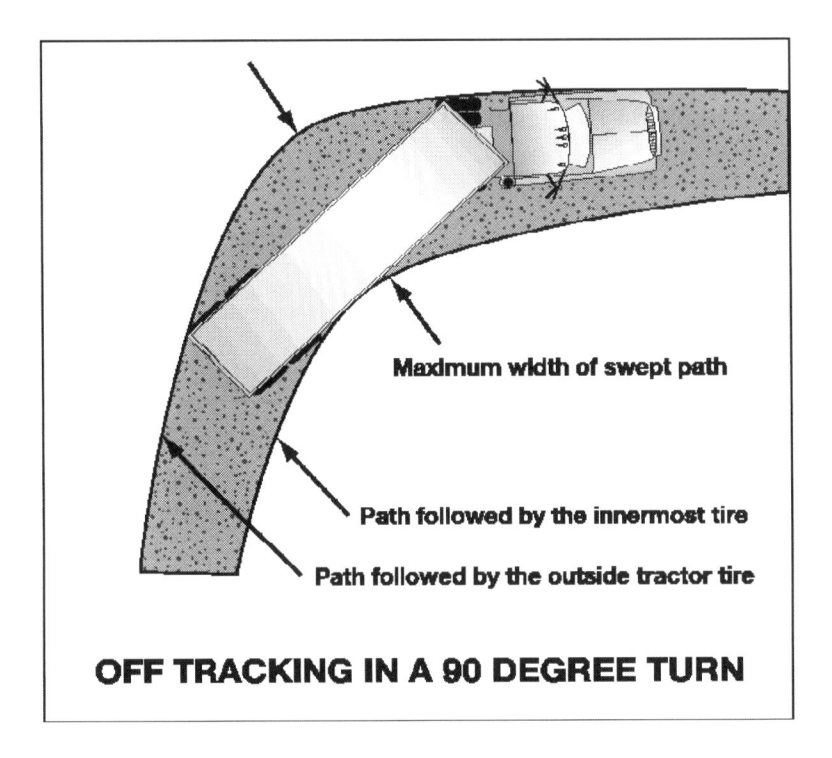

**OFF TRACKING IN A 90 DEGREE TURN**

## STEERING

Steer the front end wide enough around a corner so the rear end does not run over the curb, pedestrians, etc. However, keep the rear of your vehicle close to the curb. This will stop other drivers from passing you on the right. If you cannot complete your turn without entering another traffic lane, turn wide as you complete the turn. This is better than swinging wide to the left before starting the turn because it will keep other drivers from passing you on the right.

## PULLING DOUBLE/TRIPLE TRAILERS

Prevent roll-overs:

- Double and triple tractor-trailer combinations are less stable than other commercial vehicles. Therefore, steer gently and go slowly around curves, corners, on ramps, and off ramps.
- Remember, a safe speed on a curve for a straight truck or a single trailer combination vehicle may be too fast for a set of double or triple trailers.

Beware of the crack-the-whip effect:

- Doubles and triples are more likely to turn over than other combination vehicles because of the crack the-whip effect. You must steer gently when pulling trailers. The last trailer in a combination is the most likely one to turn over.

Look ahead:

- You must drive doubles and triples very smoothly to prevent a rollover or jackknife. Therefore, look far ahead so you can slow down or change lanes gradually if necessary.

Manage your space:

- Doubles and triples take up more room than other commercial vehicles. They are longer and also need additional space because you cannot turn or stop them suddenly.
- Allow more following distance.
- Make sure you have large enough gaps before entering or crossing traffic.
- Be sure you are clear on the side before you change lanes.

Be even more careful in adverse conditions:

- In bad weather, slippery conditions or when driving in the mountains, you must be very careful when driving doubles and triples.

# Combination Vehicles Endorsement Practice Test #1

1. Why must you be extra careful when bobtailing?
   a. Bobtails may not be equipped with splash guards or back bumpers.
   b. Bobtails stop more smoothly but take longer to stop.
   c. Bobtails can be hard to stop smoothly and take longer to stop than a loaded tractor-semi trailer.

2. Which of the following would have the least rearward amplification in a quick lane change?
   a. Turnpike, double 45-foot trailers
   b. Rocky mountain double—45 feet
   c. Triple 27-foot trailers

3. What is the earliest and best way to recognize that your trailer has started to skid?
   a. Hearing the tires strain
   b. Feeling the trailer wheels lose grip on the road
   c. Seeing it in your mirrors

4. Which of the following is another name for the service air line?
   a. Control line
   b. Supply line
   c. Vent line

5. How do you prevent a rollover or jackknife while driving doubles and triples?
   a. Ensure that your sides are clear at all times.
   b. Drive very smoothly.
   c. Accelerate into curves.

6. Before backing up how should you position the tractor in relation to the trailer?
   a. Slightly to the left of the trailer.
   b. Slightly to the left of the center of the trailer.
   c. Directly in front of the trailer.

7. Why should you check your mirrors whenever you apply the brakes hard?
   a. This is the best way to recognize if the trailer has started to skid.
   b. To tell if the mirrors are still in adjustment.
   c. To tell if your cargo door comes open.

8. To ease the pressure on the locking jaws, when preparing to uncouple a trailer, you should:
   a. Remove the trailer wheel chocks and store them in a safe place.
   b. Put the parking brakes on while the tractor is pushing against the kingpin.
   c. Raise the landing gear all the way up and secure the crank handle.

9. **Why do large combination vehicles that are empty take longer to stop than when they are fully loaded?**
    a. When lightly loaded, stiff suspension springs and strong brakes give poor traction and make it easy to lock up the wheels.
    b. Combination vehicles are longer than bobtails and therefore require more length to stop.
    c. Empty trucks are harder to control and the brake connections are more likely to come loose.

10. **Which of the following is NOT one of the two air lines that every combination vehicle has?**
    a. Service line
    b. Emergency line
    c. Return line

11. **When inspecting a sliding fifth wheel, ensure that it is not too far forward, because during turns, that could:**
    a. Cause the air power to cut out
    b. Cause the cab to hit the trailer
    c. Cause damage to the slide

12. **What makes lightly loaded combination vehicles have poor traction and easily locking wheels?**
    a. Rearward amplification
    b. Over-pressurized tanks and emergency brakes
    c. Stiff suspension springs and strong brakes

13. **After raising the landing gear, putting the full weight of the trailer on the tractor, you should check that:**
    a. The air and electrical lines will not hit any moving parts of the vehicle.
    b. The surface of the parking area can support the weight of the trailer.
    c. There is enough clearance between the top of the tractor tires and the nose of the trailer.

14. **When is it okay to back under a trailer at an angle?**
    a. Never
    b. Only when circumstances require it
    c. Anytime there is limited space and you have a spotter

15. **When the wheels of a trailer lock up, what will the trailer tend to do?**
    a. The trailer will immediately stop.
    b. The trailer will tend to jackknife or swing around.
    c. The trailer will automatically break loose from the fifth wheel assembly.

16. **More than half of truck driver deaths in crashes are the result of:**
    a. Rollovers
    b. Skids
    c. Jackknifes

**17. What happens when you push in the trailer air supply control knob and what happens when you pull it out?**
   a. Push it in to supply the trailer with air. Pull it out to release all air to the trailer.
   b. Pull it out to release all air to the trailer. Do not push it in when the vehicle is underway.
   c. Push it in to supply the trailer with air. Pull it out to shut the air off and put on the trailer emergency brakes.

**18. When backing to couple your trailer, which of the following is most likely if the trailer is too high?**
   a. It may not couple correctly.
   b. The tractor may strike and damage the trailer nose.
   c. The air lines may be crushed or caught.

**19. For the coupling to be complete for a fifth wheel with a locking lever, where must the safety catch for the fifth wheel locking lever be?**
   a. Over the locking lever.
   b. Level with the locking lever.
   c. Under the locking lever.

**20. The fifth wheel jaws should be locked around the:**
   a. Kingpin head
   b. Kingpin shank
   c. Kingpin base

# Answer Key and Explanations for Test #1

**1. C**: Bobtails can be hard to stop smoothly and take longer to stop than a loaded tractor-semi trailer.

**2. A:**

### INFLUENCE OF COMBINATION TYPE ON REARWARD AMPLIFICATION

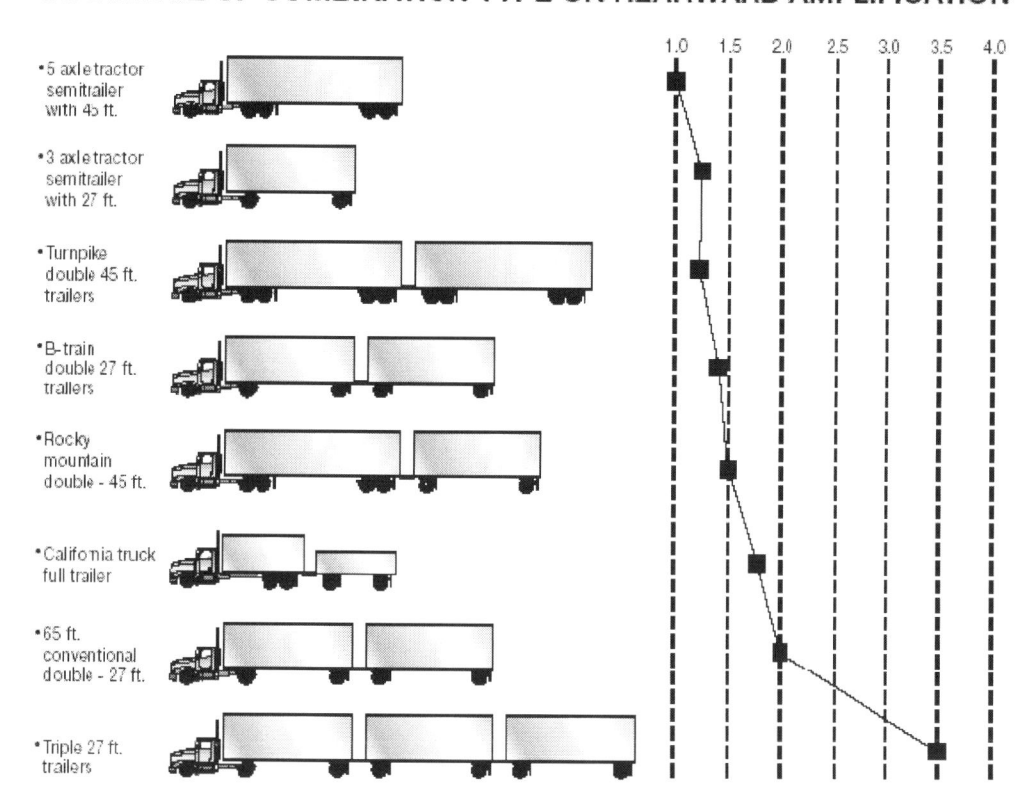

- 5 axle tractor semitrailer with 45 ft.
- 3 axle tractor semitrailer with 27 ft.
- Turnpike double 45 ft. trailers
- B-train double 27 ft. trailers
- Rocky mountain double - 45 ft.
- California truck full trailer
- 65 ft. conventional double - 27 ft.
- Triple 27 ft. trailers

**3. C**: The earliest and best way to recognize that the trailer has started to skid is by seeing it in your mirrors. Any time you apply the brakes hard, check the mirrors to make sure the trailer is staying where it should be. Once the trailer swings out of your lane, it's very difficult to prevent a jackknife.

**4. A**: The service line (also called the control line or signal line) carries air, which is controlled by the foot brake or the trailer hand brake. Depending on how hard you press the foot brake or hand valve, the pressure in the service line will similarly change. The service line is connected to relay valves. These valves allow the trailer brakes to be applied more quickly than would otherwise be possible.

**5. B**: You must drive doubles and triples very smoothly to prevent a rollover or jackknife. Therefore, look far ahead so you can slow down or change lanes gradually if necessary.

**6. C**: Directly in front of the trailer.

**7. A**: This is the best way to recognize if the trailer has started to skid.

**8. B:** To ease the pressure on the locking jaws: Shut off the trailer air supply to lock the trailer brakes. Ease pressure on the fifth wheel locking jaws by backing up gently. This will help you release the fifth wheel locking lever. And put the parking brakes on while the tractor is pushing against the kingpin. This will hold the rig with pressure off the locking jaws.

**9. A**: When lightly loaded, stiff suspension springs and strong brakes give poor traction and make it easy to lock up the wheels.

**10. C:** Every combination vehicle has two air lines: the service line and the emergency line. They run between each vehicle (tractor to trailer, trailer to dolly, dolly to second trailer, etc.).

**11. B:** When checking the sliding fifth wheel, check that the fifth wheel is not so far forward that the tractor frame will hit the landing gear, or that the cab will hit the trailer, during turns.

**12. C:** When lightly loaded, the very stiff suspension springs and strong brakes give poor traction and make it very easy to lock up the wheels. Your trailer can swing out and strike other vehicles. Your tractor can jackknife very quickly.

**13. C:** After raising the landing gear, secure the crank handle. When the full weight of the trailer is resting on the tractor, check that there is enough clearance between the rear of the tractor frame and the landing gear. When the tractor turns sharply, it must not hit the landing gear. And check that there is enough clearance between the top of the tractor tires and the nose of the trailer.

**14. A:** Put the tractor directly in front of the trailer. Never back under the trailer at an angle. This could cause the trailer to move sideways and break the landing gear.

**15. B**: The trailer will tend to jackknife or swing around.

**16. A:** More than half of truck driver deaths in crashes are the result of truck rollovers. When more cargo is piled up in a truck, the center of gravity moves higher up from the road. The truck becomes easier to turn over. Fully loaded rigs are ten times more likely to roll over in a crash than empty rigs.

**17. C**: Push it in to supply the trailer with air. Pull it out to shut the air off and put on the trailer emergency brakes.

**18. A:** The trailer should be low enough that it is raised slightly by the tractor when the tractor is backed under it. Raise or lower the trailer as needed. (If the trailer is too low, the tractor may strike and damage the trailer nose; if the trailer is too high, it may not couple correctly.)

**19. A**: Over the locking lever.

**20. B:** Check the fifth wheel (lower) locking jaws around the shank, not the head of the kingpin. Make sure the fifth wheel jaws have closed around the shank of the kingpin.

# Combination Vehicles Endorsement Practice Test #2

1. What are "dead end" or dummy couplers for?
    a. To prevent water and dirt from getting into unused couplers and air lines
    b. To support or back the glad hands while hauling multiple trailers
    c. To stop the service and emergency air lines from shifting

2. When the emergency line loses pressure, what happens to the tractor protection value?
    a. The valve will open.
    b. The valve will close.
    c. The valve will pop out.

3. With the trailer handbrake or the service brake pedal on, after opening and closing the service line valve, what will indicate that you have air all the way to the back?
    a. Air escaping from both lines
    b. The trailer air supply control popping out
    c. The air pressure falling

4. When can you utilize the trailer hand valve for parking a combination vehicle?
    a. Always.
    b. When the emergency brake is not working.
    c. Never.

5. When inspecting doubles and triples, make sure the pintle eye of your dolly is in place in the:
    a. Pintle hook of your trailer
    b. Glad hand of your trailer
    c. Sockets of your trailer

6. To stop other drivers from passing you on the right, while making a right turn, you should:
    a. Swing wide to the left before starting the turn.
    b. Keep the rear of your vehicle close to the curb.
    c. Go slow and turn on your flashers.

7. Which of the following is NOT an example of a low-slung unit, likely to get stuck on raised railroad crossings?
    a. Car carrier
    b. Bobtail
    c. Moving van

8. The tractor protection valve will close automatically if air pressure is within the range of:
    a. 0-20 psi
    b. 20-45 psi
    c. 45-70 psi

**9. After you lock the kingpin into the fifth wheel how can you check the connection?**
   a. By tapping it with a rubber hammer.
   b. By pulling the tractor ahead gently with the trailer brakes locked.
   c. By pulling it by hand.

**10. Before you back under a semi-trailer in coupling your tractor at what height should the trailer be?**
   a. Four feet eight inches.
   b. Well above the top of the fifth wheel.
   c. Just below the middle of the fifth wheel.

**11. When colors are used to differentiate between air line types, what color is used for the supply lines?**
   a. Blue
   b. Yellow
   c. Red

**12. What are two reasons why doubles and triples take up more space than other commercial vehicles?**
   a. They are longer and they cannot be turned or stopped suddenly.
   b. They are longer and weave from side to side.
   c. They are longer and are taller than tractors.

**13. When hauling multiple trailers, you must ensure that all shut-off valves in the service and supply air lines are in the open position, EXCEPT the ones:**
   a. At the front or on the tractor
   b. In between the tractor and first trailer
   c. At the back of the last trailer

**14. On older vehicles there may be a lever, rather than a knob, for the tractor protection valve. What are the normal and emergency positions?**
   a. The normal position is used for pulling a trailer. The emergency position is used to shut air off to the trailer.
   b. The normal position is horizontal. The emergency position is vertical.
   c. The normal position is used for supplying air to the drive wheel brakes. The emergency position is used to substitute for the emergency brakes.

**15. How much visible space should be between the upper and lower fifth wheel?**
   a. About $\frac{1}{4}$ inch or enough for easy pivoting
   b. Just enough to see light through it
   c. No visible space

**16. What is it called when the rear wheels follow a different path than the front wheels when a vehicle goes around a corner?**
   a. A close fit.
   b. Offtracking.
   c. Crack-the-whip effect.

**17. When inspecting a combination vehicle's air brakes, how will you know if the entire emergency (supply) system is charged?**
   a. Step on and off the brake pedal several times to ensure the air pressure does not drop too quickly.
   b. Listen carefully; air audibly escapes from both the service line and the supply line when the valves are closed.
   c. Listen carefully; air audibly escapes when the emergency line shut-off valve at the rear of the last trailer is open.

**18. Inspect the coupling. You must make certain that there is enough clearance between which two of the following?**
   a. Between the fifth wheel and the floor of the trailer.
   b. Between the tractor taillights and the landing gear.
   c. Between the tops of the tractor tires and the nose of the trailer.

**19. Fully loaded rigs are how many times more likely to roll over in a crash than empty rigs?**
   a. Five times more likely
   b. Ten times more likely
   c. Twenty times more likely

**20. Large combination vehicles take longer to stop when they are:**
   a. Empty
   b. Half full
   c. Fully loaded

# Answer Key and Explanations for Test #2

**1. A:** Some vehicles have "dead end" or dummy couplers to which the hoses may be attached when they are not in use. This will prevent water and dirt from getting into the coupler and the air lines. Use the dummy couplers when the air lines are not connected to a trailer. If there are no dummy couplers, the glad hands can sometimes be locked together (depending on the couplings). It is very important to keep the air supply clean.

**2. B**: The valve will close.

**3. A:** Use the trailer handbrake to provide air to the service line. Open the service line valve to check that service pressure goes through all the trailers (this test assumes that the trailer handbrake or the service brake pedal is on), and then close the valve. If you do not hear air escaping from both lines, check that the shut-off valves on the trailers and dollies are in the open position. You must have air all the way to the back for all the brakes to work.

**4. C**: Never.

**5. A:** When inspecting double and triple trailers, be sure the pintle eye of the dolly is in place in the pintle hook of the trailer(s). Make sure the pintle hook is latched.

**6. B:** Steer the front end wide enough around a corner so the rear end does not run over the curb, pedestrians, etc. However, keep the rear of your vehicle close to the curb. This will stop other drivers from passing you on the right. If you cannot complete your turn without entering another traffic lane, turn wide as you complete the turn. This is better than swinging wide to the left before starting the turn because it will keep other drivers from passing you on the right.

**7. B:** Railroad-highway crossings can cause problems, particularly when pulling trailers with low underneath clearance. Examples of low-slung units include the lowboy, car carrier, moving van, and possum-belly livestock trailer.

**8. B:** The tractor protection valve will close automatically if air pressure is low (in the range of 20-45 psi). When the tractor protection valve closes, it stops any air from going out of the tractor. It also lets the air out of the trailer emergency line. This causes the trailer emergency brakes to come on, with possible loss of control.

**9. B**: By pulling the tractor ahead gently with the trailer brakes locked.

**10. C**: Just below the middle of the fifth wheel.

**11. C:** When coupling, make sure to couple the proper glad hands together. To help avoid mistakes, colors are sometimes used. Blue is used for the service lines and red for the emergency (supply) lines. Sometimes, metal tags are attached to the lines with the words "service" and "emergency" stamped on them.

**12. A:** They are longer and they cannot be turned or stopped suddenly.

**13. C:** Shut-off valves (also called cut-out cocks) are used in the service and supply air lines at the back of trailers used to tow other trailers. These valves permit closing the air lines off when another trailer is not being towed. You must check that all shut-off valves are in the open position except the ones at the back of the last trailer, which must be closed.

**14. A**: The normal position is used for pulling a trailer. The emergency position is used to shut air off to the trailer.

**15. C:** There should be no visible space between the upper and lower fifth wheel.

**16. B**: Offtracking.

**17. C:** Wait for air pressure to reach normal, then push in the trailer air supply knob, which is red. This will supply air to the emergency (supply) lines. Go to the rear of the rig. Open the emergency line shut-off valve at the rear of the last trailer. You should hear air escaping, showing the entire system is charged. Close the emergency line valve.

**18. C**: Between the tops of the tractor tires and the nose of the trailer.

**19. B:** More than half of truck driver deaths in crashes are the result of truck rollovers. When more cargo is piled up in a truck, the center of gravity moves higher up from the road. The truck becomes easier to turn over. Fully loaded rigs are ten times more likely to roll over in a crash than empty rigs.

**20. A:** Large combination vehicles take longer to stop when they are empty than when they are fully loaded. When lightly loaded, the very stiff suspension springs and strong brakes give poor traction and make it very easy to lock up the wheels. Your trailer can swing out and strike other vehicles. Your tractor can jackknife very quickly.

# Combination Vehicles Endorsement Practice Test #3

1. Why should you never unlock the pintle hook with the dolly still under the rear trailer?
   a. The dolly tow bar may fly up.
   b. There may not be enough grease on the pintle hook to enable it to ride smoothly.
   c. It may be too hard to unlock it next time.

2. What is one purpose of the emergency air line?
   a. It allows you to continue your trip when the primary system is malfunctioning.
   b. It activates an emergency locator transmitter.
   c. It supplies air to the trailer air tanks.

3. After you have coupled the tractor with a trailer where should the landing gear be before driving away?
   a. Raised at least six inches above the ground.
   b. Raised at least one foot above the ground with the crank handle secured in its bracket.
   c. Fully raised with the crank handle secured in its bracket.

4. What tells how much pressure the relay valves should send to the trailer brakes?
   a. The position of the foot pedal.
   b. The position of the brake linings.
   c. The pressure in the service line.

5. What two things can a driver do to prevent rollovers?
   a. Keep the cargo as close to the ground as possible. Go slowly around turns.
   b. Go slowly around turns. Try to raise the center of gravity of your load.
   c. Accelerate slowly. Slow down quickly.

6. When you are hauling double trailers, what is the most likely to turn over?
   a. Tractor
   b. First trailer
   c. Second trailer

7. Since a sudden movement with your steering wheel can tip a trailer over, how far behind other vehicles should you follow when pulling trailers.
   a. At least one second for each unit of your vehicle plus another second if going over 45 miles per hour.
   b. At least one second for each 20 feet of your vehicle length, plus another second if going over 35 miles per hour.
   c. At least one second for each ten feet of your vehicle length, plus another second if going over 40 miles per hour.

8. If the air lines on a truck are color coded, which lines are blue?
   a. The emergency lines.
   b. The spring line.
   c. The service line.

9. How are the air tanks on trailers and converter dollies filled?
    a. By the tractor protection valve.
    b. By the air compressor cut off valve.
    c. By the emergency supply line from the tractor.

10. Which valves on the service line on the trailer connect the trailer air tanks to the trailer air brakes?
    a. One-way check valves.
    b. Relay valves.
    c. Automatic valves.

11. When you are hauling multiple semi-trailers, where should the heaviest one be positioned?
    a. Immediately behind the tractor
    b. In the rear/farthest from the tractor
    c. Weight does not matter when positioning trailers

12. In what situation should the trailer hand valve be utilized?
    a. When parking
    b. To test the trailer brakes
    c. For emergency stops

13. Do trailers made before 1975 have spring brakes?
    a. Most of them do.
    b. All of them do.
    c. Many do not.

14. Before you back under the trailer, you should be sure that the trailer brakes are?
    a. Disengaged (Unapplied).
    b. Locked (Applied).
    c. Unhooked.

15. What happens to the trailer emergency brakes if there is a loss of pressure in the emergency line?
    a. The emergency trailer brakes will fail.
    b. The emergency trailer brakes will fade.
    c. The emergency trailer brakes will come on.

16. In normal driving, should you ever use the trailer hand valve before the brake pedal to prevent trailer skids?
    a. Always
    b. When the brake pedal does not work.
    c. Never.

17. What is the cause of over half of truck driver deaths in accidents?
    a. Rush hour traffic.
    b. Truck rollovers.
    c. Heart attacks.

**18. If the tractor protection valve closes, letting air out of the trailer emergency line, which brakes should come on?**
   a. The trailer handbrake.
   b. The trailer emergency brakes.
   c. The brakes on the front axle.

**19. Why must the fifth wheel plate have enough grease?**
   a. To prevent sparks - and smoke.
   b. To prevent squealing.
   c. To prevent steering problems.

**20. Which of the following is NOT one of the emergency line's two primary purposes?**
   a. Carry air to brake relay valves
   b. Supply air to the trailer air tanks
   c. Control the emergency brakes on combination vehicles

# Answer Key and Explanations for Test #3

**1. A**: The dolly tow bar may fly up.

**2. C**: It supplies air to the trailer air tanks.

**3. C**: Fully raised with the crank handle secured in its bracket.

**4. C**: The pressure in the service line.

**5. A**: Keep the cargo as close to the ground as possible. Go slowly around turns.

**6. C**: Doubles and triples are more likely to turn over than other combination vehicles because of the crack the-whip effect. You must steer gently when pulling trailers. The last trailer in a combination is the most likely one to turn over.

**7. C**: At least one second for each ten feet of your vehicle length, plus another second if going over 40 miles per hour.

**8. C**: The service line.

**9. C**: By the emergency supply line from the tractor.

**10. B**: Relay valves.

**11. A**: The semi-trailer with the heaviest load should be immediately behind the tractor. The lighter trailer should be in the rear.

**12. B**: The trailer hand valve (also called the trolley valve or Johnson bar) works the trailer brakes. The trailer hand valve should be used only to test the trailer brakes. Do not use it in driving because of the danger of making the trailer skid. The foot brake sends air to all of the brakes on the vehicle, including the trailer(s). There is much less danger of causing a skid or jackknife when using just the foot brake. Never use the hand valve for parking because all the air might leak out, unlocking the brakes (in trailers that don't have spring brakes). Always use the parking brakes when parking. If the trailer does not have spring brakes, use wheel chocks to keep the trailer from moving.

**13. C**: Many do not.

**14. B**: Locked (Applied).

**15. C**: The emergency trailer brakes will come on.

**16. C**: Never.

**17. B**: Truck rollovers.

**18. B**: The trailer emergency brakes.

**19. C**: To prevent steering problems.

**20. A**: The emergency line (also called the supply line) has two purposes. First, it supplies air to the trailer air tanks. Second, the emergency line controls the emergency brakes on combination vehicles.

# Combination Vehicles Endorsement Practice Test #4

1. What is another name for the emergency air line?
   a. Control line
   b. Signal line
   c. Supply line

2. You can release the dolly brakes by opening what part of the dolly air tank?
   a. Petcock
   b. Pintle hook
   c. Slack adjusters

3. If your trailer has started to skid, what should you do to get traction back?
   a. Release the brakes. Don't use the trailer handbrake.
   b. Press harder on the brake pedal to stop the vehicle faster.
   c. Set the trailer handbrake.

4. What should you use to be safe when you park trailers that don't have spring brakes?
   a. Use wheel chocks
   b. Use available rocks.
   c. Use the curb.

5. Which valve keeps air in the tractor or truck if the trailer breaks away or develops a bad leak?
   a. The one-way check valve.
   b. The relay valve.
   c. The tractor protection valve.

6. If a set speed on a curve is safe for a straight truck or a single trailer combination, then it may be:
   a. Too slow for a set of double or triple trailers
   b. Just as safe for a set of double or triple trailers
   c. Too fast for a set of double or triple trailers

7. When backing to couple your trailer, which of the following is most likely if the trailer is too low?
   a. It may not couple correctly.
   b. The tractor may strike and damage the trailer nose.
   c. The air lines may be crushed or caught.

8. If you will be pulling doubles where one trailer is more heavily loaded than the other, where should the heavier loaded trailer be placed?
   a. It should always be behind the lighter trailer.
   b. It should always be in front of the lighter trailer
   c. It should be placed where it will have the least wind resistance.

9. **What is a reason why there is more chance of skids with doubles and triples in bad weather, slippery conditions and mountain driving?**
    a. Your drive wheels provide security for the pulling unit only.
    b. Your front wheels may not be equipped with brakes.
    c. You have more length and additional dead axles to pull.

10. **When coupling triple trailers, what group should you couple first?**
    a. Tractor, first trailer, and second trailer
    b. Tractor, second trailer, and third trailer
    c. First trailer, second trailer, and third trailer

11. **In trailers that don't have spring brakes, why should you never use the hand valve for parking?**
    a. All the air might leak out, unlocking the brakes.
    b. They can freeze up, making the vehicle immobile.
    c. It can cause slackening in the brake system.

12. **Shut-off valves are also called:**
    a. Supply dampers
    b. Cut-out cocks
    c. Block-off taps

13. **If the spring brakes do not release when you push the trailer air supply control, what should you do?**
    a. Unhook the air line connections.
    b. Check the air line connections.
    c. Tighten the air line connections.

14. **In what position should the air line shut off valves be when you check them?**
    a. They should be in the open position except at the back of the last trailer.
    b. They should be in the open position.
    c. They should be in the closed position.

15. **Which of the following is NOT the proper procedure when preparing for fifth wheel coupling?**
    a. The jaws should be closed.
    b. The wheel should be tilted down toward the rear of the tractor.
    c. The safety unlocking handle should be in the automatic lock position.

16. **To connect the glad hands, the tow seals are pressed together with the couplers at what kind of angle to each other?**
    a. A 45-degree angle.
    b. A 90-degree angle.
    c. A 180-degree angle.

17. **Which of the following is a coupling device with one or two axles and a fifth wheel?**
    a. Trailer support
    b. Glide plate
    c. Dolly

**18. When closed, which of the following lets the air out of the trailer emergency line, causing the trailer emergency brakes to come on?**
   a. Tractor protection valve
   b. Foot brake or hand valve
   c. Air tank drain valve

**19. Suppose you do the following: You charge the trailer air brake system. You ensure the trailer rolls freely. You stop, and then pull out the trailer air supply control. What should now be on?**
   a. The air tank drain
   b. The trailer emergency brakes
   c. The hand valves

**20. When you park trailers without spring brakes, you should always use:**
   a. Emergency brakes
   b. Parking brakes
   c. Wheel chocks

# Answer Key and Explanations for Test #4

**1. C:** The emergency line (also called the supply line) has two purposes. First, it supplies air to the trailer air tanks. Second, the emergency line controls the emergency brakes on combination vehicles. Loss of air pressure in the emergency line causes the trailer emergency brakes to come on.

**2. A:** Release the dolly brakes by opening the dolly air tank petcock. If the dolly has spring brakes, use the dolly parking brake control.

**3. A:** Release the brakes. Don't use the trailer handbrake.

**4. A:** Use wheel chocks

**5. C:** The tractor protection valve.

**6. C:** Double and triple tractor-trailer combinations are less stable than other commercial vehicles. Therefore, steer gently and go slowly around curves, corners, on ramps, and off ramps. Remember, a safe speed on a curve for a straight truck or a single trailer combination vehicle may be too fast for a set of double or triple trailers.

**7. B:** The trailer should be low enough that it is raised slightly by the tractor when the tractor is backed under it. Raise or lower the trailer as needed. (If the trailer is too low, the tractor may strike and damage the trailer nose; if the trailer is too high, it may not couple correctly.)

**8. B:** It should always be in front of the lighter trailer

**9. C:** You have more length and more dead axles to pull.

**10. B:** To couple triple trailers: Couple the tractor to the second (middle) and third (rear) trailers using the steps outlined for coupling doubles. Then uncouple the tractor and pull away from the second and third trailers. Couple the tractor to the first (front) trailer using the steps outlined previously. Then move the converter dolly into position and attach the first trailer to the second trailer using the steps outlined for coupling doubles. The coupling is now finished.

**11. A:** Never use the hand valve for parking because all the air might leak out, unlocking the brakes (in trailers that don't have spring brakes). Always use the parking brakes when parking. If the trailer does not have spring brakes, use wheel chocks to keep the trailer from moving.

**12. B:** Shut-off valves (also called cut-out cocks) are used in the service and supply air lines at the back of trailers used to tow other trailers. These valves permit closing the air lines off when another trailer is not being towed.

**13. B:** Check the air line connections.

**14. A:** They should be in the open position except at the back of the last trailer.

**15. A:** The fifth wheel's proper position for coupling is as follows: The wheel should be tilted down toward the rear of the tractor. The jaws should be open. And the safety unlocking handle should be in the automatic lock position.

**16. B:** A 90-degree angle.

**17. C:** A converter gear, or dolly, is a coupling device with one or two axles and a fifth wheel. It is used to couple a semi-trailer to the rear of a tractor-trailer combination, forming twin trailers.

**18. A:** When the tractor protection valve closes, it stops any air from going out of the tractor. It also lets the air out of the trailer emergency line. This causes the trailer emergency brakes to come on, with possible loss of control.

**19. B:** Test the trailer emergency brakes as follows: Charge the trailer air brake system and check that the trailer rolls freely. Then stop and pull out the trailer air supply control (also called the tractor protection valve control or trailer emergency valve) or place it in the "emergency" position. Pull gently on the trailer with the tractor to check that the trailer emergency brakes are on.

**20. C:** Converter dollies and trailers built before 1975 are not required to have spring brakes. Trailers that do not have spring brakes have emergency brakes that work from the air stored in the trailer air tank. The emergency brakes come on whenever air pressure in the emergency line is lost. These trailers do not have a parking brake. The emergency brakes come on whenever the air supply knob is pulled out or the trailer is disconnected. But the brakes will not hold if there is not sufficient air pressure in the trailer air tank. Eventually, the air will leak away and there will be no brake. Therefore, always use wheel chocks when you park trailers without spring brakes.

# Combination Vehicles Endorsement Practice Test #5

1. **What happens if (only) the service line comes apart while you are driving?**
   a. You may not notice anything until you try to put the brakes on when air loss from the leak will quickly lower the air tank pressure.
   b. Nothing will happen.
   c. You will hear a loud explosion.

2. **What should the trailer height be before you connect a converter dolly to a second or third trailer?**
   a. Five feet eight inches.
   b. It must be slightly lower than the center of the fifth wheel.
   c. Four feet eight inches.

3. **You have connected the air lines but have not yet backed under the trailer. What should you do?**
   a. Check the light connections.
   b. Supply air to the trailer electrical system.
   c. Supply air to the trailer system.

4. **What are some things that you can do to avoid getting surprised and having to make a sudden lane change?**
   a. Use your high-beam headlights at all times. Look far ahead all the time.
   b. Slow down to a safe speed before going into a turn. Focus your attention on the taillights of the vehicle ahead.
   c. Look far enough down the road and allow lots of following distance.

5. **Which of the following is a coupling device used to connect the service and emergency air lines from the truck or tractor to the trailer?**
   a. Lower plate
   b. Glad hands
   c. Relay valves

6. **Why should you lock the glad hands to each other when you are not towing trailers?**
   a. To prevent brake fade.
   b. To keep the brakes from overheating.
   c. To keep dirt and water out the lines.

7. **Which of the following is true about maintaining air tanks that have automatic drains?**
   a. Automatic drains will keep all moisture out.
   b. You should open the drains to make sure that all water is drained.
   c. New tanks with automatic drains are not equipped with manual drains.

8. When connecting twin trailers, which of the following is NOT the appropriate positioning for a shut-off valve?
   a. Open the shut-off valve located in the rear of the first trailer.
   b. Open the shut-off valve located on the dolly.
   c. Open the shut-off valve located in the rear of the second trailer.

9. To prevent friction between the tractor and trailer, always be sure that the fifth wheel plate is:
   a. Unlocked
   b. Cracked
   c. Greased

10. Which of the following is NOT another name for the trailer hand valve?
    a. Trolley valve
    b. Johnson bar
    c. Brake rod

11. To position the converter dolly in front of a second trailer that's far away, you should:
    a. Wheel the dolly into position by hand.
    b. Use the tractor and first semi-trailer to pick up the dolly.
    c. Use the second trailer to move the dolly.

12. Are fully loaded rigs more likely to roll over in a crash than empty rigs?
    a. There is no difference as to the load so far as rolling over is concerned.
    b. Fully loaded rigs are less likely to roll over in a crash.
    c. Fully loaded rigs are 10 times more likely to roll over in a crash.

13. Which of the following is true when preparing the fifth wheel for coupling?
    a. The jaws should be closed.
    b. The wheel should be tilted down toward the front of the tractor.
    c. The safety unlocking handle should be in the automatic lock position.

14. How can you check that the trailer is locked onto the tractor?
    a. Put the tractor into neutral while releasing the spring brakes.
    b. Drive slowly in reverse and watch for the landing gear to rise.
    c. Pull the tractor gently forward while the trailer brakes are locked.

15. What does the trailer air supply control look like on newer vehicles?
    a. A lever with normal and emergency settings
    b. A red eight-sided knob
    c. An orange switch with three positions

16. Which of the following will offtrack more?
    a. Longer vehicles
    b. Bobtail tractors
    c. Shorter vehicles

**17. When colors are used to differentiate between air line types, what color is used for the service lines?**

a. Blue
b. Yellow
c. Red

**18. When a tractor and a trailer are coupled, how much space should there be between the upper and lower fifth wheel.**

a. No space.
b. Space enough to allow air to flow freely.
c. Seven eighths inch.

**19. What is the tractor protection valve's primary function?**

a. To connect the service line and the emergency line between each vehicle
b. To safeguard the trailer air supply control valve in the cab
c. To keep air in the tractor brake system in case the trailer breaks away or develops a bad leak

**20. Looking into the back of the fifth wheel, which part of the kingpin should the locking jaws close around?**

a. The skid plate.
b. The pickup ramp.
c. The shank of the kingpin.

# Answer Key and Explanations for Test #5

**1. A**: You may not notice anything until you try to put the brakes on when air loss from the leak will quickly lower the air tank pressure.

**2. B**: It must be slightly lower than the center of the fifth wheel.

**3. C**: Supply air to the trailer system.

**4. C**: Look far enough down the road and allow lots of following distance.

**5. B**: Glad hands are coupling devices used to connect the service and emergency air lines from the truck or tractor to the trailer. The couplers have a rubber seal, which prevents air from escaping. Clean the couplers and rubber seals before a connection is made. When connecting the glad hands, press the two seals together with the couplers at a 90-degree angle to each other. A turn of the glad hand attached to the hose will join and lock the couplers. It helps if you moisten the rubber seals.

**6. C**: To keep dirt and water out the lines.

**7. B**: It is important that you don't let water and oil build up in the air tanks. If you do, the brakes may not work correctly. Each tank has a drain valve on it, and you should drain each tank every day. If your tanks have automatic drains, they will keep most moisture out. But you should still open the drains to make sure.

**8. C**: Close the converter dolly air tank petcock and shut-off valves at the rear of the second trailer. The service and emergency line shut-off valve at the rear of the second trailer should be closed.

**9. C**: Be sure that the fifth wheel plate is greased. Failure to keep the fifth wheel plate greased could cause steering problems because of friction between the tractor and trailer.

**10. C**: The trailer hand valve (also called the trolley valve or Johnson bar) works the trailer brakes. The trailer hand valve should be used only to test the trailer brakes. Do not use it in driving because of the danger of making the trailer skid.

**11. B**: If it isn't too far, wheel the dolly into position by hand, lining it up with the kingpin. Otherwise, use the tractor and first semi-trailer to pick up the converter dolly.

**12. C**: Fully loaded rigs are 10 times more likely to roll over in a crash.

**13. C**: The fifth wheel's proper position for coupling is as follows: The wheel should be tilted down toward the rear of the tractor. The jaws should be open. And the safety unlocking handle should be in the automatic lock position.

**14. C**: To check the connection for security: Raise the trailer landing gear slightly off the ground. Pull the tractor gently forward while the trailer brakes are locked to be sure that the trailer is locked onto the tractor.

**15. B**: The trailer air supply control on newer vehicles is a red eight-sided knob, which you use to control the tractor protection valve. You push it in to supply the trailer with air, and pull it out to shut off the air and put on the trailer emergency brakes. The valve will pop out (thus closing the tractor protection valve) when the air pressure drops into the range of 20-45 psi. Tractor protection valve controls, or "emergency" valves on older vehicles, may not operate automatically. There may be a lever rather than a knob. The "normal" position is used for pulling a trailer. The "emergency" position is used to shut off the air and put on the trailer emergency brakes.

**16. A:** When a vehicle goes around a corner, the rear wheels follow a different path than the front wheels. This is called "offtracking" or "cheating." Longer vehicles will offtrack more. The rear wheels of the powered unit (truck or tractor) will offtrack some, and the rear wheels of the trailer will offtrack even more. If there is more than one trailer, the rear wheels of the last trailer will offtrack the most.

**17. A:** When coupling, make sure to couple the proper glad hands together. To help avoid mistakes, colors are sometimes used. Blue is used for the service lines and red for the emergency (supply) lines. Sometimes, metal tags are attached to the lines with the words "service" and "emergency" stamped on them.

**18. A**: No space.

**19. C:** The tractor protection valve keeps air in the tractor or truck brake system in case the trailer breaks away or develops a bad leak. The tractor protection valve is controlled by the trailer air supply control valve in the cab. The control valve allows you to open and shut the tractor protection valve. The tractor protection valve will close automatically if air pressure is low (in the range of 20-45 psi). When the tractor protection valve closes, it stops any air from going out of the tractor. It also lets the air out of the trailer emergency line. This causes the trailer emergency brakes to come on, with possible loss of control.

**20. C**: The shank of the kingpin.

# Hazardous Materials Endorsement

## FEDERAL MOTOR CARRIER SAFETY REGULATIONS

"...a motor carrier or other person to whom this part is applicable must comply with the rules in parts 390 through 397, inclusive, of this subchapter when he/she is transporting hazardous materials by a motor vehicle which must be marked or placarded in accordance with § 177.823 of this title."

## HAZARDOUS MATERIALS

Hazardous materials are products that pose a risk to health, safety, and property during transportation. The term often is shortened to HAZMAT, which you may see on road signs, or to HM in government regulations. Hazardous materials include explosives, various types of gas, solids, flammable and combustible liquids, and other materials. Because of the risks involved and the potential consequences these risks impose, all levels of government regulate the handling of hazardous materials. HAZMAT endorsements are not transferable from state to state. Hazardous materials are categorized into nine major hazard classes. The following chart shows the classes and categories and gives examples of materials in each one.

| Class | Class Name | Example |
|---|---|---|
| 1 | Explosives | Ammunition Dynamite Fireworks |
| 2 | Gases | Propane Oxygen Helium |
| 3 | Flammable and Combustible Liquids | Gasoline Alcohol Diesel Fuel Fuel Oils |
| 4 | Flammable Solids | Matches Magnesium |
| 5 | Oxidizers | Ammonium Nitrate Hydrogen Peroxide |
| 6 | Poisons | Pesticides Arsenic |
| 7 | Radioactive | Uranium Plutonium |
| 8 | Corrosives | Hydrochloric Acid Battery Acid, Formaldehyde |
| 9 | Miscellaneous Hazardous Materials | Asbestos Airbag Inflators & Modules |

## Hazardous Materials Regulations

The Code of Federal Regulations gives regulations for hazardous materials. These regulations are located in title 49, parts 171-180. You will hear these regulations referred to as 49 CFR 171-180. The Hazardous Materials Table in the regulations includes a list of hazardous materials. However, this table does not show all hazardous materials. A material is considered hazardous based on its characteristics. A shipper decides if a product meets the definition of a hazardous material in the regulations. Because the federal regulations change often, be sure that your copy is up to date. You may get a copy from your local Government Printing Office bookstore and various publishers. Union or company offices often have copies for drivers to use.

## Intent of Federal Regulations

Transporting hazardous materials can be risky. Federal regulations tell you how to contain the material and communicate the risk. They also assure safe drivers and equipment. Packaging rules tell shippers how to package the materials safely. They also tell drivers how to load, transport and unload the material. To communicate the risk, shippers use hazard warning labels and markings on packages. They also provide shipping papers, emergency response information and placards. These labels and papers communicate the hazard to the shipper, the carrier, and the driver. To ensure safe drivers, anyone who transports hazardous materials must have a commercial driver's license (CDL) and a hazardous materials endorsement. To pass the test for the hazardous materials endorsement, a driver must know how to:

- Identify hazardous materials
- Safely load shipments
- Placard a vehicle in accordance with federal regulations
- Safely transport shipments

## Following Regulations

Learn the regulations and follow them. Following the regulations reduces the risk of injury from hazardous materials. Taking shortcuts and breaking the rules is unsafe and could be deadly. Additionally, drivers who violate the regulations can be fined and put in jail.

Inspect your vehicle before and during each trip. Police may stop and inspect your vehicle. When stopped, they may check your shipping papers, vehicle placards, the hazardous materials endorsement on your driver's license and your knowledge of hazardous materials.

## Licensing and Endorsements

You must have a commercial driver's license (CDL) with a hazardous materials endorsement to drive a vehicle carrying hazardous materials that requires placards. You must pass a written test to get this endorsement. Everything you need to know to pass the written test is in this section. However, this is just the beginning. You can learn more by reading the federal and state regulations for hazardous materials and by attending training courses.

## Training Requirements

Hazardous materials courses are offered by transportation employers, colleges, universities, and associations. In fact, the federal regulations require training and testing for all drivers who transport hazardous materials. You must be trained and tested at least once every 3 years. Your employer must provide this training and testing. Your employer must also keep a record of the training completed by each employee who works with hazardous materials.

Federal regulations also require that drivers receive special training before driving a vehicle transporting certain flammable gas materials or highway/route-controlled radioactive materials. Drivers transporting cargo tanks and portable tanks must also receive specialized training. Your employer must provide this training.

## PERMITS

The majority of states and some localities require registrations or permits to transport hazardous material or subsets of such materials. States and counties may also require drivers to follow special hazardous materials routes. The federal government may require permits or exemptions for special hazardous materials cargo such as rocket fuel. Find out about permits, exemptions, and special routes for the places that you drive.

## ROLES IN TRANSPORTING HAZARDOUS MATERIALS

The shipper sends hazardous products from one place to another by truck, rail, ship, or airplane. The shipper:

- Uses hazardous materials regulations to determine the product's:
    - proper shipping name
    - hazard class
    - identification number
    - correct packaging
    - correct label and markings
    - correct placards
- Prepares products for shipping. The shipper:
    - packages, marks, and labels all materials
    - prepares shipping papers
    - provides emergency response information
    - supplies placards
- Certifies on the shipping paper that the shipment has been prepared according to federal regulations. If you are pulling cargo tanks supplied by you or your employer, the certification statement is not required.

The carrier is a person or company engaged in the transportation of passengers or property as a for-hire or private carrier. The carrier:

- Takes the shipment from the shipper to its destination
- Refuses improper shipments
- Reports accidents and incidents involving hazardous materials to the proper government agency

The driver safely transports the shipment without delay. The driver:

- Makes sure the shipper has identified, marked, and labeled the hazardous materials
- Refuses leaking packages and shipments
- Placards his vehicle when loading, if required
- Follows all regulations about transporting hazardous materials
- Keeps hazardous materials shipping papers and emergency response information in the proper place

## COMMUNICATION RULES

A material's hazard class shows the risks associated with it. There are 9 different hazard classes. The chart below gives the meaning of each hazard class and lists the types of materials included in each class.

| Class | Division | Name of Class or Division | Example |
|---|---|---|---|
| 1 | 1.1 | Explosives (Mass Detonations) | Dynamite |
|   | 1.2 | Projection Hazards | Ammunition for Cannons |
|   | 1.3 | Mass Fire Hazards | Display Fireworks |
|   | 1.4 | Minor Hazards | Small Arms Ammunition |
|   | 1.5 | Very Insensitive | Blasting Agents |
|   | 1.6 | Extremely Insensitive | Explosive Devices |
| 2 | 2.1 | Flammable Gases | Propane |
|   | 2.2 | Non-Flammable Gases | Helium |
|   | 2.3 | Poisonous/Toxic Gases | Fluorine, Compressed |
| 3 | --- | Flammable and Combustible Liquids | Gasoline, Diesel Fuel, Fuel Oil |
| 4 | 4.1 | Flammable Solids | Ammonium Picrate, Wetted |
|   | 4.2 | Spontaneous Combustible | White Phosphorus |
|   | 4.3 | Dangerous When Wet | Sodium |
| 5 | 5.1 | Oxidizers | Ammonium Nitrate |
|   | 5.2 | Organic Peroxides | Methyl Ethyl Ketone Peroxide |
| 6 | 6.1 | Poison (Toxic Material) | Potassium Cyanide |
|   | 6.2 | Infectious Substances | Anthrax Virus |
| 7 | --- | Radioactive | Uranium |
| 8 | --- | Corrosives | Battery Fluid |
| 9 | --- | Miscellaneous Hazardous Materials | Polychlorinated Biphenyls (PCB) |

Hazardous Materials Table in the federal regulations:

- Appendix A to the Hazardous Materials Table-the List of Hazardous Substances and Reportable Quantities, and
- Appendix B to the Hazardous Materials Table-the List of Marine Pollutants
- Before transporting any material, look for the name of the material on these three lists. Some materials may be on all lists. Others may be on only one.

Appendix A-List of Hazardous Substances and Reportable Quantities the Department of Transportation (DOT) and the Environmental Protection Agency (EPA) need to know about all spills of any hazardous substances. These substances are named in **Appendix A of the federal regulations**. Part of this list is shown below.

| Hazardous Substance | Other Names for the Substance | Reportable Quantity in Pounds (kilograms) |
|---|---|---|
| Phenyl mercaptan | Benzenethiol | 100 (45.4) |
|  | Thiophenol |  |
| Phenylmercuric acetate | Mercury, (acetate-0) phenyl | 100 (45.4) |
| N-Phenylthiourea | Thiourea, phenyl | 100 (45.4) |
| Phorate | Phosphorothioic acid, O, O-diethyl | 10 (4.54) |
|  | S-(ethyl thio), Methyl ester |  |
| Phosgene | Carbonyl chloride | 10 (4.54) |
| Phosphine* | Hydrogen phosphide | 100 (45.4) |
| Phosphoric acid* |  |  |
| Phosphoric acid, diethyl |  |  |
| 4-nitrophenyl ester | Diethyl-p-nitrophenyl | 100 (45.4) |
| Phosphoric acid, lead salt | Lead phosphate | 1 (0.454) |

- Column 1 shows names of elements and compounds that are hazardous substances.
- Column 2 shows other names that these substances may be called.
- Column 3 shows the reportable quantity for each product. If you spill this amount of the material or more, you or your employer must notify the appropriate authorities regarding the spill. Packages that contain a reportable quantity of the material will show the letters RQ. The letters RQ will also show on the shipping paper.
- If the term "INHALATION HAZARD" appears on the shipping forms or the package itself, you must use the "POISON" or "POISON GAS" placards. These placards are not to be used solely, but in addition to other placards required according to the product's hazard class. Always use all necessary placards, even if you are only carrying a very small amount.
- Appendix B shows the lists of marine pollutants.

## Shipping Papers

A shipping paper describes the hazardous materials being transported. Shipping papers include shipping orders, bills of lading and manifests. After an accident or hazardous materials accident or spill, you may be injured and unable to tell others about your hazardous cargo. Firefighters and police can prevent or reduce the amount of damage and injury if they know about the hazardous materials you are carrying. Your life and the lives of others could depend on quickly locating hazardous materials shipping papers. Shippers must describe hazardous materials correctly and include an emergency response telephone number on the shipping papers. Carriers and drivers must tab hazardous materials shipping papers or keep them on top of other shipping papers. They must also keep the emergency response information with the shipping papers. Drivers must keep hazardous materials shipping papers in one of these locations:

- In a pouch on the driver's door
- In clear view within immediate reach while the driver's seat belt is fastened
- On the driver's seat when the driver is out of the vehicle

The shipping paper shown below shows a detailed description of a shipment:

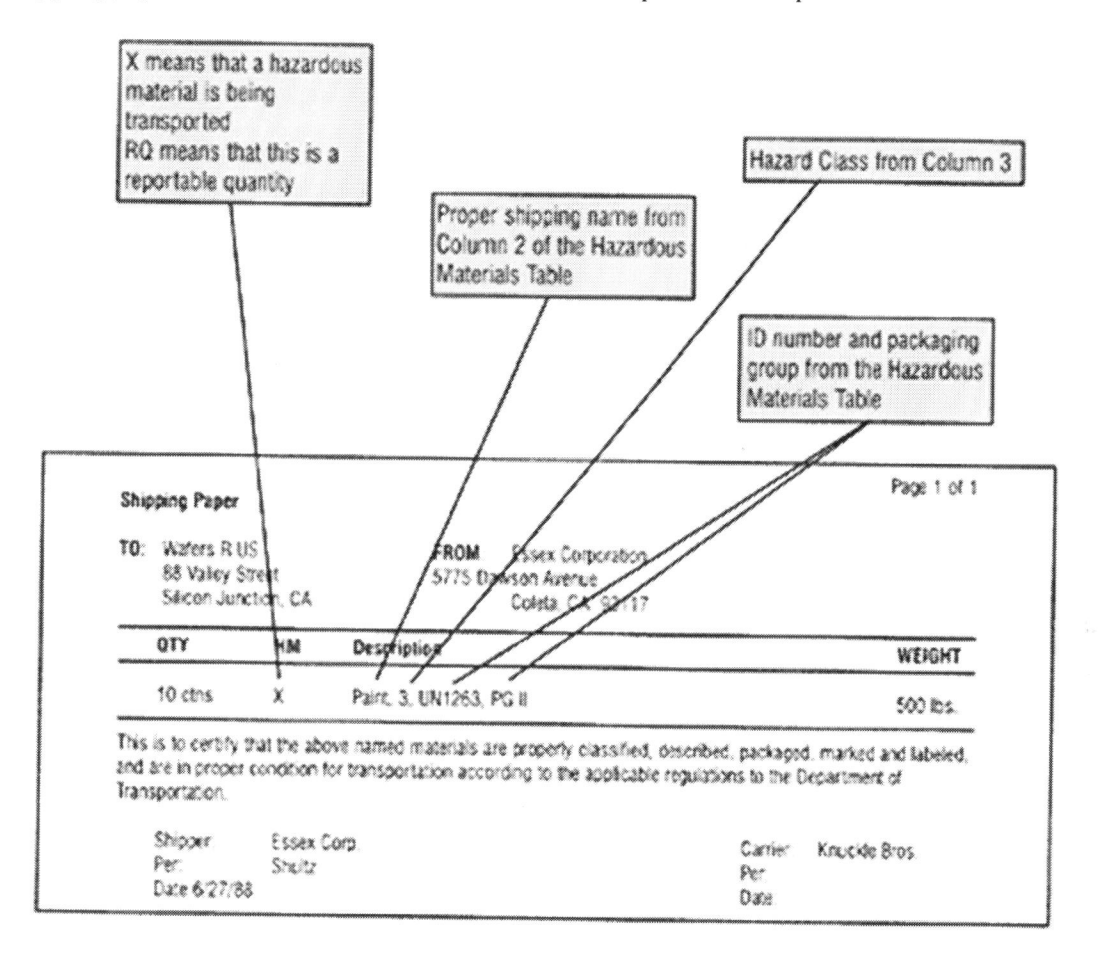

[Shipping paper diagram with callouts:
- "X means that a hazardous material is being transported. RQ means that this is a reportable quantity" → points to HM column
- "Proper shipping name from Column 2 of the Hazardous Materials Table" → points to Description
- "Hazard Class from Column 3" → points to Description
- "ID number and packaging group from the Hazardous Materials Table" → points to Description

Shipping Paper — Page 1 of 1
TO: Wafers R US, 88 Valley Street, Silicon Junction, CA
FROM: Essex Corporation, 5775 Dawson Avenue, Goleta, CA 93717

| QTY | HM | Description | WEIGHT |
|---|---|---|---|
| 10 ctns | X | Paint, 3, UN1263, PG II | 500 lbs. |

This is to certify that the above named materials are properly classified, described, packaged, marked and labeled, and are in proper condition for transportation according to the applicable regulations to the Department of Transportation.

Shipper: Essex Corp
Per: Shultz
Date: 6/27/88

Carrier: Knuckle Bros
Per:
Date:]

A shipping paper for hazardous materials must include:

- page numbers if the shipping paper has more than one page. The first page must show the total number of pages. For example, "page 1 of 4."
- a proper shipping description for each hazardous material. See below for a list of items in the shipping description.
- a shipper's certification signed by the shipper. This certification states that the shipper prepared the shipment according to the federal regulations.

If the shipping paper describes hazardous and non-hazardous products, the hazardous materials will be:

- described first, or
- highlighted in a contrasting color, or
- identified by an X placed before the shipping name in a column labeled HM. If a reportable quantity is present in one package, the letters RQ may be used instead of X.

## Package Labels

Package labels are diamond-shaped hazard warning labels found on most hazardous materials packages. These labels inform others of the hazard. If the diamond label does not fit on the package, shippers may put the label on a tag attached to the package. For example, compressed gas cylinders often have tags or decals.

## Placards

Placards warn others of hazardous materials. They are placed on the outside of the vehicle and identify the hazard class of the cargo. A placarded vehicle must have at least 4 identical placards. Placards must be readable from all four directions. Therefore, they are put on the front, rear and both sides of the vehicle. Placards measure 10 ¾ inches square and are turned in a diamond shape. Cargo tanks and other bulk packaging display the identification number of their contents on placards. Or they may use orange panels or white diamond-shape displays the same size as placards.

## Shipping Description

The shipping description for a hazardous material includes (in this order):

- Proper shipping name
- Hazard class or division
- The identification number
    - Shipping name, hazard class, and ID number must not be abbreviated unless authorized in the federal regulations.
- The packing group
    - The group is displayed in Roman numerals (for example, I, II, III). The numerals may be preceded by the letters PG.
- The total quantity of each hazardous product and the unit of measure
    - Total quantity must appear before or after the basic description. The packaging type and unit of measure may be abbreviated. For example: "10 ctns. Paint, 3, UN1263, PG II, 500 lbs"
- The letters RQ if a reportable quantity is present
- The name of the hazardous substance if the letters RQ appear
- For n.o.s. (not otherwise specified) and generic descriptions, the technical name of the hazardous material must be shown.
    - Example: Weed killer is a generic name; paraquat is a technical name.
- The shipper of hazardous wastes must put the word WASTE before the name of the material on the shipping paper (hazardous waste manifest).
    - Example: Waste Acetone, 3, PGII, UN1090, PG II

You may not use a hazard class or ID number to describe a non-hazardous material.

Shippers must list an emergency response telephone number on the shipping paper. The number can be used by emergency workers to get information about any hazardous materials involved in a spill or fire. Shippers must also provide emergency response information to the motor carrier for each hazardous material being shipped. The driver must carry this information. You must be able to use this information away from the motor vehicle and it must provide information on how to safely handle incidents involving the materials shipped. It must include the shipping name of the hazardous material and information about the risks of fire and explosion and risks to health. It must also include information about initial methods for handling fires, spills, and leaks of materials.

The emergency information may be included on the shipping paper or another document that includes the basic description and technical name of the hazardous material, or it may be in a guidance book such as the Emergency Response Guide (ERG). The driver must provide the emergency response information to any federal, state, or local authority responding to or investigating a hazardous materials incident.

A hazard class indicates the general nature of the hazard. Within some classes, divisions exist to indicate additional hazards. For example, Class 2 covers all compressed gases. Within Class 2:

- Division 2.1 = Flammable Gas
- Division 2.2 = Non-Flammable Gas
- Division 2.3 = Poison Gas

## CERTIFICATION STATEMENT

When the shipper packages hazardous materials, he certifies that the package has been prepared according federal regulations. The signed shipper's certification appears on the original shipping paper. Exceptions: A shipper does not have to sign a certification statement if the shipper is a private carrier transporting its own product and the product will not be transported by another carrier. The shipper does not have to sign a certification statement if the material is transported in a cargo tank supplied by the carrier. Unless a package is clearly unsafe, you may accept the shipper's certification concerning proper packaging. Some carriers have additional rules about transporting hazardous materials. Follow your employer's rules when accepting shipments.

## PACKAGE MARKINGS AND LABELS

Shippers print required markings directly on the package, an attached label or tag. The most important package marking is the name of the hazardous material. It is the same name as the one used on the shipping paper. The shipper will put the following information on the package:

- The name and address of the shipper or consignee (the business or person to whom the shipment is being sent)
- The hazardous material's shipping name and identification number

## REQUIRED LABELS

If a reportable quantity or inhalation hazardous is being shipped, the shipper will also put RQ or INHALATION HAZARD on the package. Packages with liquid containers inside will have arrows pointing in the corrected upright direction. The labels used always reflect the hazard class of the product. Labels should appear near the proper shipping name.

## RECOGNIZING HAZARDOUS MATERIALS

Learn to recognize shipments of hazardous materials. To find out if the shipment includes hazardous materials, look for these clues:

- An entry with a proper shipping name, hazard class and ID number.
- A highlighted entry or one with an X or RQ in the hazardous materials column.
- Look for other clues and ask:
  - What business is the shipper in? Paint dealers, chemical suppliers, scientific supply houses, pest control or agricultural suppliers, and explosives, munitions, or fireworks dealers are all likely sources for hazardous materials.
  - Do you see tanks with diamond labels or placards around the business?
  - What type of package is being shipped? Cylinders and drums are often used for hazardous materials shipments.
  - Is a hazard class label, proper shipping name and ID number on the package?
  - Does the package have handling precautions?

## HAZARDOUS WASTE MANIFEST

When transporting hazardous wastes, you must sign and carry a Uniform Hazardous Waste Manifest. The name and EPA identification number of the shippers, carriers and destination must appear on the manifest. Shippers must prepare, date, and sign the manifest. Treat the manifest as a shipping paper when transporting the waste. Only give the waste shipment to a carrier with an EPA identification number or an EPA permitted treatment, storage, or disposal facility. Each carrier/driver transporting the shipment must sign the manifest. After you deliver the shipment, keep your copy of the manifest. Each copy must have all needed signatures and dates. It must include the signature of the person to whom you delivered the waste.

## PLACARDING

Attach the appropriate placards to the vehicle before you drive it. If you find that your vehicle is not placarded or placarded improperly, you may move it only during an emergency to protect life or property. To decide which placards to use, you must know:

- The hazard class of the materials
- The quantity of each hazardous material
- The total weight of all hazardous materials in your vehicle

Placard tables: There are two placard tables that tell you how to placard your vehicle.

- Placard Table 1: Any Amount. Table 1 materials must be placarded whenever any amount is transported.

| If your vehicle contains any amount of: | Placard as: |
| --- | --- |
| 1.1 | EXPLOSIVE 1.1 |
| 1.2 | EXPLOSIVE 1.2 |
| 1.3 | EXPLOSIVE 1.3 |
| 2.3 | POISON GAS |
| 4.3 | DANGEROUS WHEN WET |
| 6.1 (PG 1, inhalation hazard only) | POISON, INHALATION HAZARD REF. 172.55c |
| 7 (Radioactive Yellow III label only) | RADIOACTIVE |

- Placard Table 2: More than 1,000 lb. Except for bulk packaging, the hazard classes in Table 2 need placards only if the total amount transported exceeds 1,000 lb including packaging. To find out if you need a placard, add the amounts from all shipping papers for all the Table 2 products that you have on board.

| Category of Material (Hazard class or division number and description as appropriate) | Placard Name |
|---|---|
| 1.4 | EXPLOSIVES 1.4 |
| 1.5 | EXPLOSIVES 1.5 |
| 1.6 | EXPLOSIVES 1.6 |
| 2.1 | FLAMMABLE GAS |
| 3 | FLAMMABLE |
| 3 | COMBUSTIBLE |
| 4.1 | FLAMMABLE SOLID |
| 4.2 | SPONTANEOUS COMBUSTIBLE |
| 5.1 | OXIDIZER |
| 5.2 | ORGANIC PEROXIDE |
| 6.1 (PG I or II, other than PG I inhalation hazard) If ZONE A or B | POISON INHALATION |
| 6.1 (PG III) | KEEP AWAY FROM FOOD |
| 6.2 | (no placard required) |
| 8 | CORROSIVE |
| 9 | CLASS 9** |

- You may use DANGEROUS placards instead of separate placards for each Table 2 hazard class if both of the following apply:
    o you have loaded two or more Table 2 hazard classes that weigh more than 1,000 lb and which require different placards
    o you have not loaded more than 1,000 kg of any Table 2 hazard class material from any one shipper.
- If you have loaded more than 1,000 kg of a hazardous material from any one shipper, you must use the specific placard for this material
- If the words INHALATION HAZARD are on the shipping paper or package, you must display POISON or POISON GAS placards, as appropriate, in addition to other placards required by the products hazard class.
- If the vehicle contains division 1.1 or 1.2 explosives and is placarded with EXPLOSIVES 1.1 or EXPLOSIVES 1.2 and you are also carrying EXPLOSIVES 1.5, OXIDIZER or DANGEROUS placard materials, you may use DANGEROUS placards instead of separate placards for each Table 2 Hazard you have loaded.
- If the vehicle displays a Division 2.1 FLAMMABLE GAS or a Division 2.2 OXYGEN placard, you do not need to use a Division 2.2 NON-FLAMMABLE GAS placard.
- Placards that identify the primary hazard class of a material must show the hazard class or division number in the lower corner of the placard. Placards that identify a secondary hazard class of a material may not show the hazard class or division number.
- You may display a placard for a hazardous material, even if it is not required, as long as the placard identifies the hazard of the material being transported.

## LOADING AND UNLOADING HAZARDOUS MATERIALS
### GENERAL LOADING REQUIREMENTS

- Do everything you can to protect containers of hazardous materials. Don't use tools which might damage containers or packaging during loading. Don't use hooks.
- Before loading or unloading, set the parking brake. Make sure the vehicle will not move.
- Many products become more hazardous when exposed to heat. Load hazardous materials away from heat sources.
- Watch for signs of leaking or damaged containers. **Do not transport leaking packages.** You, your truck, and others could be placed in danger.
- To prevent movement during transit, brace packages containing:
  - Class 1 (explosives)
  - Class 2 (gases)
  - Class 3 (flammable liquids)
  - Class 4 (flammable solids)
  - Class 5 (oxidizers)
  - Division 6.1 (poisons)
  - Class 8 (corrosives)
- When loading or unloading hazardous materials, keep fire away.
- Never allow smoking near:
  - Class 1 (explosives)
  - Division 2.1 (flammable gas)
  - Class 3 (flammable liquids)
  - Class 4 (flammable solids)
  - Class 5 (oxidizers)
- Be careful when loading containers with valves or other fittings.
- After loading, do not open any package during your trip. Never transfer hazardous materials from one package to another during the trip. You may empty a cargo tank, but do not empty any other package while it is on the vehicle.
- Cargo heater rules. There are special cargo heater regulations found in the Code of Federal Regulations for loading:
  - Class 1 (explosives)
  - Division 2.1 (flammable gas)
  - Class 3 (flammable liquids)
- The regulations generally forbid use of cargo heaters, including automatic cargo heating/refrigeration units. Unless you have read all the related regulations, do not load these products in a cargo space that has a heater.
- You must use closed cargo space for the following materials unless all packages are in fire- and water-resistant packaging or covered with a fire- and water-resistant tarp:
  - Class 1 (explosives)
  - Class 4 (flammable solids)
  - Class 5 (oxidizers)
- You also may not have overhang or tailgate loads of these materials.

## PRECAUTIONS FOR SPECIFIC HAZARDS

Class 1 (explosive) materials:

- Turn off your engine before loading or unloading explosives. Then check the cargo space. You must:
  - Disable cargo heaters. Disconnect heater power sources and drain heater fuel tanks.
  - Make sure there are no sharp points that might damage cargo. Look for bolts, screws, nails, broken side panels and broken floor boards.
- Use a floor lining with Division 1.1, 1.2 or .1.3 explosives. The floors must be tight and the liner must be either non-metallic material or non-ferrous metal (metal that does not contain iron).
- Use extra care to protect explosives. Never use hooks or other metal tools. Never drop, throw, or roll packages. Protect explosive packages from other cargo that might cause damage.
- Do not transfer a Division 1.1, 1.2, or 1.3 explosive from one vehicle to another on a public roadway except in an emergency. If you must make an emergency transfer, set out red warning reflectors, flags or electric lanterns. You must warn others on the road.
- Never transport damaged packages of explosives. Do not take a package that shows dampness or an oily stain.
- Do not transport Division 1.1 or 1.2 explosives in vehicle combinations or triples if either of these apply:
  - A marked or placarded cargo tank is in the combination
  - The other vehicle in the combination contains any of the following:
    - Division 1.1 A (initiating) explosives
    - Packages of Class 7 (radioactive) materials labeled "Yellow III,"
    - Division 2.3 (poisonous gas) or Division 6.1 (poisonous) materials
    - Hazardous materials in a portable tank, a DOT Spec 106A or 110A tank

Class 2 (compressed gasses) including cryogenic liquids:

- Cryogenic liquids are liquids carried at very cold temperatures. See 49 CFR 177 for additional details.
- If your vehicle doesn't have racks to hold cylinders, the cargo space floor must be flat. The cylinders must be:
  - Held upright or braced laying down flat, or
  - In racks attached to the vehicle, or
  - In boxes that will keep them from turning over.

Division 2.3 (poisonous gas) or Division 6.1 (poisonous) materials

- Never transport these materials in containers with interconnections
- Never load a package labeled POISON or POISON GAS in the driver's cab, sleeper or with food material for human or animal consumption.

Class 7 (radioactive) materials. Some packages of Class 7 (radioactive) materials show a number called the transport index. The shipper labels these packages Radioactive II or Radioactive III and prints the package's transport index on the label.

- Radiation surrounds each package and passes through all nearby packages. As a result, the number of packages you can load together is controlled. Their closeness to people, animals and unexposed film is also controlled.
- The transport index (shown below) shows how close you can load Class 7 (radioactive) materials to people, animals, or film. For example, you can't leave a package with a transport index of 1.1 within 2 feet of people or cargo space walls during transit. The total transport index of all packages in a single vehicle must not exceed 50. Single vehicles include automobiles, vans, trucks tractors and semi-trailers.

Class 8 (corrosive) materials:

- If loading by hand, load breakable containers of corrosive liquid one by one. Keep them right side up. Do not drop or roll the containers. Load them on an even floor surface. Stack carboys only if the lower tiers can bear the weight of the upper tiers safely. (Carboys are portable tanks that may be metal or plastic and are placed in a special cage.)
- Do not load nitric acid above any other product or stack more than 2 high.
- Load charged storage batteries so their liquid won't spill. Keep them right side up. Make sure other cargo won't fall against or short circuit them.
- Never load corrosive liquids next to or above:
    - Division 1.4
    - Class 4 (flammable solids)
    - Class 5 (oxidizers)
    - Division 2.3, Zone B gases
- Never load corrosive liquids with:
    - Division 1.1, 1.2, or 1.3
    - Division 1.5 (blasting agents)
    - Division 2.3, Zone A, gases
    - Division 4.2 (spontaneously combustible materials)
    - Division 6.1, PGI, Zone A (poison liquids)

## RADIOACTIVE TRANSPORT INDEX

Do not leave radioactive yellow-II or yellow-III labeled packages near people, animals, or film longer than shown in this table.

| TOTAL TRANSPORT INDEX | MINIMUM DISTANCE IN FEET TO NEAREST UNDEVELOPED FILM ||||| TO PEOPLE OR CARGO COMPARTMENT PARTITIONS |
|---|---|---|---|---|---|---|
|  | 0-2 Hours | 2-4 Hours | 4-8 Hours | 8-12 Hours | Over 12 Hours |  |
| None | 0 | 0 | 0 | 0 | 0 | 0 |
| 01. to 1.0 | 1 | 2 | 3 | 4 | 5 | 0 |
| 1.1 to 5.0 | 3 | 4 | 6 | 8 | 11 | 2 |
| 5.1 to 10.0 | 4 | 6 | 9 | 11 | 15 | 3 |
| 10.1 to 20.0 | 5 | 8 | 9 | 11 | 15 | 3 |
| 20.1 to 30.0 | 7 | 10 | 15 | 20 | 29 | 5 |
| 30.1 to 40.0 | 8 | 11 | 17 | 22 | 33 | 6 |
| 40.1 | 9 | 12 | 19 | 24 | 36 |  |

Federal regulations stipulate that certain products cannot be carried together in the same cargo space. The table below lists some examples. The Segregation and Separation chart names other materials that you must keep apart.

| DO NOT LOAD... | IN THE SAME VEHICLE WITH... |
|---|---|
| Division 6.1 or 2.3 POISON or poison gas labeled material | Animal or human food unless the poison package is overpacked in an approved way. Foodstuffs are anything you swallow. However, mouthwash, toothpaste, and skin creams are not foodstuff. |
| Division 2.3 (poisonous) gas Zone A or Division 6.1 (poisonous) gas Zone A or Division 6.1 (poison) liquids, PGI Zone A | Division 5.1 (oxidizers), Class 3 (flammable liquids), Class 8 (corrosive liquids) Division 5.2 (organic peroxides), Division 1.1, 1.2, 1.3 (Class A or B explosives) Division 1.5 (blasting agents) Division 2.1 (flammable gasses), Division 4.1 (flammable solids) Division 4.2 (spontaneously combustible). Division 4.3 (dangerous when wet). See 49 CFR 177 for additional details. |
| Charged storage batteries | Division 1.1 Class A (explosives) |
| Class 1 (detonated primers) | Any other explosives unless in authorized containers or packaging |
| Division 6.1 (cyanides or cyanide mixtures) | Acids, corrosive materials, or other acidic materials which could release hydrocyanic acid from cyanides. For example: Cyanides, inorganic, n.o.s. Silver Cyanide Sodium Cyanide |
| Nitric acid (Class 8) | Other materials unless the nitric acid is not loaded above any other material and not more than two tiers high. |

## Marking, Loading, and Unloading Packaging
### Bulk Packaging

Bulk packaging is any packaging in which hazardous materials are loaded with no intermediate form of containment and which:

- As a receptacle for liquid holds 450 liters or 119 gallons or more
- As a receptacle for solids holds 400 kilograms/882 pounds or 450 liters/119 gallons or more
- As a receptacle for gas has a water capacity greater than 454 kilograms/1000 pounds (refer to the definition in 49 CFR 173, 115)

Bulk packaging includes transport vehicles and freight containers. A cargo tank is a bulk packaging which is:

- A tank intended primarily for carrying liquids or gases and includes appurtenances, reinforcements, fittings, and closures
- Permanently attached to or forms a part of a motor vehicle (or if not permanently attached to a motor vehicle, it is loaded or unloaded without being removed from the motor vehicle)
- Not made according to specifications for cylinders, portable tanks, tank cars, or multi-unit tank car tanks

Portable tanks are bulk containers which are permanently attached to a vehicle. The product is loaded or unloaded while the portable tanks are off the vehicle. Many types of cargo tanks are in use. The most common cargo tanks are MC306/406 for flammable liquids and MC331 for Bulk gases. Other liquid hazardous materials must be transported in other types of specification tanks such as MC307/407 or MC312/412.

### Markings

You must display the ID number of the hazardous materials in portable tanks, cargo tanks and intermediate bulk packaging containers. ID numbers are shown in column 4 of the Hazardous Materials Table. Federal regulations require black 100 mm (3.9 inch) numbers on orange panels, placards, or a white diamond-shaped background if placards are not required. Specification cargo tanks must show retest date markings. In addition, portable tanks:

- Must show the lessee or owner's name
- Must display the shipping name of the contents on two opposite sides

The letters of the shipping name must be at least 2 inches tall on portable tanks with capacities of more than 1,000 gallons and 1 inch tall on portable tanks with capacities of less than 1,000 gallons. The ID number must appear on each side and each end of a portable tank or other bulk packaging that holds 1,000 gallons or more. The ID number must appear on two opposite sides if the portable tank holds less than 1,000 gallons. The ID numbers must be visible when the portable tank is on the motor vehicle. If they are not visible, you must display the ID number on both sides and on both ends of the motor vehicle. If the identification numbers cannot be seen from outside the vehicle, additional numbers must be affixed to the exterior-front, rear and both sides.

## Tank Loading and Unloading

The person in charge of loading and unloading a cargo tank must make sure a qualified person is always watching. The person watching must:

- Be alert
- Have a clear view of the cargo tank
- Be within 100 feet of the tank (397.5 D 1)
- Know the hazards of the materials involved
- Know procedures to follow in an emergency
- Be authorized and able to move the cargo tank

Close all manholes and valves before moving a tank of hazardous materials, no matter how small the amount in the tank or how short the distance. Manholes and valves must be closed to prevent leaks.

### Flammable Liquids

Turn off your engine before loading or unloading any flammable liquids. Run the engine only if you need it to operate a pump. Ground a cargo tank correctly before filling through an open filling hole. Ground the tank before opening the filling hole and maintain the ground until after you close the filling hole.

### Compressed Gas

Keep liquid discharge valves on a compressed gas tank closed except when loading and unloading. Run the engine only if you need it to operate a pump. If you run your engine, turn it off after transferring the product and before you unhook the hose. Unhook all loading/unloading connections before coupling, uncoupling, or moving a chlorine tank. Always chock trailers and semi-trailers to prevent motion when uncoupled from the tractor or power unit.

## Parking and Driving Rules

### Parking with Division 1.1, 1.2 or 1.3 Explosives

Never park with Division 1.1, 1.2, or 1.3 explosives within 5 feet of the operating roadway. Do not park within 300 feet of the following:

- A bridge, tunnel, or building
- A place where people gather
- An open fire

If you must park, for example to refuel, be as quick as possible. Do not park on private property unless the owner is aware of the danger. Someone must always watch the parked vehicle. You may let someone else watch the vehicle only if it is:

- On the shipper's property
- On the carrier's property
- On the consignee's property

### Safe Havens

You may leave your vehicle unattended in a safe haven. A safe haven is an approved place for parking unattended vehicles loaded with explosives. Local or state and federal authorities identify areas for safe havens.

## Parking a Placarded Vehicle Not Carrying Division 1.1, 1.2 or 1.3 Explosives

You may park a placarded vehicle (not carrying explosives) within 5 feet of the traveled part of the road only if your work requires it. Move the vehicle as soon as possible. Someone must always watch the vehicle when parked on a public road or shoulder. Do not uncouple a trailer with hazardous materials and leave it on a public street. Do not park within 300 feet of an open fire.

## Attending Parked Vehicles

The person watching a placarded vehicle must:

- Be in the vehicle and awake. He cannot be in the sleeper berth. Or, the person must be within 100 feet of the vehicle and have it within clear view.
- Be aware of the hazards of the materials being transported.
- Know what to do in an emergency.
- Be able to move the vehicle if needed.

## Flares

If you need to use warning devices, use reflective triangles or red electric lights. NEVER use burning signals, such as flares or fuses, around a:

- Tank used for Class 3 (flammable liquids) or Division 2.1 (flammable gas) whether loaded or empty.
- Vehicle loaded with Division 1.1, 1.2 or 1.3 explosives.

## Smoking

Do not smoke while driving or within 25 feet of a placarded cargo tank used for Class 3 (flammable liquids) or Division 2.1 (gases). Do not smoke or carry a lighted cigarette, cigar or pipe while driving or within 25 feet of any vehicle which contains:

- Class 1 Explosives
- Class 3 Flammable Liquids
- Class 4 Flammable Solids Class 5 Oxidizers

## Refuel with the Engine Off

Turn off your engine before fueling a motor vehicle carrying hazardous materials. Someone must always be at the nozzle controlling the fuel flow.

## Carry a 10 B:C Fire Extinguisher

The tractor or power unit or placarded vehicles must have a fire extinguisher with a UL rating of 10 B:C or more. Make sure the extinguisher is fully charged. Know how to operate it before you need it!

## Equipment for Chlorine

A driver transporting chlorine in cargo tanks must have an approved gas mask in the vehicle. The driver must also carry an emergency kit for controlling leaks in the dome cover plate fittings on the cargo tank.

## Permit and Route Restrictions

Most states and some localities require permits to transport hazardous materials and wastes. Rules about permits can change. Make sure you have all the needed permits before you start. Many states and localities have either route restrictions or designated routes for the transportation of hazardous materials. These restrictions and designations can change often. If you work for a carrier, ask your dispatcher about route restrictions or permits. If you are an independent trucker and are planning a new route, check with agencies where you plan to travel. Some localities prohibit transportation of hazardous materials through tunnels, over bridges or other roadways. Check before you start. Whenever you drive a placarded vehicle, avoid heavily populated areas, crowds, tunnels, narrow streets, and alleys. Take other routes, even if they are more inconvenient. Never drive a placarded vehicle near open fires unless you can safely pass without stopping.

## Carrying Division 1.1, 1.2, or 1.3 Explosives

If you are carrying Division 1.1, 1.2, or 1.3 explosives:

- You must have a written route plan and must follow that plan.
- Keep a copy of the plan with you while transporting the explosives.
- Carriers prepare the route plan ahead of time and give the driver a copy.
- You may plan the route yourself if you pick up the explosives somewhere other than at your employer's terminal. If you plan the route, write it out in advance and keep it with you while transporting the explosives.
- Deliver shipments of explosives only to authorized persons or leave them in locked rooms designed for explosives storage.
- A carrier must choose the safest route to transport placarded radioactive materials. After choosing the route, the carrier must tell the driver about the radioactive materials and tell him the route plan.

## Shipping Papers and Emergency Response Information

Do not accept a hazardous materials shipment without a properly prepared shipping paper.

A shipping paper for hazardous materials must always be easily recognized. Other people must be able to find it quickly after an accident. Put hazardous materials shipping papers on top of your stack of shipping papers or tab them so that they stand out from other papers. When you are driving, keep shipping papers within your reach (with your seat belt on) or in a pouch on the driver's door. They must be seen easily by someone entering the cab. When you are not behind the wheel, leave the shipping papers in the driver's pouch or on the driver's seat. Emergency response information must be kept with the shipping paper.

## Papers for Division 1.1, 1.2, or 1.3 Explosives

A carrier must give each driver transporting Division 1.1, 1.2 or 1.3 explosives a copy of Federal Motor Carrier Safety Regulations (FMCSR), Part 397. The carrier must also give the driver written instructions about what to do if the driver is delayed or in an accident. These instructions must include:

- Names and contact numbers of appropriate people to contact (i.e., agents or shippers).
- Information about the explosives being transported
- Information about what to do in emergencies such as accidents, fires, or leaks.

The driver must sign showing receipt for these documents. When you are driving, you must have and be familiar with:

- The shipping papers
- The written emergency instructions
- The written route plan
- A copy of FMCSR, part 397

## Check Your Tires Every 2 Hours/100 Miles

Ensure your tires are inflated properly before you begin your trip. Check placarded vehicles with dual tires at the start of each trip and when you park. You must stop and check the tires every 2 hours or 100 miles, whichever comes first. Use a tire pressure gauge to check the pressure. This is the only acceptable way to check pressure. Do not drive with a tire that is leaking or flat except to the nearest safe place to fix it. Remove any overheated tire. Place it a safe distance from your vehicle. Don't drive until you correct the cause of overheating. Follow the rules about parking and attending placarded vehicles. They apply even when you are checking, repairing, or replacing tires.

## Stop Before Railroad Crossings (392.10)

Always stop before a railroad crossing if your vehicle:

- Is placarded
- Carries any amount of chlorine
- Is a cargo tank used for hazardous materials, whether empty or loaded

You must stop 15-50 feet prior to reaching the nearest rail. Proceed with caution, only when you are positive that no train is coming. Never shift gears while crossing the tracks.

# Hazardous Materials Endorsement Practice Test #1

**1. Packages that contain a reportable amount of a hazardous material will have what identifying marker on them?**

   a. The letters RQ
   b. A DOT placard
   c. A health hazard symbol

**2. If a label will not fit on a hazardous materials package?**

   a. The driver may use a bright red marking pen to mark the package.
   b. The package will not have to be labeled if it weighs less than 100 pounds.
   c. The label must be put on a tag which is then wired to the package.

**3. Which is not part of a correct shipping name?**

   a. NOS
   b. The technical name of the product
   c. The brand name of the product

**4. Which of the following contains the List of Marine Pollutants?**

   a. The Hazardous Materials Table
   b. Appendix A to the Hazardous Materials Table
   c. Appendix B to the Hazardous Materials Table

**5. Which requires a placard even if there is only one pound of it on board?**

   a. Flammable Liquids
   b. Corrosives
   c. Class A Explosives

**6. What hazard class contains gases, like propane, oxygen, and helium?**

   a. Class 1
   b. Class 2
   c. Class 3

**7. Two letters that may be shown before the name of a hazardous substance?**

   a. AD
   b. PX
   c. RQ

**8. To transport hazardous materials, you must receive training and testing at least every:**

   a. 2 years
   b. 3 years
   c. 4 years

9. Which of the following is NOT an appropriate location for the person watching a placarded vehicle?
    a. Within the driver's cab
    b. In the sleeper berth
    c. Within 100 feet of the vehicle

10. Information on a hazardous materials shipping paper must be shown?
    a. Proper shipping name, then packing group, then ID number
    b. Proper shipping name, then hazard class, ID number, packing group
    c. Hazard class first followed by shipping name, ID and packing group

11. You should always stop before a railroad crossing if your vehicle:
    a. Is not placarded
    b. Carries any chlorine
    c. Is a bobtail

12. If the vehicle displays a Division 2.1 "FLAMMABLE GAS" or a Division 2.2 "OXYGEN" placard, you do NOT need to use a:
    a. Division 2.2 "NON-FLAMMABLE GAS" placard
    b. Division 2.3 "POISON GAS" placard
    c. Division 3 "FLAMMABLE" placard

13. Which of the following is the List of Hazardous Substances and Reportable Quantities?
    a. The Hazardous Materials Table
    b. Appendix A to the Hazardous Materials Table
    c. Appendix B to the Hazardous Materials Table

14. What materials have a numerical transport index?
    a. Class 4 (flammable solids)
    b. Class 7 (radioactive)
    c. Class 9 (miscellaneous hazardous materials)

15. In bulk quantities only on highways marine pollutants are regulated?
    a. In interstate commerce
    b. In foreign commerce within all countries
    c. In intrastate and interstate commerce

16. A commodity named in Placard Table I requires a placard for?
    a. Any quantity
    b. A shipment that weighs more than a thousand pounds
    c. A shipment that contains more than one class of hazardous materials

17. Poisons must not be transported with which of the following?
    a. Carcinogens
    b. Foods, animal feed or medicines
    c. Fungicides, pesticides or liquid fertilizers

**18. Where must the ID number appear on a portable tank, if the portable tank holds less than 1,000 gallons?**

   a. On two opposite sides
   b. On each side and each end
   c. Once, anywhere visible

**19. Where must the ID number appear on a portable tank or other bulk packaging that holds 1,000 gallons or more?**

   a. On two opposite sides
   b. On each side and each end
   c. Once, anywhere visible

**20. When is the only time you should run the engine while loading and unloading compressed gas?**

   a. To unhook the hose
   b. While opening or closing liquid discharge valves
   c. To operate a pump

**21. How should each trailer be placarded in a combination unit?**

   a. At the front of the first trailer and the back of the last trailer
   b. For the class of hazardous material contained in that trailer
   c. On the sides of the trailers only with a placard on the power unit

**22. When hauling Division 1.1, 1.2, or 1.3 explosives, the driver must sign to show receipt of what documents?**

   a. A copy of FMCSR Part 397, and written emergency instructions
   b. Properly prepared shipping papers
   c. A copy of the written route plan, and a liability agreement

**23. When fueling a placarded vehicle, someone must be?**

   a. Supervising the fueling from a safe distance
   b. Supervising the fueling from at least 25 feet away
   c. At the nozzle, controlling the fuel flow

**24. What is the most common cargo tank for hauling bulk gases?**

   a. MC306/406
   b. MC312/412
   c. MC331

**25. Class 8 refers to which hazardous materials?**

   a. Miscellaneous hazardous materials
   b. Explosives
   c. Corrosives

**26. The Hazardous Materials Table is organized?**

   a. In alphabetical order by the proper shipping name
   b. In numerical order by the hazard class number only
   c. In the same order as the listings in the placard tables

**27. You may let someone else watch your vehicle containing Division 1.1, 1.2, or 1.3 explosives if:**
   a. They know the procedures to follow in an emergency.
   b. It is parked away from major roadways.
   c. It is parked on the shipper's or carrier's property.

**28. When placards are required, they should be placed?**
   a. On the rear and both sides of the vehicle
   b. On the front, the rear, and both sides of the vehicle
   c. As long as four placards are displayed they may be placed as wanted

**29. Who is responsible for providing the emergency response information to any federal, state, or local authority responding to or investigating a hazardous materials incident?**
   a. Shipper
   b. Carrier
   c. Driver

**30. While carrying hazardous materials, what should you do when a tire overheats?**
   a. Avoid routes with highways and curves.
   b. Remove the tire and place it a safe distance from your vehicle.
   c. Drive until the cause is evident.

# Answer Key and Explanations for Test #1

**1. A:** If you spill the reportable quantity (or more) of a material, you or your employer must notify the appropriate authorities regarding the spill. Packages that contain a reportable quantity of the material will show the letters RQ. The letters RQ will also show on the shipping paper.

**2. C:** The label must be put on a tag which is then wired to the package.

**3. C:** The brand name of the product

**4. C:** Appendix B to the Hazardous Materials Table contains the List of Marine Pollutants.

**5. C:** Class A Explosives

**6. B:** Class 2 contains gases (for example, propane, oxygen, and helium).

**7. C:** RQ

**8. B:** Federal regulations require training and testing for all drivers who transport hazardous materials. You must be trained and tested at least once every 3 years. Your employer must provide this training and testing. Your employer must also keep a record of the training completed by each employee who works with hazardous materials.

**9. B:** The person watching a placarded vehicle must either be in the vehicle and awake (they cannot be in the sleeper berth), or be within 100 feet of the vehicle and have it within clear view.

**10. B:** Proper shipping name, then hazard class, ID number, packing group

**11. B:** Always stop before a railroad crossing if your vehicle is placarded, carries any amount of chlorine, or is a cargo tank used for hazardous materials, whether empty or loaded.

**12. A:** If the vehicle displays a Division 2.1 "FLAMMABLE GAS" or a Division 2.2 OXYGEN placard, you do not need to use a Division 2.2 "NON-FLAMMABLE GAS" placard.

**13. B:** Appendix A to the Hazardous Materials Table is the List of Hazardous Substances and Reportable Quantities.

**14. B:** Some packages of Class 7 (radioactive) materials show a number called the transport index. The shipper labels these packages "Radioactive II" or "Radioactive III" and prints the package's transport index on the label.

**15. C:** In intrastate and interstate commerce

**16. A:** Any quantity

**17. B:** Foods, animal feed or medicines

**18. A:** The ID number must appear on two opposite sides if the portable tank holds less than 1,000 gallons.

**19. B:** The ID number must appear on each side and each end of a portable tank or other bulk packaging that holds 1,000 gallons or more.

**20. C:** Keep liquid discharge valves on a compressed gas tank closed except when loading and unloading. Run the engine only if you need it to operate a pump. If you run your engine, turn it off after transferring the product and before you unhook the hose. Unhook all loading/unloading connections before coupling, uncoupling, or moving a chlorine tank.

**21. B**: For the class of hazardous material contained in that trailer

**22. A:** A carrier must give each driver transporting Division 1.1, 1.2, or 1.3 explosives a copy of the Federal Motor Carrier Safety Regulations (FMCSR) Part 397. The carrier must also give the driver written instructions about what to do if the driver is delayed or in an accident. The driver must sign showing receipt of these documents. When you are driving, you must have and be familiar with the shipping papers, written emergency instructions, and written route plan, as well as a copy of FMCSR Part 397.

**23. C**: At the nozzle, controlling the fuel flow

**24. C:** The most common cargo tanks are MC306/406 for flammable liquids and MC331 for bulk gases. Other liquid hazardous materials must be transported in other types of specification tanks, such as MC307/407 or MC312/412.

**25. C:** Class 8 contains corrosives (for example, hydrochloric acid, battery acid, and formaldehyde).

**26. A**: In alphabetical order by the proper shipping name

**27. C:** Never park with Division 1.1, 1.2, or 1.3 explosives within 5 feet of the operating roadway. Do not park within 300 feet of the following: a bridge, tunnel, building, place where people gather, or open fire. If you must park, for example to refuel, be as quick as possible. Do not park on private property unless the owner is aware of the danger. Someone must always watch the parked vehicle. You may let someone else watch the vehicle only if it is on the shipper's property, the carrier's property, or the consignee's property.

**28. B**: On the front, the rear, and both sides of the vehicle

**29. C:** The emergency information may be included on the shipping paper or another document that includes the basic description and technical name of the hazardous material, or it may be in a guidance book such as the Emergency Response Guidebook (ERG). The driver must provide the emergency response information to any federal, state, or local authority responding to or investigating a hazardous materials incident.

**30. B:** Do not drive with a tire that is leaking or flat, except to the nearest safe place to fix it. Remove any overheated tire. Place it a safe distance from your vehicle. Don't drive until you correct the cause of overheating. Follow the rules about parking and attending placarded vehicles. They apply even when you are checking, repairing, or replacing tires.

# Hazardous Materials Endorsement Practice Test #2

**1. When you are driving a placarded vehicle, which of the following is the safest and most advisable route?**
   a. A route that goes through heavily populated areas
   b. A path with tunnels and alleys
   c. An inconvenient route with no restrictions

**2. If you find that your vehicle is not placarded or is placarded improperly, you may move it:**
   a. Less than 1,000 feet
   b. During an emergency to protect life or property
   c. To get to the closest location with the appropriate placards

**3. N.O.S. (not otherwise specified) and generic hazardous material shipping descriptions must include:**
   a. Information about the risks of generic damage
   b. The word "WASTE" before the name of the material
   c. The technical name of the hazardous material

**4. Which of the following is displayed in Roman numerals on the shipping description?**
   a. The identification number
   b. The total quantity of each hazardous product
   c. The packing group

**5. Which of the following is true of bulk packaging?**
   a. Bulk packaging containers are permanently attached to a vehicle.
   b. When functioning as a receptacle for liquid, it holds at most 450 liters, or 119 gallons.
   c. It is packaging in which hazardous materials are loaded with no intermediate form of containment.

**6. If required to stop for a railroad crossing you must stop?**
   a. Twenty to forty feet before the nearest rail
   b. Fifteen to fifty feet before the nearest rail
   c. Wherever you can plainly see any approaching train

**7. The total transport index of all radioactive packages in a vehicle can't exceed?**
   a. 25
   b. 50
   c. 100

**8. With tank vehicles the Identification (ID) Number must appear on?**
   a. The tanks and the placards.
   b. The shipping papers.
   c. The placards and the shipping papers.

**9. Which of the following lists materials that you must keep apart?**
   a. Placard Tables 1 and 2
   b. The Hazardous Materials Table
   c. The Segregation and Separation chart

**10. What do the majority of states require you to have in order to transport hazardous materials?**
   a. Registrations or permits
   b. Route restrictions
   c. Pilot escorts

**11. Transporters must retain a copy of hazardous waste manifests for at least?**
   a. One year
   b. Two years
   c. Three years

**12. To pass the test for the hazardous materials endorsement, a driver must know how to:**
   a. Identify hazardous materials
   b. Load shipments quickly
   c. Create shipping papers

**13. You may load cylinders of compressed gas without racks if the cylinders?**
   a. Can be loaded in rounded containers
   b. Can be loaded in an upright position without supports
   c. Can be loaded on the vehicle laying down flat and braced

**14. Which word is a hazardous class description found on labels?**
   a. Corrosive
   b. Fragile
   c. Cancer

**15. If special permits or special routes are required, who is responsible for this?**
   a. Owner of the vehicle
   b. The company dispatcher
   c. Driver of the vehicle

**16. When should a driver have all needed placards in place for packaged freight?**
   a. Before loading
   b. After loading each commodity that requires a certain placard
   c. After the vehicle is loaded but before it goes out onto the highway

**17. What is the intent of the hazardous materials regulations?**
   a. To communicate risk, to protect all, and to contain the product.
   b. To reduce the costs of transportation.
   c. To raise funds for the government through fines for violations.

**18. An X or an RQ shown in the HM column of a shipping paper means?**
   a. The material in the shipment is a hazardous material.
   b. This is a hazardous material that any driver can transport.
   c. This material is an exception to the hazardous material rules.

**19. You should NOT transport Division 1.1 or 1.2 explosives in vehicle combinations or triples if:**
   a. The other vehicle in the combination is an unmarked cargo tank.
   b. The other vehicle in the combination is carrying Class 3 materials.
   c. The other vehicle in the combination contains hazardous materials in a portable tank.

**20. Which is not the proper four-digit Identification (ID) Number?**
   a. USA number
   b. NA number
   c. UN number

**21. A driver transporting hazardous materials should keep those materials?**
   a. Away from other packages
   b. Away from moisture
   c. Away from walls or side racks

**22. Which of the following is NOT information the shipper will put on hazardous material packaging?**
   a. The certification statement saying that the package was prepared correctly
   b. The hazardous material's shipping name and identification number
   c. The name and address of the shipper or consignee

**23. What is a marking that must be shown on liquid hazardous materials packages?**
   a. This Side Up
   b. This Package May Leak
   c. This Package Opens at the Bottom

**24. Diamond-shaped hazard warning labels, found directly on or attached to hazardous material packages, are:**
   a. Highlighted shipping papers
   b. Package labels
   c. Placards

**25. The transport index shows how close you can load Class 7 (radioactive) materials to:**
   a. People, animals, or film
   b. Explosives, gases, or biofuels
   c. Other hazardous materials, living organisms, or water

**26. The tractor, power unit, or placarded vehicles must have a fire extinguisher with a minimum UL rating of:**
   a. 10 B:C
   b. 40 B:C
   c. 60 B:C

**27. When stopping for a railroad crossing, you must stop how many feet prior to reaching the first rail?**
   a. 1-15 feet prior
   b. 15-50 feet prior
   c. 50-100 feet prior

**28. What is a way to determine if two materials are not compatible to transport?**
   a. Study the charts that are available.
   b. Use the trial and error method.
   c. Phone the local police or sheriff's office.

**29. Which of the following is NOT a qualification to use "DANGEROUS" placards instead of separate placards for each Table 2 hazard class material?**
   a. If you have loaded two or more Table 2 hazard classes that weigh more than 1,000 lb and require different placards
   b. If the words "INHALATION HAZARD" are on the shipping paper or package
   c. If you have not loaded more than 1,000 kg of any Table 2 hazard class material from any one shipper

**30. How many placarding tables are there to tell you how to placard your vehicle?**
   a. 2
   b. 3
   c. 4

# Answer Key and Explanations for Test #2

**1. C:** Most states and some localities require permits to transport hazardous materials and wastes. If you work for a carrier, ask your dispatcher about route restrictions or permits. If you are an independent trucker and are planning a new route, check with agencies where you plan to travel. Some localities prohibit transportation of hazardous materials through tunnels, or over bridges or other roadways. Check before you start. Whenever you drive a placarded vehicle, avoid heavily populated areas, crowds, tunnels, narrow streets, and alleys. Take other routes, even if they are more inconvenient.

**2. B:** Attach the appropriate placards to the vehicle before you drive it. If you find that your vehicle is not placarded or is placarded improperly, you may move it only during an emergency to protect life or property.

**3. C:** For N.O.S. (not otherwise specified) and generic descriptions, the technical name of the hazardous material must be shown. For example, "weed killer" is a generic name; "paraquat" is a technical name.

**4. C:** The packing group is displayed in Roman numerals (for example, I, II, III). The numerals may be preceded by the letters PG.

**5. C:** Bulk packaging is any packaging in which hazardous materials are loaded with no intermediate form of containment, and that meets the following criteria: as a receptacle for liquid, it holds at least 450 liters (119 gallons); as a receptacle for solids, it holds at least 400 kilograms (882 pounds) or 450 liters (119 gallons); and as a receptacle for gas, it has a water capacity greater than 454 kilograms (1,000 pounds) (refer to the definition in 49 CFR 173, 115). Bulk packaging includes transport vehicles and freight containers.

**6. B**: Fifteen to fifty feet before the nearest rail

**7. B**: 50

**8. C**: The placards and the shipping papers.

**9. C:** Federal regulations stipulate that certain products cannot be carried together in the same cargo space. The Segregation and Separation chart names materials that you must keep apart.

**10. A:** The majority of states, and some localities, require registrations or permits to transport hazardous materials or subsets of such materials. States and counties may also require drivers to follow special hazardous-material routes. The federal government may require permits or exemptions for special hazardous materials cargo such as rocket fuel. Find out about permits, exemptions, and special routes for the places that you drive.

**11. C**: Three years

**12. A:** To ensure safe driving, anyone who transports hazardous materials must have a commercial driver's license (CDL) and a hazardous materials endorsement. To pass the test for the hazardous materials endorsement, a driver must know how to identify hazardous materials, safely load shipments, placard a vehicle in accordance with federal regulations, and safely transport shipments.

**13. C**: Can be loaded on the vehicle laying down flat and braced

**14. A**: Corrosive

**15. C**: Driver of the vehicle

**16. C**: After the vehicle is loaded but before it goes out onto the highway

**17. A**: To communicate risk, to protect all, and to contain the product.

**18. A**: The material in the shipment is a hazardous material.

**19. C:** Do not transport Division 1.1 or 1.2 explosives in vehicle combinations or triples if either of these apply:

- A marked or placarded cargo tank is in the combination.
- The other vehicle in the combination contains any of the following:
  - Division 1.1 A (initiating) explosives
  - Packages of Class 7 (radioactive) materials labeled "Yellow III"
  - Division 2.3 (poisonous gas) or Division 6.1 (poisonous) materials
  - Hazardous materials in a portable tank, or a DOT Spec 106A or 110A tank

**20. A**: USA number

**21. B**: Away from moisture

**22. A:** Shippers print required markings directly on the package, or an attached label or tag. The shipper will put the following information on the package: the name and address of the shipper or consignee (the business or person to whom the shipment is being sent), and the hazardous material's shipping name and identification number. If a reportable quantity or inhalation hazard is being shipped, the shipper will also put "RQ" or "INHALATION HAZARD" on the package. Packages with liquid containers inside will have arrows pointing in the correct upright direction. The labels used always reflect the hazard class of the product. Labels should appear near the proper shipping name.

**23. A**: This Side Up

**24. B:** Package labels are diamond-shaped hazard warning labels found on most hazardous materials packages. These labels inform others of the hazard. If the diamond label does not fit on the package, shippers may put the label on a tag attached to the package. For example, compressed gas cylinders often have tags or decals.

**25. A:** The transport index shows how close you can load Class 7 (radioactive) materials to people, animals, or film. For example, you can't leave a package with a transport index of 1.1 within 2 feet of people or cargo space walls during transit. The total transport index of all packages in a single vehicle must not exceed 50. Single vehicles include automobiles, vans, trucks, tractors, and semi-trailers.

**26. A:** The tractor, power unit, or placarded vehicles must have a fire extinguisher with a UL rating of 10 B:C or more. Make sure the extinguisher is fully charged. Know how to operate it before you need it!

**27. B:** You must stop 15-50 feet prior to reaching the nearest rail. Proceed with caution, only when you are positive that no train is coming. Never shift gears while crossing the tracks.

**28. A**: Study the charts that are available.

**29. B:** You may use "DANGEROUS" placards instead of separate placards for each Table 2 hazard class if both of the following apply: You have loaded two or more Table 2 hazard classes that weigh more than 1,000 lb and that require different placards. And you have not loaded more than 1,000 kg of any Table 2 hazard class material from any one shipper.

**30. A:** There are two placard tables that tell you how to placard your vehicle. The first is Placard Table 1: Any Amount. Table 1 materials must be placarded whenever any amount is transported. The second is Placard Table 2: More than 1,000 lb. Except for bulk packaging, the hazard classes in Table 2 need placards only if the total amount transported exceeds 1,000 lb, including packaging.

# Hazardous Materials Endorsement Practice Test #3

1. Which is an acceptable quantity shown on a hazardous materials bill of lading?
   a. 2,100 pounds
   b. 2100
   c. 2,100

2. Poisons belong to what hazard class?
   a. Class 6
   b. Class 7
   c. Class 8

3. When can Division 6.1 or 2.3 material, labeled as poison or poison gas, be loaded in the same vehicle as foodstuffs?
   a. Only for short amounts of time
   b. When overpacked in an approved way
   c. Never

4. Class 4 of hazardous materials contains:
   a. Flammable solids
   b. Flammable combustible liquids
   c. Oxidizers

5. Which of the following would NOT be classified as foodstuffs?
   a. Alcohol
   b. Toothpaste
   c. Grains and cereals

6. Which must be shown on a hazardous materials bill of lading?
   a. The shipper's permit number
   b. The quantity of hazardous materials
   c. All of the carrier's state and federal permit numbers

7. What type of warning device should you NOT utilize around tanks used for Class 3 or Division 1.1, 1.2, 1.3, or 2.1 materials?
   a. Reflective triangles
   b. Red electric lights
   c. Flares or fuses

8. Before transporting certain radioactive materials a route restriction?
   a. May be required if the shipper tells you about it
   b. Should be obtained
   c. May be necessary

9. Labels on hazardous materials must measure?
   a. At least two inches on each side
   b. At least three inches on each side
   c. At least four inches on each side

10. Which of the following lists all parties who must sign the Uniform Hazardous Waste Manifest when hazardous waste is transported?
    a. The shipper
    b. The shipper and driver
    c. The shipper, the driver, and the person who receives the delivery

11. What placard may be used for Table 2 materials if none of them equal 1,000 lbs?
    a. Dangerous
    b. Dangerous When Wet
    c. Hazardous

12. What are placards?
    a. Diamond-shaped warning signs placed on vehicles
    b. Warning signs that are placed on boxes and other packages
    c. Stickers that must be displayed in the lower right side of windshields

13. Which of the following is NOT an appropriate destination to deliver shipments of explosives?
    a. Within 5 feet of an operating roadway
    b. In locked rooms designed for explosives
    c. With authorized persons

14. Which of the following is NOT true when hauling Class 1 (explosives), Class 4 (flammable solids), and Class 5 (oxidizers) materials?
    a. Only use closed cargo space for transport, unless packages have fire and water protection.
    b. You may not have overhang or tailgate loads.
    c. After loading, you should open and inspect packages regularly.

15. Never park with Division 1.1, 1.2, or 1.3 explosives within 300 feet of:
    a. Operating roadways
    b. Bridges or tunnels
    c. Water

16. When is the certification statement, saying that the shipment has been prepared according to federal regulations, NOT required on the shipping papers?
    a. When the shipper is a verified hazardous materials producer
    b. When the vehicle has already been properly placarded
    c. When you are pulling cargo tanks supplied by you or your employer

17. Which is correct about listing hazardous materials on a bill of lading?
    a. The commodity is named in the hazardous materials column.
    b. All commodities must be named with large letters.
    c. The proper shipping name of the commodity is listed first.

18. When a vehicle is parked the hazardous material shipping papers must be?
    a. Kept on the seat or in a pocket in the left door
    b. Kept under the seat
    c. In the glove compartment or in the driver's possession

19. Which of the following is a person or company engaged in the transportation of passengers or property as a for-hire or private carrier?
    a. Shipper
    b. Carrier
    c. Driver

20. Cargo tanks or portable tanks loaded with hazardous materials must show?
    a. The ID Number of the product
    b. A label on each side
    c. Warning: Flammable

21. Which of the following is NOT an appropriate place to keep hazardous materials shipping papers?
    a. In a pouch in the sleeper berth
    b. In clear view within immediate reach while the driver's seat belt is fastened
    c. On the driver's seat when the driver is out of the vehicle

22. When may you park a placarded vehicle (not carrying explosives) within 5 feet of the traveled part of the road?
    a. Never
    b. If your work requires it
    c. When there is low traffic

23. The letters of the shipping name must be at least how tall on portable tanks with capacities of more than 1,000 gallons?
    a. 1 inch
    b. 2 inches
    c. 3 inches

24. If the term "INHALATION HAZARD" appears on the shipping forms or the package itself, you must use what placard in addition to your regular placard(s)?
    a. "OXIDIZER" or "AIR HAZARD"
    b. "POISON" or "POISON GAS"
    c. "OXYGEN" or "CLASS 2"

25. In government regulations, the term "hazardous materials" is shortened to what?
    a. HM
    b. HAZMAT
    c. Haz. Matter

26. Which of the following is NOT required on shipping papers for hazardous materials?
    a. A shipper's certification signed by the shipper
    b. A diamond-shaped hazard warning label next to each item
    c. Page numbers if the shipping paper has more than one page

### 27. Drivers who transport highway route-controlled radioactive materials must have?
   a. Had special training within the past two years
   b. Special training from their local union every three years
   c. Special training before each trip

### 28. An exception to the rule for trailer placarding for semis is?
   a. There is no exception to the rule that trailers must be placarded all around.
   b. Instead of the trailer, a placard may be placed on the front side of the tractor.
   c. At least one placard must be placed on the front of any semi trailer.

### 29. Corrosives could require more than one label because they could also be?
   a. Asbestos
   b. Cancer-inducing in rats
   c. Poison by inhalation

### 30. Which of the following is more likely to ship hazardous materials?
   a. Textile suppliers
   b. Pest control or agricultural suppliers
   c. Fresh-produce suppliers

# Answer Key and Explanations for Test #3

**1. A**: 2,100 pounds

**2. A:** Class 6 contains poisons (for example, pesticides and arsenic).

**3. B:** Do not load Division 6.1 or 2.3 material, labeled as poison or poison gas, in the same vehicle with animal or human food unless the poison package is overpacked in an approved way. Foodstuffs are anything you swallow.

**4. A:** Class 4 contains flammable solids (for example, matches and magnesium).

**5. B:** Foodstuffs are anything you swallow. Mouthwash, toothpaste, and skin creams are not foodstuffs.

**6. B**: The quantity of hazardous materials

**7. C:** If you need to use warning devices, use reflective triangles or red electric lights. Never use burning signals, such as flares or fuses, around a tank used for Class 3 (flammable liquids) or Division 2.1 (flammable gas), whether loaded or empty, or a vehicle loaded with Division 1.1, 1.2 or 1.3 explosives.

**8. C**: May be necessary

**9. C**: At least four inches on each side

**10. C:** When transporting hazardous wastes, you must sign and carry a Uniform Hazardous Waste Manifest. The name and EPA identification number of the shippers, carriers, and destination must appear on the manifest. Shippers must prepare, date, and sign the manifest. Treat the manifest as a shipping paper when transporting the waste. Only give the waste shipment to a carrier with an EPA identification number or to an EPA-permitted treatment, storage, or disposal facility. Each carrier/driver transporting the shipment must sign the manifest. After you deliver the shipment, keep your copy of the manifest. Each copy must have all needed signatures and dates. It must include the signature of the person to whom you delivered the waste.

**11. A**: Dangerous

**12. A**: Diamond-shaped warning signs placed on vehicles

**13. A:** Deliver shipments of explosives only to authorized persons or leave them in locked rooms designed for explosives storage.

**14. C:** You must use closed cargo space for the following materials, unless all packages are in fire- and water-resistant packaging or covered with a fire- and water-resistant tarp: Class 1 (explosives), Class 4 (flammable solids), and Class 5 (oxidizers). You also may not have overhang or tailgate loads of these materials. After loading, do not open any package during your trip. Never transfer hazardous materials from one package to another during the trip. You may empty a cargo tank, but do not empty any other package while it is on the vehicle.

**15. B:** Never park with Division 1.1, 1.2, or 1.3 explosives within 5 feet of the operating roadway. Do not park within 300 feet of the following: a bridge, tunnel, building, place where people gather, or open fire.

**16. C:** The shipper certifies on the shipping paper that the shipment has been prepared according to federal regulations. If you are pulling cargo tanks supplied by you or your employer, the certification statement is not required.

**17. C:** The proper shipping name of the commodity is listed first.

**18. A:** Kept on the seat or in a pocket in the left door

**19. B:** The carrier is a person or company engaged in the transportation of passengers or property as a for-hire or private carrier. The carrier takes the shipment from the shipper to its destination, refuses improper shipments, and reports accidents and incidents involving hazardous materials to the proper government agency.

**20. A:** The ID Number of the product

**21. A:** Your life and the lives of others could depend on quickly locating hazardous materials shipping papers. Shippers must describe hazardous materials correctly and include an emergency response telephone number on the shipping papers. Carriers and drivers must tab hazardous materials shipping papers or keep them on top of other shipping papers. They must also keep the emergency response information with the shipping papers. Drivers must keep hazardous materials shipping papers in one of these locations: in a pouch on the driver's door; in clear view within immediate reach while the driver's seat belt is fastened; or on the driver's seat when the driver is out of the vehicle.

**22. B:** You may park a placarded vehicle (not carrying explosives) within 5 feet of the traveled part of the road only if your work requires it. Move the vehicle as soon as possible. Someone must always watch the vehicle when it is parked on a public road or shoulder. Do not uncouple a trailer with hazardous materials and leave it on a public street.

**23. B:** The letters of the shipping name must be at least 2 inches tall on portable tanks with capacities of more than 1,000 gallons, and 1 inch tall on portable tanks with capacities of less than 1,000 gallons.

**24. B:** If the term "INHALATION HAZARD" appears on the shipping forms or the package itself, you must use the "POISON" or "POISON GAS" placards. These placards are not to be used alone, but in addition to other placards required according to the product's hazard class. Always use all necessary placards, even if you are only carrying a very small amount.

**25. A:** Hazardous materials are products that pose a risk to health, safety, and property during transportation. The term is often shortened to HAZMAT, or HM, which you may see on road signs or in government regulations.

**26. B:** A shipping paper for hazardous materials must include page numbers if the shipping paper has more than one page. The first page must show the total number of pages—for example, "page 1 of 4." A shipping paper for hazardous materials must also include a proper shipping description for each hazardous material and a shipper's certification signed by the shipper. This certification states that the shipper prepared the shipment according to federal regulations.

**27. A**: Had special training within the past two years

**28. B**: Instead of the trailer, a placard may be placed on the front side of the tractor.

**29. C**: Poison by inhalation

**30. B:** Learn to recognize shipments of hazardous materials. Look for clues, and ask: What business is the shipper in? Paint dealers, chemical suppliers, scientific supply houses, and pest control or agricultural suppliers, as well as explosives, munitions, or fireworks dealers, are all likely sources for hazardous materials.

# Hazardous Materials Endorsement Practice Test #4

**1. If a shipper's certification is signed, must you accept a leaking package?**
   a. You must accept the package, but report it to your dispatcher immediately.
   b. You must refuse the shipment.
   c. You must place the shipment inside a larger container that is not leaking.

**2. Which Code of Federal Regulations requires that placards be used?**
   a. Title 13, CFR
   b. Title 27, CFR
   c. Title 49, CFR

**3. When is it safe to leave manholes or valves ajar while moving a tank of hazardous materials?**
   a. Never
   b. When the tank is low
   c. When only moving a short distance

**4. For the placards to use with packaged freight you must know the hazard class?**
   a. The amount shipped and the total weight of hazardous materials on board
   b. The amount shipped and the ID Number
   c. The amount shipped, the ID Number and the NMFC classification

**5. You should not park a vehicle hauling Division 1.1, 1.2, or 1.3 explosives on private property unless:**
   a. The owner is aware of the danger.
   b. Someone is watching the parked vehicle.
   c. It is 300 ft away from any place where people gather.

**6. Which is an acceptable method of showing shipper's certification on papers?**
   a. Longhand
   b. Printed
   c. Red Ink

**7. You can load nitric acid above what other products?**
   a. Division 1.1, 1.2, or 1.3
   b. Storage batteries
   c. None

**8. What is the most common cargo tank for hauling flammable liquids?**
   a. MC306/406
   b. MC312/412
   c. MC331

**9. Which of the following is NOT true about loading and unloading hazardous materials?**
   a. You should use hooks to safely load hazardous materials.
   b. Many products become more hazardous when exposed to heat.
   c. You should never transfer hazardous materials from one package to another during the trip.

**10. If you are moving breakable containers of corrosive liquids by hand, you should load them:**
   a. Upside-down
   b. One by one
   c. By rolling them

**11. A vehicle carrying hazardous materials must be parked at least?**
   a. 300 feet away from an open fire
   b. 600 feet away from an open fire
   c. 900 feet away from an open fire

**12. Who needs to know about all spills of any hazardous substances?**
   a. CFR and HFR
   b. CMV and PCB
   c. DOT and EPA

**13. A driver should count the total number of packages loaded and should count?**
   a. The number of damaged packages
   b. The number of packages with reinforcement
   c. The number of packages of hazardous materials.

**14. When are you allowed to have overhang (tailgate) loads of Explosives?**
   a. Never
   b. When there are two escort vehicles with one following
   c. During daylight hours and the overhang does not exceed five feet

**15. Who is responsible for certifying on the shipping paper that a shipment has been prepared according to federal regulations?**
   a. Shipper
   b. Carrier
   c. Driver

**16. What is the status of vehicle brakes when hazardous materials are being loaded?**
   a. All brakes should be released.
   b. The parking brakes should be set.
   c. All brakes should be locked.

**17. What is a "safe haven"?**
   a. A restricted area for leaking HAZMAT vehicles
   b. Local, state, or federal authorities' private parking
   c. A place for parking unattended vehicles loaded with explosives

18. Which of the following must show retest date markings?
    a. California truck—full trailer
    b. Specification cargo tanks
    c. Moving vans

19. Which of the following is from Placard Table 1 and must be placarded if any amount is being transported?
    a. Hazard class 1.6 explosives
    b. Hazard class 2.1 flammable gas
    c. Hazard class 2.3 poison gas

20. At what temperatures are cryogenic liquids carried?
    a. Very cold temperatures
    b. Midrange temperatures
    c. Very hot temperatures

21. Who is responsible for choosing the safest route to transport placarded radioactive materials?
    a. Shipper
    b. Carrier
    c. Driver

22. Which of these is true?
    a. With hazardous materials there are no regulations against smoking.
    b. You may smoke around Flammables if there is a fire extinguisher handy.
    c. Do not smoke when around Explosives, Flammables and Oxidizers.

23. When driving a placarded vehicle, how often must you stop and check the tires?
    a. Every 200 miles
    b. Every two hours or 100 miles
    c. Every hour or 55 miles

24. Which may be exempt from labeling rules when transported in small quantities?
    a. Consumer products
    b. Class A Explosives
    c. Poison Gas

25. The EPA registration numbers of the carrier, shipper and destination must be on?
    a. All bills of lading
    b. Safety data sheets
    c. Hazardous Waste Manifests

26. Which of the following must NOT be abbreviated in the shipping description for a hazardous material, unless authorized in federal regulations?
    a. The unit of measure
    b. The packing type
    c. The hazard class

**27. What hazard class contains miscellaneous hazardous materials, like asbestos?**
   a. Class 7
   b. Class 8
   c. Class 9

**28. Who decides if a product meets the definition of a hazardous material?**
   a. Shipper
   b. Carrier
   c. Driver

**29. Who is responsible for providing the federally required training and testing for drivers that transport hazardous materials?**
   a. Government
   b. Employer
   c. Employees

**30. Which of the following is NOT included in the shipping papers?**
   a. Bills of lading
   b. Manifests
   c. Accident record

# Answer Key and Explanations for Test #4

**1. B**: You must refuse the shipment.

**2. C**: Title 49, CFR

**3. A:** Close all manholes and valves before moving a tank of hazardous materials, no matter how small the amount in the tank or how short the distance. Manholes and valves must be closed to prevent leaks.

**4. A**: The amount shipped and the total weight of hazardous materials on board

**5. A:** If you must park, for example to refuel, be as quick as possible. Do not park on private property unless the owner is aware of the danger.

**6. B**: Printed

**7. C:** Do not load nitric acid above any other product, or stack more than two high.

**8. A:** The most common cargo tanks are MC306/406 for flammable liquids and MC331 for bulk gases. Other liquid hazardous materials must be transported in other types of specification tanks, such as MC307/407 or MC312/412.

**9. A:** Do everything you can to protect containers of hazardous materials. Don't use tools that might damage containers or packaging during loading. Don't use hooks.

**10. B:** If loading by hand, load breakable containers of corrosive liquid one by one. Keep them right side up. Do not drop or roll the containers. Load them on an even floor surface. Stack carboys only if the lower tiers can bear the weight of the upper tiers safely. (Carboys are portable tanks that may be metal or plastic and are placed in a special cage.)

**11. A**: 300 feet away from an open fire

**12. C:** The Department of Transportation (DOT) and the Environmental Protection Agency (EPA) need to know about all spills of any hazardous substances. These substances are named in Appendix A of the federal regulations.

**13. C**: The number of packages of hazardous materials.

**14. A**: Never

**15. A:** The shipper certifies on the shipping paper that the shipment has been prepared according to federal regulations. If you are pulling cargo tanks supplied by you or your employer, the certification statement is not required.

**16. B**: The parking brakes should be set.

**17. C:** You may leave your vehicle unattended in a safe haven. A safe haven is an approved place for parking unattended vehicles loaded with explosives. Local or state and federal authorities identify areas for safe havens.

**18. B:** You must display the ID number of the hazardous materials in portable tanks, cargo tanks, and intermediate bulk packaging containers. ID numbers are shown in column 4 of the Hazardous Materials Table. Federal regulations require black 100 mm (3.9 inch) numbers on orange panels, placards, or a white diamond-shaped background if placards are not required. Specification cargo tanks must show retest date markings.

**19. C:** Refer to Placard Table 1: Any Amount. Table 1 materials must be placarded whenever any amount is transported.

| If your vehicle contains any amount of: | Placard as: |
| --- | --- |
| 1.1 | EXPLOSIVE 1.1 |
| 1.2 | EXPLOSIVE 1.2 |
| 1.3 | EXPLOSIVE 1.3 |
| 2.3 | POISON GAS |
| 4.3 | DANGEROUS WHEN WET |
| 6.1 (PG 1, inhalation hazard only) | POISON, INHALATION HAZARD REF. 172.55c |
| 7 (Radioactive Yellow III label only) | RADIOACTIVE |

**20. A:** Class 2 (compressed gases) includes cryogenic liquids. Cryogenic liquids are liquids carried at very cold temperatures. See 49 CFR 177 for additional details. If your vehicle doesn't have racks to hold cylinders, the cargo space floor must be flat. The cylinders must be stored in one of the following ways: held upright or braced lying down flat, or in racks attached to the vehicle, or in boxes that will keep them from turning over.

**21. B:** A carrier must choose the safest route to transport placarded radioactive materials. After choosing the route, the carrier must tell the driver about the radioactive materials and tell him or her the route plan.

**22. C:** Do not smoke when around Explosives, Flammables and Oxidizers.

**23. B:** Every two hours or 100 miles

**24. A:** Consumer products

**25. C:** Hazardous Waste Manifests

**26. C:** In the shipping description, the shipping name, hazard class, and ID number must not be abbreviated unless authorized in federal regulations.

**27. C:** Class 9 contains miscellaneous hazardous materials (for example, asbestos, airbag inflators, and airbag modules).

**28. A:** The Code of Federal Regulations gives regulations for hazardous materials. These regulations are located in title 49, parts 171-180. You will hear these regulations referred to as 49 CFR 171-180. The Hazardous Materials Table in the regulations includes a list of hazardous materials. However, this table does not show all hazardous materials. A material is considered hazardous based on its characteristics. A shipper decides if a product meets the definition of a hazardous material in the regulations. Because the federal regulations change often, be sure that your copy is up to date.

**29. B:** Hazardous materials courses are offered by transportation employers, colleges, universities, and associations. In fact, the federal regulations require training and testing for all drivers who transport hazardous materials. You must be trained and tested at least once every 3 years. Your employer must provide this training and testing. Your employer must also keep a record of the training completed by each employee who works with hazardous materials.

**30. C:** A shipping paper describes the hazardous materials being transported. Shipping papers include shipping orders, bills of lading and manifests.

# Passenger and School Bus Endorsements

## School Buses

In order to operate a school bus, you must be at least 18 years of age. You must also hold a valid commercial driver's license. Depending on the weight and size of the bus that you will drive, you will be issued a Class B or Class C license. Additionally, you must have a passenger bus endorsement and a school bus endorsement on your CDL. School bus endorsements are not transferable from state to state. To get your CDL and the endorsements to operate a school bus, you must pass:

- The written general knowledge test
- The written passenger bus test
- The written school bus test
- The written air brakes test (if applicable to your vehicle type);
- The practical skills test associated with the type/class of vehicle that you plan to operate
    - If you plan to drive a bus equipped with air brakes, you must take the skills test in a bus equipped with air brakes.

If you plan to operate a school bus designed to carry no more than 15 passengers, including the driver, you do not need to obtain a CDL, Class B or C, or the passenger bus endorsement. However, you must have the school bus endorsement on your driver's license. Therefore, you will need to take the school bus knowledge and skills tests. You will be restricted to driving buses designed to carry no more than 15 passengers and this restriction will be printed on your license.

# Operating the Bus Safely

## Loading and Unloading Passengers

Turn on your school bus traffic warning lights:

- You must turn on the warning lights before you stop to load or unload students.
- If the posted speed limit is less than 35 mph, turn on the warning lights at least 100 feet before the stop.
- If the posted speed is 35 mph or more, turn on the warning lights at least 200 feet before the stop.
- Do not use the warning lights except when loading and unloading.
- Extend the warning sign and crossing control arm only when the bus is stopped to load and unload passengers.

When loading or unloading students:

- Do not use the emergency four-way hazard flashers.
- Stop in the right lane of the road.
- On divided highways, five lane roads where the middle lane is used for turning, or heavily traveled roads, unload the students on the side of the road where they live.
- Stop only when the bus can be seen clearly at a safe distance.
- Make sure all students are on the bus and seated before driving or reversing. Most injuries occur when the bus is stopped to load or unload students.
- Never park the bus so that the emergency exit will be blocked while students are on board.
- Report drivers who illegally pass a bus that is stopped to load or unload passengers. Make a note of:
    - The license plate number and state
    - The make, type, and color of the vehicle
    - The date, time, and location of the incident

## Backing the Bus

Do not back the bus unless there is no other safe way to move the vehicle. Drive around the block or make a detour rather than backing the bus. Post a lookout on the inside, back of the bus to warn of obstacles, approaching persons, or other vehicles. Check your mirrors constantly while backing. Pick up passengers *before* backing or turning. Unload passengers *after* backing or turning.

## Passing and Turning

Do not pass or run side-by-side with another bus on the highway. Keep a safe distance between vehicles if you must pass. When turning left, get into the left lane (if there is one) in plenty of time to make the turn safely.

## Following Other Vehicles

- Always leave at least a bus length between you and the vehicle in front of you.
- Outside of cities and towns, keep at least 200 feet between you and the vehicle in front of you.

## Railroad Crossings

As you approach a railroad crossing, tap your brakes lightly to warn other drivers that the bus is about to stop. Turn on your four-way hazard lights. Come to a full stop 15-50 feet from the nearest rail. Open the entrance door and driver's window. Turn off the warning lights unless you are loading and unloading passengers. Listen and look carefully in both directions. When it is safe for you to cross, close the entrance door and turn off the four-way hazard lights. Cross the railroad tracks in a gear which allows you to cross the rails completely without changing gears.

## Speed Limits for Buses

When traveling on interstate highways, you may drive 55 mph. You must travel 35 mph or less on all other highways. If you are driving on a highway where the posted speed limit is 45 mph or higher and you are not loading or unloading passengers between your place of departure and your destination, you may travel 45 mph. You must travel 25 mph in school, business, and residential areas. Remember that weather, road, and traffic conditions may require you to travel slower than these speed limits. When in doubt, slow down.

# Handling Emergencies

## EMERGENCY DRILLS

Most state laws require that you hold an emergency exit drill at least once during the first 90 calendar days of the school year or more often if needed. Your local school board or board of education may require more frequent drills.

## EMERGENCY SITUATIONS

### BUS ACCIDENTS

- Do not move the bus until police or school officials arrive.
- Check the bus for injured students.
- Protect the crash scene by setting out flares or reflectors.
- Do not leave students unattended. Have a responsible student or passing motorist notify the authorities.
- Keep students on the bus unless there is extensive damage or danger of further injury or fire.
- If another vehicle is involved, make note of:
  - The driver's name, address, phone number, driver's license number, insurance company name, and policy number
  - The vehicle's license plate number, the state, and the type of vehicle
  - The name, address, and phone number of witnesses or other drivers involved in the crash

### BREAK DOWNS

- Turn on the emergency four-way hazard lights.
- Set out flares or reflectors.

*Keep the students on the bus until other transportation arrives unless there is danger of injury.*

# Transporting Passengers

You must have a commercial driver's license if you plan to drive a vehicle that seats more than 15 persons, including the driver. You must also have a passenger endorsement on your CDL. To get the endorsement, you must pass:

- The written general knowledge exam
- The written passenger bus exam
- The written air brakes exam if your vehicle is equipped with air brakes
- The skills test required for the class of vehicle that you plan to drive

## PRE-TRIP INSPECTION

Before driving your bus, make sure it is safe:

- Review the inspection report made by the previous driver.
- Sign the previous driver's report only if the defects reported earlier have been certified as repaired or certified as not needing repair. By signing this report, you certify that the defects reported earlier have been fixed.
- Conduct a pre-trip inspection.
- Follow the inspection method outlined in the General Knowledge portion of the CDL.

Also check:

- Access doors and panels:
    - Close any emergency exits that are open as well as access panels (for baggage, restroom service, engine, etc.) before driving.
- Bus interior:
    - Aisles and stairways should always be clear.
    - Be sure that handholds and railings, floor covering, signaling devices (including the restroom emergency buzzer) and emergency exit handles are in good working order.
    - Be sure that all seats are securely fastened to the bus.
    - Never drive with an open emergency exit door or window.
    - The emergency exit sign on an emergency door must work. If the door has a red emergency light, the light must work. Turn it on at night and whenever you use your outside lights.
- Roof hatches:
    - You may lock some emergency roof hatches in a partly open position for fresh air. However, do not leave them open all the time.
    - Remember that the bus will have a higher clearance when the hatches are open.
- Safety equipment:
    - Be sure your bus has a fire extinguisher and emergency reflectors as required by law.
    - The bus must also have spare electrical fuses unless equipped with circuit breakers.

Always fasten your safety belt when you drive.

## LOADING THE BUS

Secure all baggage and freight so that:

- You can move freely and easily
- Riders sitting by any window or door can exit in an emergency
- Riders will not be injured if baggage falls or shifts
- All aisles and doorways are clear (Temporary seating in the aisles is not allowed.)

Watch for cargo or baggage containing hazardous materials. Hazardous materials pose a risk to health, safety, and property. Most hazardous materials cannot be carried on a bus. Federal regulations require shippers to mark containers of hazardous materials with the material's name, ID number, and hazard label. There are nine different hazard labels. The labels are diamond-shaped, four inches on each side. Do not transport hazardous materials unless you are sure federal regulations allow it.

Buses may never carry:

- Class 2 poison, liquid Class 6 poison, tear gas, or other irritating material
- More than 100 pounds of solid Class 6 poisons
- Explosives in the space occupied by people, except small arms ammunition
- Labeled radioactive materials in the space occupied by people
- More than 500 pounds total of allowed hazardous materials and no more than 100 pounds of any one class

Riders may sometimes board a bus carrying an unlabeled hazardous material. Do not allow riders to carry on common hazards such as car batteries or gasoline.

Do not allow riders to stand forward of the rear of the driver's seat. Buses designed to allow standing must have a 2-inch line on the floor or some other marking that shows riders where they cannot stand. This is called the standee line. All standing riders must stay behind it.

# Safe Driving with Buses

## Passenger Supervision

Many charter and intercity carriers have passenger comfort and safety rules. Mention rules about smoking, drinking, and use of audio devices at the start of the trip. Explaining the rules at the beginning could help avoid trouble later on. Charter bus drivers should not allow passengers on the bus until departure time. While driving, scan the interior of your bus, as well as the road ahead. You may need to remind riders to keep their arms and heads inside the bus. Occasionally, you may have a drunk or disruptive rider. You must ensure this rider's safety as well as the safety of others. Don't discharge disruptive riders where it would be unsafe for them. It may be safer to wait until you reach the next scheduled stop or well-lighted area where there are other people. Many carriers have guidelines for handling disruptive riders. When you stop the bus, announce the location, reason for stopping, departure time, and bus number. Caution riders to watch their step when leaving the bus. Wait for riders to sit down or brace themselves before starting the bus. Starting and stopping should be as smooth as possible to avoid rider injury.

## Avoiding Accidents

Use caution at all intersections, even if a signal or stop sign controls the intersection. Bus crashes often happen at intersections. Remember the clearance your bus needs. Watch for poles and tree limbs when you stop. Know the size of the gap your bus needs to accelerate and merge with traffic. Never assume other drivers will brake to give you room when you signal or begin to pull out. Reduce speed on curves. Crashes on curves result from excessive speed. In good weather, the posted speed on a curve is safe for cars, but may be too high for buses. If your bus leans toward the outside on a banked curve, you are driving too fast. Stop at railroad crossings:

- Stop your bus 15-50 feet before railroad crossings.
- Listen and look in both directions for trains.
- Improve your ability to see or hear an approaching train by opening your forward door.
- If a train has just passed, make sure that another train isn't coming from the opposite direction.
- If your bus has a manual transmission, never shift gears while crossing the tracks.

Slow down and check for other vehicles:

- At street car crossings
- At railroad tracks used only for industrial switching within a business district
- At green traffic lights
- At crossings marked "exempt" or abandoned"
- Anywhere a police officer or flag person is directing traffic

Stop at all drawbridges that do not have a traffic light or attendant:

- Stop at least 50 feet before where the bridge begins to draw.
- Make sure the draw is fully closed before attempting to cross.

Slow down at drawbridges that show a green traffic light or that have an attendant that controls traffic when the bridge opens.

## After-Trip Vehicle Inspection

Inspect your bus at the conclusion of each shift. If you are working for an interstate carrier, you must fill out an inspection form for all buses driven. It must show each bus's details and list all defects that may have an effect on safety or cause a breakdown. The report must also state if there are no defects. Report damage to hand-holds, seats, emergency exits, and windows at the end of your shift. Mechanics will repair the bus before it is used again. City transit drivers should make sure all passenger signaling devices work properly, as well as brake-door interlocks.

## Prohibited Practices

Avoid fueling your bus while passengers are on board unless it is absolutely necessary. Never refuel the bus inside a closed area with passengers aboard. Don't engage in conversation with passengers, or any other distracting activity while operating the bus. Never push or tow a disabled bus with passengers on board unless leaving the bus would be unsafe. If necessary, push or tow the disabled bus to the closest safe area to allow passengers to debark. Consult your employer's guidelines on when towing or pushing disabled buses is necessary and allowed.

City transit buses may have a brake and accelerator interlock system equipped. The interlock applies the brakes and maintains the throttle in an idle position while the rear door is open. It releases when the rear door closes. Never use this safety feature in lieu of the parking brake.

# Passenger and School Bus Endorsement Practice Test #1

1. **Why is smooth handling of transmission and clutch a safety factor on busses?**
   a. Smooth handling always reduces driver fatigue.
   b. Quick stops or sharp turns can cause injuries to passengers.
   c. Both of the above.

2. **Which of the following is a characteristic of the standee line?**
   a. It is a 12-inch line on the floor.
   b. It is meant to show riders where they cannot stand.
   c. It is located forward of the rear of the driver's seat.

3. **Which of these two items can be carried on a bus by a rider?**
   a. Car batteries.
   b. Gasoline.
   c. Neither one.

4. **You are stopped for a railroad crossing. When may you open your doors?**
   a. You should open your front door if that helps you see and hear.
   b. Never.
   c. You may open your emergency doors if it improves your view of the train.

5. **Chains are required to be installed on which wheels?**
   a. The front wheels
   b. The drive wheels.
   c. The back wheels of a tandem.

6. **Can your performance be affected the day after you have been drinking?**
   a. Yes.
   b. No.
   c. Only if you drank a large amount.

7. **How far must you stop from the draw of a drawbridge?**
   a. At least 15 feet
   b. At least 25 feet.
   c. At least 50 feet.

8. **What is a yield sign?**
   a. A yield sign tells you to stop.
   b. A yield sign tells you to slow down with caution and be prepared to stop.
   c. A yield sign tells you to slow to ten miles per hour.

9. **If you have to move quickly to avoid an accident you want to know?**
   a. Whether all of your passengers are wearing seat belts.
   b. Where your passengers are seated.
   c. Where other vehicles are around your bus.

10. How fast can you drive on interstate highways?
    a. 35 mph
    b. 45 mph
    c. 55 mph

11. Should you cross over to the far-left lane as soon as you enter a freeway?
    a. Yes, as long as you are careful.
    b. No, work over to the left lane when it is safe to do so.
    c. Yes, but if you have an incident, it is your fault.

12. Charter bus drivers should only allow passengers on the bus:
    a. If there is a full tank of fuel
    b. At departure time
    c. If they have a valid ID

13. As you approach a railroad crossing, how should you warn other drivers that the bus is about to stop?
    a. Turn on your warning lights.
    b. Travel significantly slower than the posted speed limit.
    c. Lightly tap your brakes.

14. What is the maximum total amount of allowable hazardous materials that you can carry on a bus?
    a. 250 pounds
    b. 500 pounds
    c. 750 pounds

15. Why is it harder to pass at night?
    a. You cannot judge distance as well because of oncoming headlights.
    b. Your own headlights do not give you enough light to pass.
    c. Other drivers cannot see you at night.

16. A vehicle that is straddling lanes is a possible sign of a drunk driver?
    a. Yes.
    b. Yes, only if it is at night.
    c. No.

17. During a pre-trip inspection what are some items that you must check?
    a. The standee line.
    b. The service brakes - parking brake - steering - lights - reflectors - tires.
    c. The number of bandages in first aid kits.

18. By signing the inspection report made by the previous driver, you certify that:
    a. You read the report.
    b. The defects reported earlier have been fixed, or do not need repair.
    c. Any special instructions previously given have been noted.

**19. What is a drawback to locking some emergency roof hatches in a partly open position?**
   a. Exacerbated risk of fire
   b. Altered air circulation
   c. Increased bus clearance

**20. Why should you always count the number of students waiting for your approaching bus?**
   a. The school receives state moneys based upon the number of students.
   b. You will know when everyone has boarded the bus or gotten safely away from it.
   c. You are required to make written reports.

# Answer Key and Explanations for Test #1

**1. B**: Quick stops or sharp turns can cause injuries to passengers.

**2. B:** Do not allow riders to stand forward of the rear of the driver's seat. Buses designed to allow standing must have a 2-inch line on the floor or some other marking that shows riders where they cannot stand. This is called the standee line. All standing riders must stay behind it.

**3. C**: Neither one.

**4. A**: You should open your front door if that helps you see and hear.

**5. B**: The drive wheels.

**6. A**: Yes.

**7. C**: At least 50 feet.

**8. B**: A yield sign tells you to slow down with caution and be prepared to stop.

**9. C**: Where other vehicles are around your bus.

**10. C:** When traveling on interstate highways, you may drive 55 mph. You must travel 35 mph or less on all other highways. If you are driving on a highway where the posted speed limit is 45 mph or higher and you are not loading or unloading passengers between your place of departure and your destination, you may travel 45 mph.

**11. B**: No work over to the left lane when it is safe to do so.

**12. B:** Charter bus drivers should not allow passengers on the bus until departure time.

**13. C:** As you approach a railroad crossing, tap your brakes lightly to warn other drivers that the bus is about to stop.

**14. B:** Buses may never carry more than 500 pounds total of allowed hazardous materials and no more than 100 pounds of any one class.

**15. A**: You cannot judge distance as well because of oncoming headlights.

**16. A**: Yes.

**17. B**: The service brakes - parking brake - steering - lights - reflectors - tires.

**18. B:** Review the inspection report made by the previous driver. Sign the previous driver's report only if the defects reported earlier have been certified as repaired, or certified as not needing repair. By signing this report, you certify that the defects reported earlier have been fixed.

**19. C:** You may lock some emergency roof hatches in a partly open position for fresh air. However, do not leave them open all the time. Remember that the bus will have a higher clearance when the hatches are open.

**20. B**: You will know when everyone has boarded the bus or gotten safely away from it.

# Passenger and School Bus Endorsement Practice Test #2

1. **When should you mention rules about smoking, drinking, and use of audio devices to passengers?**
    a. At the start of the trip
    b. Whenever incidents occur
    c. Near the end of the transit

2. **Which of the following is NOT safe or advisable when traveling over a drawbridge?**
    a. Ensure the draw is fully closed before trying to cross.
    b. Stop at all drawbridges that do not have a traffic light or attendant.
    c. If stopping, stop at least 20 feet before where the bridge begins to draw.

3. **Why is it often difficult to look far enough ahead when driving at night?**
    a. There is too much light inside your vehicle.
    b. The glare from oncoming headlights may force you to look to the shoulder.
    c. The pavement tends to be drier and shines more at night.

4. **Where else should you look while driving besides the road ahead?**
    a. Also scan the emergency exit door every few seconds
    b. Also scan the emergency equipment to make sure that it is in place.
    c. Also scan the inside of the bus.

5. **If you are trying to avoid the glare of oncoming headlights you?**
    a. Are looking to the right edge of the road and could miss tinted windshields.
    b. Are looking to the right edge of the road and could miss fog lights.
    c. Are looking to the right edge of the road and could miss a threat from the left.

6. **Where should you check before passing?**
    a. Check only what is in front of you.
    b. Check only what is to the side of you.
    c. Check in your mirrors and over your shoulder and behind you.

7. **Which of the following should you absolutely never do?**
    a. Ensure the function of brake-door interlocks.
    b. Push or tow a disabled bus with passengers onboard.
    c. Refuel the bus inside a closed area with passengers aboard.

8. **When are drivers more likely to be tired?**
    a. When they first get up in the morning.
    b. After lunch.
    c. At night.

9. In backing up which is more dangerous?
    a. Backing to the left.
    b. Backing to the right
    c. They are equally dangerous.

10. How is your reaction time affected by alcohol?
    a. It is speeded up.
    b. It stays the same.
    c. It slows down.

11. One rule says that you should have how much following distance?
    a. At least three seconds.
    b. At least four seconds
    c. At least five seconds.

12. What type of drug is alcohol?
    a. A stimulant.
    b. A depressant.
    c. An opiate.

13. When braking, when will a bus have the most traction?
    a. When the wheels are rolling just short of locking up.
    b. During a skid.
    c. When the wheels have locked up.

14. You must know the student loading areas on your school bus route because?
    a. You load or unload passengers only in designated areas.
    b. Loading and unloading areas are not allowed near railroad tracks.
    c. Both of these.

15. What is the largest amount of one specific class of hazardous material that you can carry on a bus?
    a. 100 pounds
    b. 300 pounds
    c. 500 pounds

16. When you make notes to report a driver who illegally passed a bus that is stopped for loading or unloading, which of the following is NOT necessary information?
    a. The make, type, and color of the vehicle
    b. The driver's ethnicity and defining features
    c. The date, time, and location of the incident

17. At the end of your shift, when checking over the bus and filling out an inspection form, which of the following is NOT your responsibility?
    a. Report any defects.
    b. Check for damage to hand-holds, seats, and windows.
    c. Make repairs to the bus before it is used again.

18. Which can cause the most dangerous driving condition in poor weather?
    a. Rain.
    b. Ice.
    c. Snow.

19. Before driving who must inspect the emergency equipment?
    a. The shop.
    b. The driver.
    c. The dispatcher.

20. Students who have to cross the road after leaving the bus should walk?
    a. Behind the bus only.
    b. Far enough ahead of the bus so that the driver can see them.
    c. In front of the bus but as close to the bus as possible.

# Answer Key and Explanations for Test #2

**1. A:** Many charter and intercity carriers have passenger comfort and safety rules. Mention rules about smoking, drinking, and use of audio devices at the start of the trip. Explaining the rules at the beginning could help avoid trouble later on.

**2. C:** Stop at all drawbridges that do not have a traffic light or attendant. Stop at least 50 feet before where the bridge begins to draw. Make sure the draw is fully closed before attempting to cross. And slow down at drawbridges that show a green traffic light, or that have an attendant that controls traffic when the bridge opens.

**3. B:** The glare from oncoming headlights may force you to look to the shoulder.

**4. C:** Also scan the inside of the bus.

**5. C:** Are looking to the right edge of the road and could miss a threat from the left.

**6. C:** Check in your mirrors and over your shoulder and behind you.

**7. C:** Avoid fueling your bus while passengers are onboard unless it is absolutely necessary. Never refuel the bus inside a closed area with passengers aboard. Don't engage in conversation with passengers, or any other distracting activity, while operating the bus. Never push or tow a disabled bus with passengers onboard unless leaving the bus would be unsafe. If necessary, push or tow the disabled bus to the closest safe area to allow passengers to debark. Consult your employer's guidelines on when towing or pushing disabled buses is necessary and allowed.

**8. C:** At night.

**9. B:** Backing to the right

**10. C:** It slows down.

**11. B:** At least four seconds

**12. B:** A depressant.

**13. A:** When the wheels are rolling just short of locking up.

**14. C:** Both of these.

**15. A:** Buses may never carry more than 500 pounds total of allowed hazardous materials and no more than 100 pounds of any one class.

**16. B:** Report drivers who illegally pass a bus that is stopped to load or unload passengers. Make a note of: the license plate number and the state; the make, type, and color of the vehicle; and the date, time, and location of the incident.

**17. C:** Inspect your bus at the conclusion of each shift. If you are working for an interstate carrier, you must fill out an inspection form for all buses driven. It must show each bus's details and list all defects that may have an effect on safety or cause a breakdown. The report must also state if there are no defects. Report damage to hand-holds, seats, emergency exits, and windows at the end of your shift. Mechanics will repair the bus before it is used again. City transit drivers should make sure all passenger signaling devices work properly, as well as brake-door interlocks.

**18. B**: Ice.

**19. B**: The driver.

**20. B**: Sufficiently far in front of the bus so that the driver can see them.

# Passenger and School Bus Endorsement Practice Test #3

1. **What should you do if you miss your freeway off ramp?**
   a. Put the vehicle in reverse and go back to the off ramp.
   b. Cross over the median and make a U-turn.
   c. Take the next off ramp.

2. **What is the total weight of hazardous materials of one class allowed on a bus?**
   a. One hundred pounds.
   b. Five hundred pounds.
   c. One thousand pounds.

3. **When the posted speed limit is 35 mph or more, what is the minimum distance, before stopping to load or unload, that you should turn on the warning lights?**
   a. 100 feet
   b. 200 feet
   c. 300 feet

4. **When may a disabled bus be towed to a safe place with passengers on board?**
   a. When the emergency exit is not working.
   b. Only if getting off the bus would be inconvenient for the passengers.
   c. Only if getting off the bus would be unsafe for the passengers.

5. **The light turns green and as the car ahead starts forward you?**
   a. Wait a moment so that you will have a safe following distance.
   b. Proceed as closely as possible behind that car.
   c. Stop at the limit line to make sure it is safe.

6. **What determines whether you will be issued a Class B or Class C license?**
   a. Your age
   b. The weight and size of the bus you will drive
   c. Whether you have a school bus endorsement on your CDL

7. **When can you park on the freeway?**
   a. When you need to stop to look at a map.
   b. When you need to get out and stretch your legs.
   c. Only in emergencies.

8. **Which of these can fully recharge the body?**
   a. Coffee and stretching your legs.
   b. Just coffee.
   c. None of these.

9. When the posted speed limit is less than 35 mph, what is the minimum distance, before stopping to load or unload, that you should turn on the warning lights?
    a. 100 feet
    b. 200 feet
    c. 300 feet

10. What shape are hazardous material labels?
    a. Diamond-shaped.
    b. Round.
    c. Rectangular.

11. What is the maximum weight of hazardous materials allowed on a bus?
    a. One hundred pounds.
    b. Five hundred pounds.
    c. One thousand pounds.

12. How does failing to look far enough ahead of you affect your driving?
    a. It can cause your vehicle to weave in and out.
    b. It can cause you to stop too smoothly.
    c. It can cause you to be in the wrong gear.

13. How many feet away must you stop your bus for railroad tracks?
    a. At least 10 feet but not more than 50 feet from the crossing.
    b. At least 15 feet from the crossing.
    c. At least 15 feet but no more than 50 feet from the crossing.

14. Where must passengers who are standing remain while the bus is underway?
    a. On buses where permitted they must stand at the back of the bus.
    b. On buses where permitted they must stand behind the standee line.
    c. Passengers are never allowed to stand on buses.

15. Which way will a bus lean if you are driving too fast on a banked curve?
    a. It will lean toward the inside
    b. It will lean in the direction of the turn.
    c. It will lean toward the outside.

16. Can the emergency exit door be opened when the bus is underway?
    a. Never drive with an open emergency exit door.
    b. The emergency exit door must be open.
    c. The emergency exit door will be opened whenever the bus is stopped.

17. If a posted speed is 45 MPH what is a safe speed for your bus?
    a. It may be 45 miles per hour or it could be more.
    b. It will be exactly 45 miles per hour
    c. It may be 45 miles per hour or it could be less.

18. **Is it OK to have a drink if you are still under the maximum allowed?**
    a. Yes, because you are not legally drunk.
    b. Yes, because you are still able to drive.
    c. No, because you do not know you can drive safely.

19. **When you are on the freeway - if you can safely do so, maintain a speed?**
    a. That is the average of other drivers.
    b. That is slower than the other drivers.
    c. That is faster than the other drivers.

20. **Interstate what kind of report must you complete at the end of your shift?**
    a. You must complete a logbook page for each bus driven.
    b. You must make a list of the names of all passengers transported.
    c. You must complete a written inspection report for each bus driven.

# Answer Key and Explanations for Test #3

**1. C**: Take the next off ramp.

**2. A**: One hundred pounds.

**3. B:** You must turn on the warning lights before you stop to load or unload students. If the posted speed is 35 mph or more, turn on the warning lights at least 200 feet before the stop.

**4. C**: Only if getting off the bus would be unsafe for the passengers.

**5. A**: Wait a moment so that you will have a safe following distance.

**6. B:** Depending on the weight and size of the bus that you will drive, you will be issued a Class B or Class C license.

**7. C**: Only in emergencies.

**8. C**: None of these.

**9. A:** You must turn on the warning lights before you stop to load or unload students. If the posted speed limit is less than 35 mph, turn on the warning lights at least 100 feet before the stop.

**10. A**: Diamond-shaped.

**11. B**: Five hundred pounds.

**12. A**: It can cause your vehicle to weave in and out.

**13. C**: At least 15 feet but no more than 50 feet from the crossing.

**14. B**: On buses where permitted, they must stand behind the standee line.

**15. C**: It will lean toward the outside.

**16. A**: Never drive with an open emergency exit door.

**17. C**: It may be 45 miles per hour or it could be less.

**18. C**: No, because you do not know you can drive safely.

**19. A**: That is the average of other drivers.

**20. C**: You must complete a written pre/post trip inspection report for each bus driven.

# Passenger and School Bus Endorsement Practice Test #4

1. **Can tear gas be transported on a bus?**
   a. No, irritating material may not be carried.
   b. Yes, if written permission is received from the DOT
   c. Yes, if the containers meet certain packaging requirements.

2. **What is a factor that most affects the amount of traction that your bus has?**
   a. The width of the road.
   b. The type and condition of the road surface.
   c. The brand name of your tires.

3. **Are you allowed to shift gears when crossing railroad tracks?**
   a. Yes.
   b. No.
   c. Only when the crossing has been marked exempt.

4. **You should never bring your bus into the stop to pick up students until?**
   a. There is no traffic in the area.
   b. A parent is present.
   c. The students have lined up properly.

5. **What should you do before the students are allowed to start toward the bus?**
   a. The bus should be stopped and the door should be opened.
   b. The students should have seen your bus and are aware that it is approaching.
   c. You should be slowing down approaching the bus stop.

6. **How often do most state laws require that you hold an emergency exit drill?**
   a. At least once during the first 90 calendar days of the school year
   b. At least once during the first 60 calendar days of the school year
   c. At least once during the first 30 calendar days of the school year

7. **If red is reflected back from pavement markings you are going?**
   a. In the right direction on the freeway.
   b. To be coming to the end of the freeway.
   c. In the wrong direction on the freeway.

8. **When following another vehicle while driving outside of cities and towns, you should keep at least how much distance between you and the vehicle in front of you?**
   a. 200 feet
   b. 300 feet
   c. 400 feet

9. When passing a vehicle at night what is important to remember?
   a. Have your high beams on.
   b. Use your low beams.
   c. Flash your lights.

10. Name a situation where you must not allow your bus to be fueled.
    a. When the air temperature is below freezing.
    b. When the engine is turned off and the driver is absent.
    c. When in a closed building with riders on board.

11. How fast should you drive in school, business, and residential areas during normal driving conditions?
    a. 25 mph
    b. 30 mph
    c. 35 mph

12. It is illegal to transport passengers if you have consumed?
    a. An intoxicating beverage within two hours.
    b. An intoxicating beverage within four hours.
    c. An intoxicating beverage within eight hours.

13. What should you do when driving for a long period?
    a. Keep the window rolled down.
    b. Take regular breaks.
    c. Drink coffee.

14. If you should discharge an unruly passenger, where should this be done?
    a. Within the city limits of an incorporated city.
    b. Only at a bus terminal.
    c. At a place that is safe for them.

15. What is the best tactic to use before crossing an intersection?
    a. Look right - then left - then right again.
    b. Look left - then right - then left again.
    c. Look to the rear - then ahead and then to the rear again.

16. At night your ability to steer a vehicle is reduced because?
    a. You cannot see as well.
    b. You may not be able to look down the road far enough.
    c. Both of the above.

17. Since you must know what is in front of you how should you use your eyes?
    a. You should be gazing straight ahead at all times.
    b. You should either be looking at your dashboard or looking straight ahead.
    c. You should be shifting your view every few seconds.

18. Which of the following is the minimum requirement to operate a school bus designed to carry no more than 15 passengers, including the driver?
    a. CDL test
    b. Passenger bus endorsement test
    c. School bus knowledge and skills tests

19. What is the only real control that you have over students leaving the school bus?
    a. Turning off the engine.
    b. Opening the door.
    c. Threatening them with punishment.

20. Which of the following is much harder to judge at night?
    a. The time.
    b. Your strength.
    c. Distance.

# Answer Key and Explanations for Test #4

**1. A**: No, irritating material may not be carried.

**2. B**: The type and condition of the road surface.

**3. B**: No.

**4. C**: The students have lined up properly.

**5. A**: The bus should be stopped and the door should be opened.

**6. A:** Most state laws require that you hold an emergency exit drill at least once during the first 90 calendar days of the school year, or more often if needed. Your local school board or board of education may require more frequent drills.

**7. C**: In the wrong direction on the freeway.

**8. A:** When following other vehicles, always leave at least a bus length between you and the vehicle in front of you. Outside of cities and towns, keep at least 200 feet between you and the vehicle in front of you.

**9. B**: Use your low beams.

**10. C**: When in a closed building with riders on board.

**11. A:** You must travel 25 mph in school, business, and residential areas. Remember that weather, road, and traffic conditions may require you to travel slower than this speed limit. When in doubt, slow down.

**12. B**: An intoxicating beverage within four hours.

**13. B**: Take regular breaks.

**14. C**: At a place that is safe for them.

**15. B**: Look left - then right - then left again.

**16. C**: Both of the above.

**17. C**: You should be shifting your view every few seconds.

**18. C:** If you plan to operate a school bus designed to carry no more than 15 passengers, including the driver, you do not need to obtain a CDL, Class B or C, or the passenger bus endorsement. However, you must have the school bus endorsement on your driver's license. Therefore, you will need to take the school bus knowledge and skills tests. You will be restricted to driving buses designed to carry no more than 15 passengers, and this restriction will be printed on your license.

**19. B**: Opening the door.

**20. C**: Distance.

# Passenger and School Bus Endorsement Practice Test #5

1. What is a warning that you are getting tired?
    a. You are watching out for everything around you.
    b. You are beginning to look in one place too long.
    c. Both of the above.

2. Why must you be careful when passing a heavy vehicle going downhill?
    a. The other driver cannot see you as easily as he can when going uphill.
    b. The heavy vehicle may be picking up speed.
    c. It is illegal to pass a vehicle going downhill.

3. If you are driving on a highway where the posted speed limit is 45 mph or higher and you are not loading or unloading passengers between your place of departure and your destination, how fast can you drive?
    a. 55 mph
    b. 45 mph
    c. 35 mph

4. When entering the freeway your best strategy is to?
    a. Try to keep your speed low.
    b. Merge at or close to the speed of traffic on the freeway.
    c. Stop until there is a spot to enter.

5. How should an intersection with flashing red lights be treated?
    a. As if it was controlled by stop signs.
    b. As if it was a two-way intersection.
    c. No special treatment must be given to the intersection.

6. You should only back the bus when:
    a. There is no other safe way to move the vehicle.
    b. Driving forward would mean a time-consuming detour.
    c. You misjudged the needed stopping distance.

7. Buses parked in line at the school should be parked so that?
    a. Evacuation drills can be held that utilize the front and back exits.
    b. Students will not have to walk very far between their classroom and the bus.
    c. No one can walk between the busses.

8. Can oxygen be carried on board by a passenger?
    a. No, gases are not permitted on board.
    b. Yes, if special written permission is received from the DOT.
    c. Yes, if medically prescribed for and in the possession of a passenger.

9. When preparing to turn left, how should you keep your wheels pointing?
    a. To the left.
    b. To the right.
    c. Straight ahead

10. Which of the following is NOT advisable when loading or unloading students?
    a. Report drivers who illegally pass a bus that is stopped to load or unload.
    b. When on heavily traveled roads, unload students on the side of the road where they live.
    c. Use the emergency four-way hazard flashers when loading or unloading.

11. Why should you be aware of a car directly in front of a car you will be passing?
    a. It may try to pass also.
    b. It might get a flat tire.
    c. To be sure you can safely return to your lane after completing the pass.

12. Which will make you tire earlier?
    a. You do not like what you are doing.
    b. You have exercised beforehand.
    c. You are hungry.

13. May passengers leave carry-on baggage or other items in a doorway or in the aisle?
    a. Yes, unless there is a printed notice prohibiting it.
    b. No, unless no other space is available.
    c. No, there should be nothing in a doorway or the aisle that could potentially trip riders.

14. Can looking ahead prevent accidents with cars going in same direction?
    a. You can see changes in the traffic flow early enough to make adjustments
    b. You can see objects that are far away better than those that are close.
    c. You can see where passengers are waiting for your bus in time to stop.

15. Usually the best position for a bus when students are crossing the road is?
    a. On the left side of the road.
    b. On the right edge of the road.
    c. In the middle of the road.

16. Why does it require more time for the eyes to adjust at night?
    a. There is less light at night.
    b. Different parts of the eyes are used.
    c. Both of the above.

17. How do you certify corrected defects on your pre-trip inspection?
    a. Skip these items on your pre-trip inspection.
    b. Sign the previous driver report.
    c. Assume that the shop has handled these items.

18. How can you know if you are driving too fast on a banked curve?
    a. If the bus leans toward the outside of the curve
    b. If you are driving below the posted speed limit
    c. If you slow down and there are no other vehicles around you

**19. What should you do about speed if the road becomes slippery?**
   a. Reduce your speed gradually.
   b. Reduce your speed quickly.
   c. Stop immediately wherever you are.

**20. Should you start to pass another vehicle before a no-passing zone?**
   a. Yes, if you begin your pass before you reach the solid yellow lines.
   b. Only if the pass can be completed safely before the no-passing zone.
   c. Yes, if no oncoming traffic is coming.

# Answer Key and Explanations for Test #5

**1. B**: You are beginning to look in one place too long.

**2. B**: The heavy vehicle may be picking up speed.

**3. B**: If you are driving on a highway where the posted speed limit is 45 mph or higher and you are not loading or unloading passengers between your place of departure and your destination, you may travel 45 mph.

**4. B**: Merge at or close to the speed of traffic on the freeway.

**5. A**: As if it was controlled by stop signs.

**6. A:** Do not back the bus unless there is no other safe way to move the vehicle. Drive around the block or make a detour rather than backing the bus. Post a lookout inside the bus at the back to warn of obstacles, approaching persons, or other vehicles. Check your mirrors constantly while backing. Pick up passengers *before* backing or turning. Unload passengers *after* backing or turning.

**7. C**: No one can walk between the busses.

**8. C**: Yes, if medically prescribed for and in the possession of a passenger.

**9. C**: Straight ahead

**10. C:** Do not use the emergency four-way hazard flashers when loading or unloading students.

**11. C**: To be sure you can safely return to your lane after completing the pass.

**12. A**: You do not like what you are doing.

**13. C**: No, there should be nothing in a doorway or the aisle that could potentially trip riders.

**14. A**: You can see changes in the traffic flow early enough to make adjustments

**15. B**: On the right edge of the road.

**16. C**: Both of the above.

**17. B**: Sign the previous driver report.

**18. A:** Crashes on curves result from excessive speed. In good weather, the posted speed on a curve is safe for cars, but may be too high for buses. If your bus leans toward the outside on a banked curve, you are driving too fast.

**19. A**: Reduce your speed gradually.

**20. B**: Only if the pass can be completed safely before the no-passing zone.

# Passenger and School Bus Endorsement Practice Test #6

1. **When can your rear-view mirrors be a handicap to you at night?**
   a. When they make other objects seem closer than they are.
   b. When the glare of other headlights in them blinds you.
   c. When they do not show your blind spots.

2. **On which wheels may buses have recapped or regrooved tires?**
   a. On all wheels.
   b. On all wheels except the front wheels
   c. On all wheels except the drivers.

3. **Which of the following can be stowed in the aisle on a school bus?**
   a. Book bags and calculators and books.
   b. Lunches and coats and jackets.
   c. None of these.

4. **Students planning to get off the school bus should not get up from their seat until?**
   a. The school bus driver has turned on the flashing red lights.
   b. The bus has come to a complete stop.
   c. The driver tells them to get up.

5. **Before passing, many drivers make the common error of?**
   a. Following too far behind.
   b. Following too closely.
   c. Turning their blinker on too soon.

6. **Employees using drugs and alcohol have how many times as many accidents as unencumbered employees?**
   a. Twice as many.
   b. Three to four times as many.
   c. Five times as many.

7. **What is the only circumstance in which you should use the bus's warning lights?**
   a. When backing the bus
   b. When pulled over for repairs
   c. When loading and unloading

8. **How often should you look in your rear-view mirrors?**
   a. Several times per minute.
   b. Only when you are changing lanes or backing up.
   c. Once a minute.

9. Which of the following is NOT a valid reason to unload students from the bus in case of an accident?
   a. Extensive damage
   b. Danger of further injury or fire
   c. Other motorists are passing

10. After loading, what should you wait for before starting the bus?
    a. Time to announce the location, reason for stopping, departure time, and bus number
    b. An improved ability to see or hear
    c. Passengers to sit down or brace themselves

11. Opening your forward door while stopped at a railroad crossing will help you:
    a. Maintain passenger awareness
    b. See or hear better
    c. Shift gears

12. Which of the following may never be carried on a bus?
    a. Prescription drugs
    b. Small-arms ammunition
    c. Tear gas

13. Why should a driver count the number of students getting on a school bus?
    a. Helps to know if the bus is overloaded.
    b. Helps to determine if some passengers will have to stand.
    c. Helps to know if everyone is on the bus or is safely away from it.

14. What may be the only notice that drivers following you have at night?
    a. Your taillights.
    b. Your back bumper.
    c. Your rear window.

15. What is a common hazard that you should not allow riders to board the bus with?
    a. Unexposed film
    b. Car batteries
    c. Raw foodstuffs

16. On a two-lane road can you pass a car that is passing another vehicle?
    a. Yes.
    b. Yes, only if the person knows you are passing them.
    c. No.

17. When driving down a steep hill which is best?
    a. Shift down to a lower gear and not use your brakes.
    b. Shift down to a lower gear so that you will not use your brakes hard.
    c. Use your brakes only.

**18. Can your ability to look around you be handicapped by what you see?**
   a. No, you will continue to keep your eyes moving at all times.
   b. No, you are only interested in the vehicles that could be a threat to you.
   c. Yes, certain things will attract your attention more than others.

**19. Why is it important to keep a safe following distance on the freeway?**
   a. So you will not get a ticket for tailgating.
   b. So you can adjust quickly if traffic comes to a complete stop.
   c. So you will save fuel.

**20. What are three items of emergency equipment you must have on a bus?**
   a. A fire extinguisher and a first aid kit and tire irons.
   b. Reflectors and stretchers and hydraulic jacks.
   c. Reflectors and a fire extinguisher and spare electric fuses.

# Answer Key and Explanations for Test #6

**1. B**: When the glare of other headlights in them blinds you.

**2. B**: On all wheels except the front wheels

**3. C**: None of these.

**4. B**: The bus has come to a complete stop.

**5. B**: Following too closely.

**6. B**: Three to four times as many.

**7. C**: Do not use the warning lights except when loading and unloading.

**8. A**: Several times per minute.

**9. C**: In an accident, keep students on the bus unless there is extensive damage or danger of further injury or fire.

**10. C:** Wait for riders to sit down or brace themselves before you start the bus. Starting and stopping should be as smooth as possible to avoid rider injury.

**11. B:** Stop your bus 15-50 feet before railroad crossings. Listen and look in both directions for trains. Improve your ability to see or hear an approaching train by opening your forward door. If a train has just passed, make sure that another train isn't coming from the opposite direction. If your bus has a manual transmission, never shift gears while crossing the tracks.

**12. C:** Buses may never carry any of the following: Class 2 poison, liquid Class 6 poison, tear gas, or other irritating material; more than 100 pounds of solid Class 6 poisons; explosives in the space occupied by people, except small-arms ammunition; labeled radioactive materials in the space occupied by people; more than 500 pounds total of allowed hazardous materials; more than 100 pounds of any one class of hazardous materials.

**13. C:** Helps to know if everyone is on the bus or is safely away from it.

**14. A**: Your taillights.

**15. B**: Riders may sometimes board a bus carrying an unlabeled hazardous material. Do not allow riders to carry on common hazards such as car batteries or gasoline.

**16. C**: No.

**17. B**: Shift down to a lower gear so that you will not use your brakes hard.

**18. C**: Yes, certain things will attract your attention more than others.

**19. B**: So you can adjust quickly if traffic comes to a complete stop.

**20. C**: Reflectors and a fire extinguisher and spare electric fuses.

# How to Overcome Test Anxiety

Just the thought of taking a test is enough to make most people a little nervous. A test is an important event that can have a long-term impact on your future, so it's important to take it seriously and it's natural to feel anxious about performing well. But just because anxiety is normal, that doesn't mean that it's helpful in test taking, or that you should simply accept it as part of your life. Anxiety can have a variety of effects. These effects can be mild, like making you feel slightly nervous, or severe, like blocking your ability to focus or remember even a simple detail.

If you experience test anxiety—whether severe or mild—it's important to know how to beat it. To discover this, first you need to understand what causes test anxiety.

## Causes of Test Anxiety

While we often think of anxiety as an uncontrollable emotional state, it can actually be caused by simple, practical things. One of the most common causes of test anxiety is that a person does not feel adequately prepared for their test. This feeling can be the result of many different issues such as poor study habits or lack of organization, but the most common culprit is time management. Starting to study too late, failing to organize your study time to cover all of the material, or being distracted while you study will mean that you're not well prepared for the test. This may lead to cramming the night before, which will cause you to be physically and mentally exhausted for the test. Poor time management also contributes to feelings of stress, fear, and hopelessness as you realize you are not well prepared but don't know what to do about it.

Other times, test anxiety is not related to your preparation for the test but comes from unresolved fear. This may be a past failure on a test, or poor performance on tests in general. It may come from comparing yourself to others who seem to be performing better or from the stress of living up to expectations. Anxiety may be driven by fears of the future—how failure on this test would affect your educational and career goals. These fears are often completely irrational, but they can still negatively impact your test performance.

> **Review Video: 3 Reasons You Have Test Anxiety**
> Visit mometrix.com/academy and enter code: 428468

## Elements of Test Anxiety

As mentioned earlier, test anxiety is considered to be an emotional state, but it has physical and mental components as well. Sometimes you may not even realize that you are suffering from test anxiety until you notice the physical symptoms. These can include trembling hands, rapid heartbeat, sweating, nausea, and tense muscles. Extreme anxiety may lead to fainting or vomiting. Obviously, any of these symptoms can have a negative impact on testing. It is important to recognize them as soon as they begin to occur so that you can address the problem before it damages your performance.

> **Review Video: 3 Ways to Tell You Have Test Anxiety**
> Visit mometrix.com/academy and enter code: 927847

The mental components of test anxiety include trouble focusing and inability to remember learned information. During a test, your mind is on high alert, which can help you recall information and stay focused for an extended period of time. However, anxiety interferes with your mind's natural processes, causing you to blank out, even on the questions you know well. The strain of testing during anxiety makes it difficult to stay focused, especially on a test that may take several hours. Extreme anxiety can take a huge mental toll, making it difficult not only to recall test information but even to understand the test questions or pull your thoughts together.

> **Review Video: How Test Anxiety Affects Memory**
> Visit mometrix.com/academy and enter code: 609003

## Effects of Test Anxiety

Test anxiety is like a disease—if left untreated, it will get progressively worse. Anxiety leads to poor performance, and this reinforces the feelings of fear and failure, which in turn lead to poor performances on subsequent tests. It can grow from a mild nervousness to a crippling condition. If allowed to progress, test anxiety can have a big impact on your schooling, and consequently on your future.

Test anxiety can spread to other parts of your life. Anxiety on tests can become anxiety in any stressful situation, and blanking on a test can turn into panicking in a job situation. But fortunately, you don't have to let anxiety rule your testing and determine your grades. There are a number of relatively simple steps you can take to move past anxiety and function normally on a test and in the rest of life.

> **Review Video: How Test Anxiety Impacts Your Grades**
> Visit mometrix.com/academy and enter code: 939819

# Physical Steps for Beating Test Anxiety

While test anxiety is a serious problem, the good news is that it can be overcome. It doesn't have to control your ability to think and remember information. While it may take time, you can begin taking steps today to beat anxiety.

Just as your first hint that you may be struggling with anxiety comes from the physical symptoms, the first step to treating it is also physical. Rest is crucial for having a clear, strong mind. If you are tired, it is much easier to give in to anxiety. But if you establish good sleep habits, your body and mind will be ready to perform optimally, without the strain of exhaustion. Additionally, sleeping well helps you to retain information better, so you're more likely to recall the answers when you see the test questions.

Getting good sleep means more than going to bed on time. It's important to allow your brain time to relax. Take study breaks from time to time so it doesn't get overworked, and don't study right before bed. Take time to rest your mind before trying to rest your body, or you may find it difficult to fall asleep.

> **Review Video: The Importance of Sleep for Your Brain**
> Visit mometrix.com/academy and enter code: 319338

Along with sleep, other aspects of physical health are important in preparing for a test. Good nutrition is vital for good brain function. Sugary foods and drinks may give a burst of energy but this burst is followed by a crash, both physically and emotionally. Instead, fuel your body with protein and vitamin-rich foods.

Also, drink plenty of water. Dehydration can lead to headaches and exhaustion, especially if your brain is already under stress from the rigors of the test. Particularly if your test is a long one, drink water during the breaks. And if possible, take an energy-boosting snack to eat between sections.

> **Review Video: How Diet Can Affect your Mood**
> Visit mometrix.com/academy and enter code: 624317

Along with sleep and diet, a third important part of physical health is exercise. Maintaining a steady workout schedule is helpful, but even taking 5-minute study breaks to walk can help get your blood pumping faster and clear your head. Exercise also releases endorphins, which contribute to a positive feeling and can help combat test anxiety.

When you nurture your physical health, you are also contributing to your mental health. If your body is healthy, your mind is much more likely to be healthy as well. So take time to rest, nourish your body with healthy food and water, and get moving as much as possible. Taking these physical steps will make you stronger and more able to take the mental steps necessary to overcome test anxiety.

# Mental Steps for Beating Test Anxiety

Working on the mental side of test anxiety can be more challenging, but as with the physical side, there are clear steps you can take to overcome it. As mentioned earlier, test anxiety often stems from lack of preparation, so the obvious solution is to prepare for the test. Effective studying may be the most important weapon you have for beating test anxiety, but you can and should employ several other mental tools to combat fear.

First, boost your confidence by reminding yourself of past success—tests or projects that you aced. If you're putting as much effort into preparing for this test as you did for those, there's no reason you should expect to fail here. Work hard to prepare; then trust your preparation.

Second, surround yourself with encouraging people. It can be helpful to find a study group, but be sure that the people you're around will encourage a positive attitude. If you spend time with others who are anxious or cynical, this will only contribute to your own anxiety. Look for others who are motivated to study hard from a desire to succeed, not from a fear of failure.

Third, reward yourself. A test is physically and mentally tiring, even without anxiety, and it can be helpful to have something to look forward to. Plan an activity following the test, regardless of the outcome, such as going to a movie or getting ice cream.

When you are taking the test, if you find yourself beginning to feel anxious, remind yourself that you know the material. Visualize successfully completing the test. Then take a few deep, relaxing breaths and return to it. Work through the questions carefully but with confidence, knowing that you are capable of succeeding.

Developing a healthy mental approach to test taking will also aid in other areas of life. Test anxiety affects more than just the actual test—it can be damaging to your mental health and even contribute to depression. It's important to beat test anxiety before it becomes a problem for more than testing.

**Review Video: Test Anxiety and Depression**
Visit mometrix.com/academy and enter code: 904704

# Study Strategy

Being prepared for the test is necessary to combat anxiety, but what does being prepared look like? You may study for hours on end and still not feel prepared. What you need is a strategy for test prep. The next few pages outline our recommended steps to help you plan out and conquer the challenge of preparation.

## STEP 1: SCOPE OUT THE TEST

Learn everything you can about the format (multiple choice, essay, etc.) and what will be on the test. Gather any study materials, course outlines, or sample exams that may be available. Not only will this help you to prepare, but knowing what to expect can help to alleviate test anxiety.

## STEP 2: MAP OUT THE MATERIAL

Look through the textbook or study guide and make note of how many chapters or sections it has. Then divide these over the time you have. For example, if a book has 15 chapters and you have five days to study, you need to cover three chapters each day. Even better, if you have the time, leave an extra day at the end for overall review after you have gone through the material in depth.

If time is limited, you may need to prioritize the material. Look through it and make note of which sections you think you already have a good grasp on, and which need review. While you are studying, skim quickly through the familiar sections and take more time on the challenging parts. Write out your plan so you don't get lost as you go. Having a written plan also helps you feel more in control of the study, so anxiety is less likely to arise from feeling overwhelmed at the amount to cover.

## STEP 3: GATHER YOUR TOOLS

Decide what study method works best for you. Do you prefer to highlight in the book as you study and then go back over the highlighted portions? Or do you type out notes of the important information? Or is it helpful to make flashcards that you can carry with you? Assemble the pens, index cards, highlighters, post-it notes, and any other materials you may need so you won't be distracted by getting up to find things while you study.

If you're having a hard time retaining the information or organizing your notes, experiment with different methods. For example, try color-coding by subject with colored pens, highlighters, or post-it notes. If you learn better by hearing, try recording yourself reading your notes so you can listen while in the car, working out, or simply sitting at your desk. Ask a friend to quiz you from your flashcards, or try teaching someone the material to solidify it in your mind.

## STEP 4: CREATE YOUR ENVIRONMENT

It's important to avoid distractions while you study. This includes both the obvious distractions like visitors and the subtle distractions like an uncomfortable chair (or a too-comfortable couch that makes you want to fall asleep). Set up the best study environment possible: good lighting and a comfortable work area. If background music helps you focus, you may want to turn it on, but otherwise keep the room quiet. If you are using a computer to take notes, be sure you don't have any other windows open, especially applications like social media, games, or anything else that could distract you. Silence your phone and turn off notifications. Be sure to keep water close by so you stay hydrated while you study (but avoid unhealthy drinks and snacks).

Also, take into account the best time of day to study. Are you freshest first thing in the morning? Try to set aside some time then to work through the material. Is your mind clearer in the afternoon or evening? Schedule your study session then. Another method is to study at the same time of day that you will take the test, so that your brain gets used to working on the material at that time and will be ready to focus at test time.

## Step 5: Study!

Once you have done all the study preparation, it's time to settle into the actual studying. Sit down, take a few moments to settle your mind so you can focus, and begin to follow your study plan. Don't give in to distractions or let yourself procrastinate. This is your time to prepare so you'll be ready to fearlessly approach the test. Make the most of the time and stay focused.

Of course, you don't want to burn out. If you study too long you may find that you're not retaining the information very well. Take regular study breaks. For example, taking five minutes out of every hour to walk briskly, breathing deeply and swinging your arms, can help your mind stay fresh.

As you get to the end of each chapter or section, it's a good idea to do a quick review. Remind yourself of what you learned and work on any difficult parts. When you feel that you've mastered the material, move on to the next part. At the end of your study session, briefly skim through your notes again.

But while review is helpful, cramming last minute is NOT. If at all possible, work ahead so that you won't need to fit all your study into the last day. Cramming overloads your brain with more information than it can process and retain, and your tired mind may struggle to recall even previously learned information when it is overwhelmed with last-minute study. Also, the urgent nature of cramming and the stress placed on your brain contribute to anxiety. You'll be more likely to go to the test feeling unprepared and having trouble thinking clearly.

So don't cram, and don't stay up late before the test, even just to review your notes at a leisurely pace. Your brain needs rest more than it needs to go over the information again. In fact, plan to finish your studies by noon or early afternoon the day before the test. Give your brain the rest of the day to relax or focus on other things, and get a good night's sleep. Then you will be fresh for the test and better able to recall what you've studied.

## Step 6: Take a practice test

Many courses offer sample tests, either online or in the study materials. This is an excellent resource to check whether you have mastered the material, as well as to prepare for the test format and environment.

Check the test format ahead of time: the number of questions, the type (multiple choice, free response, etc.), and the time limit. Then create a plan for working through them. For example, if you have 30 minutes to take a 60-question test, your limit is 30 seconds per question. Spend less time on the questions you know well so that you can take more time on the difficult ones.

If you have time to take several practice tests, take the first one open book, with no time limit. Work through the questions at your own pace and make sure you fully understand them. Gradually work up to taking a test under test conditions: sit at a desk with all study materials put away and set a timer. Pace yourself to make sure you finish the test with time to spare and go back to check your answers if you have time.

After each test, check your answers. On the questions you missed, be sure you understand why you missed them. Did you misread the question (tests can use tricky wording)? Did you forget the information? Or was it something you hadn't learned? Go back and study any shaky areas that the practice tests reveal.

Taking these tests not only helps with your grade, but also aids in combating test anxiety. If you're already used to the test conditions, you're less likely to worry about it, and working through tests until you're scoring well gives you a confidence boost. Go through the practice tests until you feel comfortable, and then you can go into the test knowing that you're ready for it.

## Test Tips

On test day, you should be confident, knowing that you've prepared well and are ready to answer the questions. But aside from preparation, there are several test day strategies you can employ to maximize your performance.

First, as stated before, get a good night's sleep the night before the test (and for several nights before that, if possible). Go into the test with a fresh, alert mind rather than staying up late to study.

Try not to change too much about your normal routine on the day of the test. It's important to eat a nutritious breakfast, but if you normally don't eat breakfast at all, consider eating just a protein bar. If you're a coffee drinker, go ahead and have your normal coffee. Just make sure you time it so that the caffeine doesn't wear off right in the middle of your test. Avoid sugary beverages, and drink enough water to stay hydrated but not so much that you need a restroom break 10 minutes into the test. If your test isn't first thing in the morning, consider going for a walk or doing a light workout before the test to get your blood flowing.

Allow yourself enough time to get ready, and leave for the test with plenty of time to spare so you won't have the anxiety of scrambling to arrive in time. Another reason to be early is to select a good seat. It's helpful to sit away from doors and windows, which can be distracting. Find a good seat, get out your supplies, and settle your mind before the test begins.

When the test begins, start by going over the instructions carefully, even if you already know what to expect. Make sure you avoid any careless mistakes by following the directions.

Then begin working through the questions, pacing yourself as you've practiced. If you're not sure on an answer, don't spend too much time on it, and don't let it shake your confidence. Either skip it and come back later, or eliminate as many wrong answers as possible and guess among the remaining ones. Don't dwell on these questions as you continue—put them out of your mind and focus on what lies ahead.

Be sure to read all of the answer choices, even if you're sure the first one is the right answer. Sometimes you'll find a better one if you keep reading. But don't second-guess yourself if you do immediately know the answer. Your gut instinct is usually right. Don't let test anxiety rob you of the information you know.

If you have time at the end of the test (and if the test format allows), go back and review your answers. Be cautious about changing any, since your first instinct tends to be correct, but make sure you didn't misread any of the questions or accidentally mark the wrong answer choice. Look over any you skipped and make an educated guess.

At the end, leave the test feeling confident. You've done your best, so don't waste time worrying about your performance or wishing you could change anything. Instead, celebrate the successful completion of this test. And finally, use this test to learn how to deal with anxiety even better next time.

> **Review Video: 5 Tips to Beat Test Anxiety**
> Visit mometrix.com/academy and enter code: 570656

## Important Qualification

Not all anxiety is created equal. If your test anxiety is causing major issues in your life beyond the classroom or testing center, or if you are experiencing troubling physical symptoms related to your anxiety, it may be a sign of a serious physiological or psychological condition. If this sounds like your situation, we strongly encourage you to seek professional help.

# Tell Us Your Story

We at Mometrix would like to extend our heartfelt thanks to you for letting us be a part of your journey. It is an honor to serve people from all walks of life, people like you, who are committed to building the best future they can for themselves.

We know that each person's situation is unique. But we also know that, whether you are a young student or a mother of four, you care about working to make your own life and the lives of those around you better.

**That's why we want to hear your story.**

We want to know why you're taking this test. We want to know about the trials you've gone through to get here. And we want to know about the successes you've experienced after taking and passing your test.

In addition to your story, which can be an inspiration both to us and to others, we value your feedback. We want to know both what you loved about our book and what you think we can improve on.

**The team at Mometrix would be absolutely thrilled to hear from you!** So please, send us an email at tellusyourstory@mometrix.com or visit us at mometrix.com/tellusyourstory.php and let's stay in touch.

# Additional Bonus Material

Due to our efforts to try to keep this book to a manageable length, we've created a link that will give you access to all of your additional bonus material:

**mometrix.com/bonus948/cdlspteall**

Made in United States
Orlando, FL
12 February 2023